The French Vineyards

DENIS MORRIS

THE FRENCH VINEYARDS

1958
EYRE & SPOTTISWOODE
LONDON

CATALOGUE NO. 6/2360

Printed in Great Britain by
Billing and Sons Limited Guildford and London

Contents

Illustrations

7

Preface

THE CELEBRATED physician looked at me quizzically, 'Mr. Morris,' he said, 'in the course of a long professional career I have often been asked for advice of the kind you are seeking. In my experience more people are unhappy about the things that they have not done than about the things that they have. My advice therefore is—take the lot—and take some Gelusil with you as a precaution.' I took the advice.

The question had been, in effect, 'I am going over to France for some months to obtain information for a book that will set out to make wine ordering and drinking more profitable and enjoyable for others like myself who are fond of it but comparatively unknowledgeable. I know the French and how well they will set out to entertain me: shall I refuse all hospitality every fourth or fifth day or shall I risk it?'

At the beginning of this gruelling experience I was forty-nine, felt older and weighed twelve and a half stone. At the end I was fifty, felt like forty, had sampled several thousand wines, and had put on seven pounds in weight despite much bathing, many singles at tennis and running into fourteen days of heat wave in the Loire Valley.

This book is, I hope, not pretentious. It draws on the experience of many far more knowledgeable than I. It seeks to lead others away from the madness of mixing incompatible drinks and consuming them to their own—and often to others'—disadvantage. It sets on record a journey through the world's most civilized country during which many sometimes priceless, sometimes very ordinary, examples of wine were tasted or consumed.

If this is a nursery slope to the pleasure of the drink so often blessed or to the fascinating literature of others far more erudite then in some very small measure I shall have said 'thank you' to the monks of old who spread the science of viticulture, to the loving vintners who followed them and, in advance, to all those who will read this book because they think that 'Good wine is a good familiar creature, if it be well used'.

DENIS MORRIS

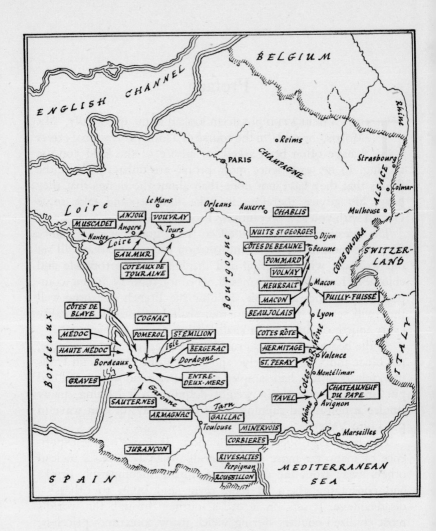

I

Starting Out

I F YOU must motor through the mists and grey horizons which so depressed Vincent Van Gogh, avoid Sundays. On a week-day streets and squares are curiously deserted, like the dying towns of Provence, or Bruges, when its citizens are away working in Brussels. Sundays are different. They are different for two reasons—bowls and bicycles.

In France bowls needs no pageantry, either of green grass or spotless white. It needs three friends, or more, the corner of a street or market place, or the spot where a motorist wants to steer or park his car. Earth must be dusty, ruts irregular, and 'boule' misshapen. The game is played more in the Rhône valley and the Midi than in the northern borders, and it is played with tremendous concentration and a deal of argument, though not perhaps with the religious fervour associated with cricket in England or base-ball in America. I remember watching with an eminent English writer a game played years ago in a typical Beaujolais village. We had lunched as guests of wine-growers, which means we had lunched well. The wines of those parts are made to be quaffed, and quaffed again and again. They are wines for love-talk and loud laughter, wines for Rabelais who praised them rather than for Montesquieu, who preferred the more intellectually demanding vintages of the Gironde.

We came upon the game in one of those unexpected tree-peopled squares which abound in provincial France; an oasis of shadow, dedicated on weekdays to morning markets, afternoon siestas and evening courtship; on Sundays to boule and promenading.

We watched enthralled. Six or seven players in the black trousers of a French Sunday; some wearing berets; all smoking hand-made cigarettes of the kind that sullenly smoulder. Expressions intense; conversation staccato; skill considerable: bad luck passing un-remarked as well-sighted boule hit tree root or pebble. Who says that the French are voluble? Suddenly they were, and with much gesticulation all the players approached the jack—a yard or so from us—and argued violently. Between us and the vociferous players was only a temporary wooden structure 2 feet high, a kind of boundary mark. The sun or the wine or both were too much for my friend. Suddenly he swayed against the board and fell into the game, scattering jack, bowls and three of the players. He was dazed and shaken. Without a word they lifted him up, humped him over the partition, bowed gravely to me and went on with their argument without even attempting to replace their woods in relatively similar positions. These mad English! Or is it the French?

Bicycling is different. Very different.

Bicycle races are to the French what Test Matches are to the English or the World Series to the Americans. If you have a hundred kilometres to motor, and three hours to catch your boat and you hit a Regional championship, you have had it. Main roads will be cordoned off—not once in a while but most summer Sundays; diversions will be long and deceitful. Gradually you worm your way out of the town and come again to a halt 4 kilometres out. Then come cars, sirens, gendarmes, more cars fitted with cameras or advertisements, and finally a string of weedy, mud-splashed, strained-looking cyclists whose trainers and friends shout imprecations and encouragement from cars running along-side. The whole procession takes about three minutes, but will have cost you half an hour. Now time presses—you press too, for ten minutes making fine time. What! You are held up again. Surely not another cycle race? You are right; not another, the same one has gone back on itself!

So we try to avoid Sundays—though this time we did not—and counsel you to also. Like most English and many Americans, we usually arrive via the night ferry from England and start off tired but excited at the very crack of dawn. Often it is wet or misty as we feel our way out of Dunkirk, but always it is France, land of contrasts, contradictions and wine.

From the coast to Cassel there is little reflection of the beauty of France or suggestion of the glories of the country as a whole, nothing but huge fields, vast open views and an under-sea-level kind of feeling. 'It's a country made for war', was once said, and its vast cemeteries mock our peacemakers, the names of its towns are printed in blood on Anglo-Saxon hearts—St Omer, Arras, Bethune, Cambrai, Vimy, St Quentin and a hundred others.

How many lives has France's eastern frontier cost? And for how far back in history? Today it is America who seeks to guard that plain. Yesterday Julius Caesar built a fort at Cassel to protect his eastern front a mile or two away. Louis XIV captured the only rising ground—hardly worthy of the name 'hill'—before commencing his ill-conceived campaign against the Low Countries, and from there also Marshal Foch directed the battle of the Yser. 'A country made for war.'

In wartime its citizens have long been renowned, as any veteran of the first World War will tell, for their ability to carry on as usual—tilling the fields, or gathering in the harvest through shell and shrapnel, bomb and blast. In peacetime they are more like their Dutch, Belgian and German neighbours than their own kith and kin of the south. Solid, industrious, worthy. But they can be gay, and many of them have traditional festivities in the spring and summer months, like the great celebrations at Cassel at Easter, when the roof-top-high figures, Father and Mother Reuza, are carried through rollicking crowds, to the accompaniment of rhythmic music as exciting to these usually serious Netherlanders as is more sensuous music to an African native.

Maybe, combining business and pleasure, you will travel towards Reims through the northernmost belt of manufacturing towns. This is too slow a process for the average holidaymaker, though Lille is really worth a detour, not for its outstanding prosperity but for the fascinating architectural memorials to its various conquerors, particularly the Spaniards whose style runs riot in the Grande Place so beloved of the people of Flanders. The old Bourse built by Julien Destre in the seventeenth century, the new Town Hall and Belfry and the Palais des Beaux Arts are all most beautiful.

The Museum is of particular interest. Some will prefer the Rubens 'Descent from the Cross', others the two Goyas, one of youth triumphant in the comely shape of two girls, the other of gnarled old women, their lustre gone, their finery pathetic, and their companion—Death. Be sure to let Franz Hals' 'Cheerful Witch' take these harridans out of your mind before leaving the Museum.

If you have to spend a night in Lille try the Strasbourg—a comfortable and welcoming hotel with the additional advantage of having no restaurant, so that you can go out with a clear conscience and treat yourself, or better still let the firm treat you (as the

French say, 'Au frais de la Princesse'), to a superb and inevitably delightful meal with M. Baillieul at the Restaurant Huîtrière. His appreciation of the nuances of flavour that can accompany his famous dishes have earned him the gratitude of many thousands of gourmets. But, unless you are particularly interested in architecture or the contents of its Museum, avoid Lille as on this trip we did.

II

Champagne: Golden and Bubbling with Pride

REIMS, TEN times the size of Epernay, became synonymous with Champagne simply because its scores of miles of tunnels provided perfect storage space for the region's Champagne makers.

The city is said to be part of the ancient inland sea which made the white cliffs of Dover chalky. Architecturally and spiritually it is dominated by its Cathedral which, with those of its near neighbours Châlons and Amiens, is one of the most perfect examples of harmonious beauty left us by the Middle Ages.

From some corners of the fertile Marne plains, the Cathedral looks squat and toad-like; from others, immense and unreal; at times a formidable railway engine, and others a ship with over-ambitious superstructure.

Approach and it becomes what it is—symbol of an enlightened architectural grace which threw off the sackcloth and ashes of twelfth-century building and gave us churches and cathedrals in which those who worshipped could feel happy. Or so it seems to me.

There is a curious affinity between Reims Cathedral and champagne, 'the world's most civilized drink' as Voltaire once called it. First of all, its angels cover the four points of the compass like the wines of its soil; secondly, these gracious figures time and time again, whether they be angel or saint, Apostle, Bishop or Prophet, are real people whose faces resemble in an astonishing degree the feelings this bubbling wine can bring.

Undoubtedly the angel Gabriel, in the group of the Annunciation on the western façade, has the same physical expression that the wine of champagne emphemerally brings; whilst that of Autumn on the south door is a profoundly disturbing warning of how it feels to abuse one of God's greatest gifts.

I soon learnt that many of the old caves, quarries, and catacombs in which the wine is stored were once filled with the stone from which the Cathedral is made, and that the early Christian monks were the first to cultivate the vine studiously and thoughtfully.

In Reims and Epernay the people and the product they make are insolubly and devotedly joined. This is a common phenomenom with those who work on the land—it is much more rarely found in townsmen.

We arrived in Reims at midday instead of the later afternoon and happened to meet our host, Etienne Lanson, in the street outside his home. He told us that he was on his way to vote, which seems a very civilized thing to be doing on a Sunday, instead of trying to run it in before or after going to work, as we do.

Etienne's father, Victor Lanson, knew that we were going to spend several days visiting a very representative number of champagne makers and had offered us a room above the offices of Lanson Père et Fils as a *pied à terre*. The room turned out to be a delightful flat which contained two particular treasures.

One, the caretaker-cum-general-handyman of the firm, dubbed Jeeves, who turned out to be a kind, friendly man—a constant car polisher and trouser presser. The other, a large ice box just by the door.

'Whilst you are here', said Etienne, 'you will be drinking a lot of different makes of champagne. It is essential for you to have a yardstick. Here it is.' And with that he opened the door of the cupboard to show us rows of Lanson 1949, 1947, and Black Label, in bottles and half bottles.

In a few minutes we were already drinking in our first lesson. Champagne should always be served cold, but not too cold, at about 44 to 48 degrees—colder, it will lose its flavour and fragrance; warmer, its sparkle becomes a rushing torrent—a real *vin du diable* as it was formerly called, before the Monk Dom Pérignon and chemists like Pasteur came to master its turbulence. We also learnt how bad the flat, cut-glass champagne tumblers, that get handed from one generation of the thriven to another, are for the wine. It takes some five years to make a high-grade champagne, and much of the time and trouble in its making is taken up by conserving the bubbles for the great moment. The wide area exposed to the air in a large open glass enables the bubbles to escape far too quickly, with the result that the second half of each glass is comparatively flat.

1   Pouring wine into tanks for blending

2 *Remuage*—shaking to bring the deposits to the necks of the bottles

Most champagne makers are convinced the right glass is a tulip-shaped one, and also that the glass should never be allowed to become quite empty until the wine is finished. If you do this the delicate bubbles that give champagne its refreshing pick-me-up, isn't-the-world-a-wonderful-place-and-aren't-I-lucky-to-be-married-to-you kind of quality will go on all the time. At least they will if you have had the wisdom or luck to be drinking your wine out of a glass that has been dried with a linen cloth after washing up—cotton is death to the wine.

All this we learnt as we sat drinking our first bottle of Black Label, and we learnt too how different it makes the world feel even when you are very tired on a wet spring morning.

Sir Harry Preston, the famous Edwardian hotelier and sportsman, used to say that champagne was the only elevenses, but he was an over-privileged man when it came to drinking: I have even had liqueur brandy and Vichy water with him as a long drink.

Maurice Healy recalled that for years he started Christmas in the right Christian spirit by attending midnight Mass and then letting a bottle of champagne and some delicious spiced beef accompany him to bed. Some have tried it—not without success—as an aphrodisiac, and others merely to blind the other sex as to the object of the exercise.

Warner Allen in his delightful book *White Wines and Champagne*, admits that 'there are few who are insensible to its peculiar charm and attraction', though he described its charms 'as being superficial, obvious, and evanescent'.

For myself, I find it the happiest of wines; it laughs its way into your heart, bursting through your blood stream, captivating your senses. It is never heavy; always gay; never dishonest. It is a wine to pet and fondle and caress, unlike Beaujolais, which calls for big gulps, or Bordeaux which demands intellectual effort. People are too frightened of champagne. Either they treat it like liquid gold—the fault of the Customs who seek to kill it—or else they guzzle it because they are really gin drinkers and fear they will not be in sufficient form for the impending celebration.

There is no need to be chi chi or obvious about Champagne, nor for that matter about any drink, though it is a great temptation. Anyhow, petting and fondling are best done in private, and not with the arrogant anonymity of a serviceman overseas. So take your glass—and if you want a fine bouquet and real finesse, let it contain dry or very dry champagne. Start by looking at it

B

reflectively. Its colour should be golden; pale rather than dark; then savour its *parfum*. It should bring you a harmony of all the delicate fragrances of which it is a symposium. If it does not, it is not good champagne, or it is too cold, or you should go and see a throat, nose and ear specialist and have those polypi removed or your sinus scraped. You do not deserve the wine that led King Wenceslas astray; which inspired Thibault, Eustache Deschamps, Voltaire, and a thousand other poets; and which has enslaved archbishops, kings and courtiers, and of which Madame Pompadour said 'it is the only drink which leaves you still beautiful after having drunk a lot'.

As you watch, you should see a continuing series of bubbles mounting like liquid escalators to Heaven. Mounting, mounting, mounting, like a troglodyte's nightmare. No bubbles—no good. They are the lightness and the gaiety of the wine hurrying shs, shs, shs, to meet you.

Like all champagne makers, Etienne Lanson absolutely loathes swizzle sticks. Years are spent getting the bubbles into champagne and in a moment or two they are taken out by stupid people who do not realize how important they are. The habit was started by German cavalry officers in their mess. The newly joined officers had to drink the equivalent of the liquid their breastplates would hold, which was judged to be about a bottle and a half. It was impossible with the bubbles in it, therefore they swished around the inside of their breastplates with their ceremonial swords and the result is swizzle sticks; so if you want to be like nineteenth-century German cavalry officers, use them.

M. Sabbe of Moët et Chandon took us to the Abbey of Hautvillers, nestling into the hill-side above the slopes and plain of the Marne valley, where the famous Dom Pérignon was Monk Cellarer for very many years. During this time he had suggested, and nearly perfected, the art of blending; had introduced the use of corks to replace the stoppers of hemp dipped in oil, had designed fluted glasses, and had gone a long way to controlling the irresponsible sparkling of the wine in the spring.

One of his contemporaries wrote of him, 'Never was there a hand more skilful in the production of wine.' Another, Frère Pierre, who became assistant to Dom Pérignon's successor, gives in the Abbé Manceaux' *History of the Abbey and Village of Hautvillers* a more complete picture of Dom Pérignon's careful methods. 'Father Pérignon never tastes the grapes straight from the vines, although he is in the vineyards almost every day, as they approach maturity, but he brings some fresh from the vines and lets them rest during the night in the fresh air on his window sill, then he tastes them after fasting; he does not then solely judge the potentiality of his *cuvée* according to the flavour of the year, but additionally takes into consideration weather conditions such as an early or late year; a cold or a wet one, and even according to the amount of leaves on the plants. All these things guide him in deciding upon the composition of the *cuvées*.'

No less care is given to the *cuvée* today: exactly how it is achieved is every individual champagne maker's secret. All we know is that it is a solemn and serious occasion in which the firm's chief directors and the *chef du cave* spend many hours experimenting with wines from the different districts—tasting, blending, rejecting, tasting again, imagining the delicacy that this wine will bring in five years and after a second fermentation, the amount of vinosity from this source, the bouquet from another, and seeking so to proportion the blending that when the wine comes to be sold it will approximate in taste and quality to the product which in past years has carried the firm's name.

It is interesting that Dom Pérignon's tombstone records only that he was 'cellarer at the Abbey for 47 years, that he was kind to the poor and full of virtue'. Perhaps he would have wished it so.

These qualities were not entirely shared by his fellows. M. Sabbe told us a story of the monks' 'rights'—a sort of *Droit de Seigneur*—which alleges that although they were very celibate officially, in fact they were allowed, as you might say, the run of the village maidens, and not only the maidens, the married women as well. So as to embarrass nobody, they always went along to their lady friends during working hours, but just in case the husbands, or any member of the family, should come back early, they left their monk's shoes outside the front door so that the poor man would know the monk was there and refrain from coming in, to save mutual embarrassment.

Moët's also own the Château de Saran overlooking the slopes and valley of the Côtes de Blancs, which they keep as a guest house and where we had a wonderful lunch with Miss Campbell as hostess. M. Sabbe had had a bottle of 1914 Domaine *dégorgé* for us several days earlier. It still had delicacy, body and bouquet, though it was much darker than a newer wine, as was a magnificent 1928 that we had with M. Jean Mark Heidsieck.

The sparkling wine of Champagne is said to have started through the woollen firm of Ruinart giving bottles away as Christmas presents—with such success that they stopped making wool and are now the oldest of the champagne makers.

Champagne was slowly attaining its present degree of perfection. By the end of the eighteenth century it was capturing the world's imagination as the symbol of gaiety and rich living—though it was still only a rich man's drink. Its sales soared, but in the process the industry was nearly ruined. Perfection was in sight but it had by no means arrived, as the wine was still uneven in quantity, sometimes oily or cloudy in substance, and frequently burst whilst awaiting *dégorgement*.

Writing in *Connaissance du Champagne*, Maurice Holland computed that losses by merchants through broken bottles amounted to 25 to 40 per cent in the eighteenth century, and instances a merchant of Epernay who had over fifty thousand burst bottles in the year 1780 alone. This continued until the beginning of the nineteenth century, and as late as 1842 M. Holland tells us that two million bottles were lost. Then better bottles, control of fermentation by the addition of appropriate amounts of sugar, and a better understanding of refrigeration, ended once and for all this appalling drain on the champagne makers. Even today there are still just occasional breakages through bursting, as anyone who spends a number of hours down in the great subterranean caves of Reims, Epernay, or Ay can vouch.

These caves—which have been vastly extended in later years—were probably formed when the Romans built the ancient Gaulish city of Durocortorum. The city's inhabitants, called Remi, numbered almost exactly as many—one hundred and twenty thousand—as those of Reims today, although they dwindled to a mere two thousand after one of the earliest German invasions—in the fifth century.

We seemed to walk along many of Reims 120 miles of caves, passing within a few feet of millions of bottles—dirty bottles, clean bottles, lying-flat bottles, sloping bottles, standing-on-their-head bottles. A world of cobwebs and fungi, of dim light, and nature in suspension. The dampness and the quiet of a tomb.

The old Roman caves have much greater depth than the more recent commercial excavations. The former are the quarries from which the Romans took enormous blocks for use in building, for repairs and ramparts. Being somewhat more cultivated than those who desecrate our modern countryside by inflicting skin deep wounds on large surfaces, they quarried intelligently, making their excavations in the form of pyramids which yielded an enormous amount of material without affecting the surface. Standing at the bottom of one of these pyramids, as I did with M. Jean Marc Heidsieck, you can just see a Dutchman's trousers patch of light some 150 feet above. Around you rest hundreds of thousands of bottles of champagne, demanding as reproachfully as a puppy under restraint when playtime begins.

The day we were there followed a spell of rainy weather, and the walls and floors were damp and moist. This does not adversely affect the wine—in fact it is best that wine should not be stored in too dry conditions, as that enables insects to flourish who will attack the cork and ultimately ruin it. So if you plan to keep wine for many years in your cellar be sure to sprinkle a bit of water on the floor from time to time.

M. Heidsieck told us that the pits were discovered by workmen digging out foundations and were first used by mushroom growers, who sold the greater part of their stock to America— one of the first considerable links between the city of Reims and the United States, a link which has been since echoed by many a million plops, except in the prohibition years which nearly ruined the champagne world.

England and the United States are the market's best customers —Belgium and England being easily first and second on a *per capita* basis.

After the American mushroom market collapsed, the pits were sold to Charles Heidsieck and two other firms. Heidsieck built a large gallery some 500 yards long to connect their fifty pits. Today they present a scene of some animation when bottles are arriving after blending or being taken away for dressing-up before their penultimate journey. Usually, though, they are enveloped in thick, quiet darkness, though in wartime they were given a supplementary existence as air-raid shelters, and in them, surrounded by millions of bottles of champagne, babies were born, old folk died, and children went to school.

These Roman caves are an oddity well worth visiting. The more usual *caves* consist of miles and miles of excavations at a depth of about 30 feet or more, with one maker's *caves* running side by side, or just above or below, his neighbour's. At one point in our walk around the *caves* of Perrier Jouet at Epernay, M. Budin pointed to the wall opposite and said, 'Do you realize that the whole of Epernay and Reims is honeycombed with these *caves*? Behind that wall and only a few feet away runs one of Moët's many miles of *caves*.' When we went to Moët and Chandon we found, in fact, that they have some 11 miles of *caves* in which they keep a stock of more than fifteen million bottles.

The champagne region is a very easy one to get to know. It has been called uninteresting—I cannot think why. Its lines are gentle and welcoming, with the vast plateau of the Mountain of Reims making place-finding easy so long as you appreciate that it curves round on itself like a verdant horseshoe. To call it a mountain is a *blague*. You soon find that these men, whose red-lined faces contrast vividly with the pallor of the soil they tend, love gentle exaggerations of this sort.

In fact the Mountain is only some 200 feet high, but in these flat lands that is a commanding height, especially as it covers an area of some 16 miles by 5, and is crowned by a thick forest where many a Champenois spends his weekend shooting.

Its slopes are covered with some of the finest vines in the world. Towards the north-east the Mountain gives place to 'The Little Mountain', whose villages give a secondary but important wine. Almost all these vineyards are planted with black grapes from one of three varieties of pinot.

The designation 'Mountain of Reims' is given to those vineyards facing north across the plain. Here one finds delightful little musical comedy villages with vines sprawling right up to the cottage doors. Villages with lingering names—Mailly Champagne, Chingy-les-Roses, Rilly-la-Montagne—all joined by vines and by a winding departmental road, D 26, which takes you from vineyard to vineyard through spruce reddish villages with here a Louis XIV château, there a fort or the ruins of an Abbey; at Verzenay the last remaining windmill of this once many-sailed plain, and a view across a vast vineyard extending to Beaumont-sur-Versle and Sillery, and at Bouzy vineyards which produce an exquisite red wine. This vineyard is marked on all local maps as the Blue Route, and all the Routes du Champagne are exceedingly well signposted. And everywhere a sense of dedication to the vine.

The vineyards of 'The Valley of the Marne'—marked as the Red Route—run from Epernay to Dormans along and close to each bank of the slow, smug river.

The gentle slopes behind the busy little market town of Ay produce the finest of all this district's grapes in a vast vineyard of 900 acres, parts of which have been owned in turn by French and English kings.

The most loved by the Champenois of all these thriving villages is undoubtedly Hautvillers, in whose famous Abbey Dom Pérignon worked for so long. In 1794 Jean Remy Moët, one of the founders of Moët and Chandon, bought the deserted ruins of the abbey, which had been nearly destroyed in the Revolution, and all the adjoining vineyards. Walking through the shaded park with one of M. Remy Moët's descendants one shares with the past something of the feeling of serene peacefulness that one associates with those more meditative times—a tranquillity of mind that is part of this vast panorama of vines and villages that mingle their way gently, unhurriedly, towards the sinuous Marne.

The third of the great winefields of Champagne is the Côte des Blancs—inappropriately marked up in green on the signposts of the Route du Champagne, though aptly named, as almost all its vineyards are planted in the white pinot or chardonnay. It is this region's grapes that bring the greatest qualities of flavour and delicacy to the wine of champagne. By a freak of nature, the contour of this vineyard weaves out on this, the other side of the Marne, an almost exact replica, but in reverse, of the horseshoe pattern of the Mountain.

The route runs from Epernay to Bergères-les-Vertus, which boasts a church built on stilts. It is maligned by the couplet which describes it as a town of shepherdesses (*Bergères*) where there are hardly any, and of virtues (*Vertus*) where there are none at all. Incidentally, the Champenois delight in leg-pulling, and to this day the men of Hautvillers are referred to as 'cocu' (deceived by their wives) in memory of the alleged scandals of the Monks' sandals; those of Tauxières have the prefix 'beggars' and of Cramant 'wicked'.

The two great *crus* of this vineyard are Cramant and Avize. Many an Anglo-Saxon has been muddled between Cramant and Cremant. Cramant is usually used as one of the most important blends in a great champagne, but occasionally, like other great *crus* of the Côte des Blancs, its white pinot grapes are made into a very delicate, light champagne which is unblended with any other wine. This wine is called Blanc des blancs, followed by the name of the commune from which it comes. It is a great favourite with champagne makers, who make some for their private cellars. We first drank it in an unlabelled bottle of '43 that M. Budin, chairman of Perriet Jouet, had sent down in advance of our lunch at the Chapon Fin restaurant at Epernay, unpretentious in appearance but with an excellent table.

Our special private Cramant was ethereally light in substance —a perfect foil to the '52 which preceded and the '43 which followed it. Earlier, in M. Budin's office, we had drunk an inspiring '49 whilst he told us tales of trick and counter-trick between the occupying German buyers and himself during the war, when he was Mayor of Epernay and they wanted champagne for the German forces.

It was a long battle, with the Germans ever trying to get more champagne and wanting to drink deep into the considerable reserves of stock which are the life blood of every champagne firm, and M. Budin and his fellows managing to find a shortage here and a bottleneck there to prevent too much going to the traditional enemy.

M. Busin pointed to a chair on the other side of his solid old-fashioned desk—'Once a German officer took out his revolver when I refused his demands. He did not point it at me—he just looked at it and talked of Concentration Camps.'

Few very alert, dapper men have an appearance of sadness, but M. Budin has. He thought the young would be grateful to him at the end of the war for preserving such a comparatively large proportion of stock through procrastination and at great personal risk. Instead the younger generation immediately relieved him of his office, unthanked and unhonoured. It is some balm to his hurt and puzzled mind that the champagne makers of Reims and Epernay have continued to honour him year after year by electing him to high office in their affairs.

The path of a distinguished and patriotic man whose country is enemy occupied is a difficult and lonely one.

So much for the countryside; quiet except at harvest time and friendly always, and somewhat surprisingly largely filled with other growing things than vines—corn, market produce and pasture land.

The produce from the three great vineyards is mostly made into champagne in the great Cathedral city and strategically important capital of the plain, Reims, or the small town of Epernay in the valley of the Marne 16 miles to the south. Epernay considers itself the true commerical centre of Champagne. It is a comfortable riverside country town blessed with deep cellars and a rather pretentious avenue called, of course, the Avenue of Champagne.

The journey from grape to glass is a long one in most wines: in none is it more complicated or crowded than in Champagne.

The quantity of a year's harvest is made in the spring and early summer and is largely concerned, particularly in the more northern vineyards of Alsace, Champagne, Burgundy and the Loire, with *la gelée*—the frost which kills the flower but seldom—though it did in February 1956 in Bordeaux—harms the vines unless it comes late in the season after the fruit has set. The danger period in Champagne, Alsace and Burgundy is the period immediately after the red moon, *La Lune Rousse*, which is related to the incidence of Easter.

Frosts during this period can ruin thousands of vineyards and decimate tens of thousands more. We were in Reims on May 6. It was bitterly cold for the time of the year and slight scudding clouds were hurrying across the reddish-brown face of a nearly full moon. Towards morning the wind fell, the frost was keener, and by daylight many a man knew that he had lost a year's income.

During the following day I motored some 80 miles with Etienne Lanson of Lanson Père et Fils. We went through the villages of the Mountain of Reims; through Mailly, Verzenay and Verzy, whence come the wines that give champagne firmness and delicacy; on through Bouzy (very badly hit) and Ambonnay, whose wines bring body; to the valley of the Marne dominated by Ay and the powerful bouquet of its wines, and to the Côte des Blancs where the villages of Cramant and Avize produce perhaps the most delicate grapes of all—wines delightful in their own right as well as when blended with others to make champagne.

Here, worried men spoke anxiously in quick, clipped Nordic French.

'All is well, thank God.' 'Oh, it's formidable—already the leaves are withered, the grape clusters ruined. . . .' 'I do not yet know—I fear that in a week . . .' So the tale unfolded—in some cases despair, in others anxiety, in just a few, relief.

Next day I went over much of the same ground with M. Sabbe of Moët and Chandon, and with M. Dargent, the Director of the Champagne Growers Association. Their tale was blacker, as estimates coming in gave figures like 50 to 80 per cent of the year's crop being ruined, with many still to show whether or not they had withstood the frost.

Vintners, like farmers, find it easy to foresee the worst, but the outlook was indeed a gloomy one.

This kind of disaster reflects just one of the many reasons why champagne will always be relatively the most costly wine, as, to guard against the years when the wine is impoverished by spring frost, summer hailstones, or lack of sun, the great champagne firms have to hold back large stocks of their precious ware, whilst in addition their plants and processes have, by law, to be of the finest.

The date of the harvest, *la vendange*, varies enormously, but is usually fairly accurately assessed some hundred days beforehand when the grape first sets. In very warm years it will usually be early—in 1947, for example, it commenced on September 8 in Cramant and certain wine growers had finished harvesting by September 10, whilst in sunless 1860 and 1938 the harvest was being gathered as late as October 25 and November 2, with snow already on the ground.

A fair average is September 24, and intending visitors can find out the approximate date weeks before this from the offices of the French Tourist Board in all the world's great capitals.

It is the Prefect, the French Departmental Head, who fixes the date of the *vendange*, and within a matter of hours the news has got around to the wandering, lusting families of the Loire and many another comparatively near community. Then, like gypsies heading for Saintes-Maries-de-Mer or intellectuals for an arts festival, they take cart, car, bicycle, train, or bus, to the scene of past lusts and longings. Some looking forward to an honest day's work; others to take what is easily given on a hot, still night. All to bend till their backs are creaking; men with berets; women with deep white bonnets. Grape cutters; sorters; lifters and carriers; men who are tramps or renegades or absentee workmen; women in trouble or seeking it—quickly; families holidaying; youths playing truant. Another invasion has come to the Marne.

In the old days this motley army, hard worked, well fed, lay down for the few hours between dusk and dawn on bundles of hay or straw in the shadow of a barn or near the supper tables. Etienne Lanson showed me how times have changed.

Today the great firms as well as some of the communes and the co-operatives have their own *Vendangeoirs* (places where the first pressing is done) to which the grapes are brought on special carts which have particularly supple springs so that the grapes are not crushed, which might well start an early and unwanted fermentation. They have already been sorted, and the over-ripe, green, or sub-standard grapes thrown out.

Some of these *vendangeoirs* have really first-class living quarters and kitchens. One of Lanson's is an old posting house called La Folie, where in their day Catherine de Medici, Voltaire, and Napoleon I had stayed. Another has a vast mess on the first floor with a huge window giving a superb but probably unappreciated view of the vineyards, and a kitchen with every kind of modern gadget. There are separate cubicles for the foremen in charge of the various *hordes* or *hordons*, which are the collective names for a complete group of grape gatherers. The remaining *vendangeurs* are housed in two or three bunkers.

The grapes, which the *vendangeurs* gather so carefully, come from a comparatively small vineyard area—only some 11,000 hectares (27,500 acres). Most come from the three districts already mentioned and owe much of their renowned quality to their temperate climate, which is the lowest at which vines can successfully be grown. The rainfall is abundant but not excessive, nor are there violent changes of temperature. The prevailing south-west wind is warm; the light is clear, and the sun's rays reflected from the chalk help the grapes towards maturity. Also, the soil with its layer of loam and gravel and its subsoil of chalk is quick draining and dry, and its elements of clay, silica and limestone give the wine flavour lightness and alcoholic quality.

Varieties of the Pinot, the Chardonnay, the Meslier and the Arbanne are the only stock allowed by law in the Champagne region, and these, in the course of time, have shown themselves to be the most perfect complement to the qualities of soil and climate that feed them.

There is a curious difference of exposure in the three great vineyards—the Pinots of the valley of the Marne prefer a southern exposure, those of the Mountain of Reims are best when facing towards the north, and the Chardonnay of the Côte des Blancs towards the east. These vines all also seem to revel in the comparatively low altitudes, averaging around 150 feet, of these gentle vineyard slopes.

In any northern wine region the best grapes come from vines on the slope of hills. For one thing, they get the optimum amount

of sun, and for another, vines on slopes are much less likely to get
the spring frost than those on the plain. Consequently, poorer
vintners who can only afford the lower ground are the most hit
by bad weather.

Despite the rose-coloured spectacles through which we regard
the past it seems that disastrous years happened just as often then
as they do now, as the records of the great chroniclers like Jean
Pussot of the sixteenth century and Pierre Dubos, the grand old
man of Bordeaux, can easily prove.

Inevitably these poorer lands with the greater financial risks
have been turned over more and more to other purposes—hence
the large patches of cereal and market garden produce at the foot
of any vineyards which have a frost danger. The champagne
vineyard has, in fact, shrunk to only around a fifth of the size it
was a hundred years ago, whilst there was even a reduction of
about 8 per cent as a result of the last war.

The Champenois are convinced that the 27,000 acres remaining
of this once immense vineyard is always in such a perfect harmony
of climate, soil, stock cultivation, and ultimately of wine making,
that it is unsurpassed in the world, though this is a claim which will
always be challenged at the Domaine de la Romaneé in the Côte
d'Or, by Château d'Yquem in Sauternes, and by the leading
crus of the Médoc.

Perfection in any form of agriculture is always pleasing to the
eye, and usually rewarding to the farmer. Grape farming in
Champagne can be immensely profitable. For instance, at Cramant
a vineyard changed hands at five and a half million francs per
hectare (2½ acres) in 1952, and at Mailly land has changed hands
recently at four and a half million francs per hectare.

Winter work consists of manuring, ploughing, replacing old
vines, making good and stocking in a central point both compost
manure and artificials. This arid, dry, thirsty soil is as changed in its
chemical content during these winter months as is any market
garden.

January and February pruning is severe, so that each plant
shall only produce a comparatively small number of grapes of the
highest quality. This close pruning also assures that the grapes
will receive the utmost possible amount of sun from above, and
sap from below.

From March onwards hoeing alternates with tying branches
back to the wires, stopping new shoots, eliminating surplus leaves,

turning the soil, cutting back superfluous shoots a second time, with spraying and more hoeing and spraying several times more.

To make things more difficult the champagne vineyards are more scattered so far as individual ownership is concerned than any others in the world—this is in the hope that if a thunderstorm hits the district at least some of any one owner's vines may have escaped damage. To run a vineyard successfully in Champagne is no easy way of life and demands intense specialization and traditional knowledge. As a consequence, very few of the 18,000 vineyard owners have either the capital or the inclination to make their grapes into wine and thence into champagne.

On the other hand, some great champagne firms like Moët and Chandon, Pommery, Lanson, and Veuve Clicquot, have many vineyards of their own, but most have none, and simply buy in the grapes or even the wine after the first fermentation.

The Wine Pressing

You soon find that the great firms much prefer to do their own pressing. It should be done quickly, particularly in the case of the black grapes, whose juice must be pressed away from the skin and the pips before the slightest fermentation or bruising has occurred, lest the juice either becomes tinted or loses its delicacy. M. Lanson emphasized time and again how important it is that the pressing should be done gently so as to avoid completely crushing the individual cells of the grape, as the best wine comes from the middle of the grape and the 'not so good' from the *tailles*.

This wine from the middle of the grapes is in fact the first ten casks of 44 gallons each, which come from 4 tons of grapes, which is always the amount pressed at one time. In all, thirteen casks are pressed out of the 4 tons—usually in hydraulic presses— ten, as said, making the best wine, the *vin de cuvée*—and taking between two and four hours to press.

The remainder of the wine that may be called champagne is much more severely pressed—almost crushed—for one and a half to two hours, until the last three barrels, called the *tailles*, are obtained.

Another way of showing how gently the original fat, luscious grapes are pressed is in the fact that you need 331 kilogrammes of grapes to make the ten barrels of the *Cuvée*; 265 kilogrammes to make the first one and a half barrels of the *taille*, and only 198 kilo- grammes to make the second barrel and a half of the *taille*.

The much more severe crushing experienced by the *taille*, especially the last barrel and a half, releases more colour from the skins of the black grapes and more tannin. There is also less tartaric acid.

It still makes a good champagne but with far less elegance and finesse, and of a slightly deeper colour than that made from the *cuvée*.

What is still left in the way of juice amongst the crushed grape pulp is crushed out for several more hours, but this is not allowed to be made into champagne. It is called the *rebêche* and is made into an ordinary nameless white wine usually drunk by workpeople of the champagne firms.

You can soon see why there are wide variations in the price and quality of champagne!

The first variation is in whether the grapes come from a grand *cru* or a lesser *cru*; second, whether or not the wine is *cuvée*—from the first pressings, or a mixture of first and *taille*, or just *taille*. Incidentally, the finest champagne makers sell the *taille* from their own pressings to the lower quality firms and it becomes perhaps the best part of a cheaper champagne such as B.O.B., which stands for 'buyer's own brand'.

You will have noticed that most merchants offer, in addition to the well-known makes of champagne, either a variant of their own name on the label or else something pretty impressive and *à la française*. This will usually be a B.O.B. made from *taille* and will contain the smallest possible amount of the most delicate and fragrant grapes, in contrast with the wines made by the great firms, who will blend only from the finest, and who, in a great year, use only the wines of that year and declare it a vintage year.

There is a final confusion in the marketing of champagne, and that is that firms may register fictitious names for marketing purposes, and in fact it is said that there are over a thousand registered names although there are only two hundred makers.

I asked one of the great ones of the champagne world what he thought of B.O.B. and the much lower quality champagne. 'You could say', he smiled, 'that they are good for launching enemy ships, but that would be cynical and unfair. All champagne is good —it has to be by the very strict law which controls its making, and the extremely strict control of every process. Some is a good deal better than others and this is reflected in its price. Besides, what should we do with our *taille* if we had not got these very good customers to sell it to? They are doing a job—everyone can't afford the best—and if there had never been African drum music Beethoven's Seventh Symphony would never have been written.'

This was pretty typical of the attitude I found throughout Reims, Epernay, and Ay. Comparative sympathy for others making a different class of wine; keen competition of a fairly tolerant kind between those making wine of similar types.

Another, more cynical, high quality man described B.O.B. simply as 'suitable for a firemen's banquet'—a phrase which sounds far more insulting in French, as said by the Priest of Guinoiseau in Maurice Brillant's fascinating description of the 'Banquet de Pompiers'.

Sixty years ago things were very different. Competition was cut-throat, with the heads of the champagne houses touring the world by steamer and carriage—Charles Heidsieck even opened up the Russian market on horseback, with an accompanying pack-horse loaded with samples by his side, with Veuve Clicquot's salesman at one time a few leagues ahead, and another 200 miles behind.

Today, established agencies and co-operative marketing has ended all that, and salesmanship consists largely of showing the flag in between innumerable aeroplane flights.

The Fermentation

The juice obtained from the pressing passes into vast vats placed immediately under the presses, and stays there for about twelve hours whilst the wine clears. It is then drawn off into 44 gallon casks and is taken as fast as possible to its home for the next five years or so, at Reims, Epernay, or Ay.

It has to be transported quickly, as the wine immediately shows its 'devil' by fermenting slightly during the journey.

Before the full fermentation or boiling (*bouillage*) a small amount of sugar is added, if this is necessary, to ensure an alcoholic content in the final wine of 10 to 12 degrees, and also a minute amount of tartaric acid to help give the wine the acidity that brings bouquet and fragrance.

The high quality firms use barrels shaped by an axe for the fermentation. They say that if they are sawn the hurt grain seeps into the wine and taints its taste. This is far more expensive than the vast glass-lined cement tanks used by some firms who still have a great name. The Champenois are quite certain, though, that fermentation is better in barrels, as the temperature can more easily be controlled. There is also no doubt in the minds of those who only use barrels that they procure a much more elegant bouquet than comes from wine which ferments in tanks.

Whatever the container, the wine 'boils' for from one to three weeks before almost calming down, though it continues to 'work' for about as long again.

The basic wine is now there. Its first heady impetuous violence has bubbled itself out. Its sugar has become alcohol or carbonic gas. In the process of tranquillization its impurities settle and the clear wine can be drawn off ready for the spring blending.

The Cuvée

Again comes a difference between the firms making a high quality champagne and those who particularly concentrate on attractive gold-foil and labels. The former always keep back very large stocks of their finest wine to blend with that of a later year, when the grape has not had enough sun. The latter are less worried about this, as their customers are far less perceptive and have a preference for sweeter champagne in which delicacy of bouquet is in any case difficult to taste.

Blending is usually associated with the mixing of wines from different vineyards but of the same year. The process differs in every firm; in some it is known to several members of the staff, whereas in others it is only known to a few members of the family.

In *Connaissance du Champagne* Maurice Holland gives an admirably clear example of the kind of process carried out. 'Take a normal year. The *cuvée* is composed of about a quarter of wines from the district of Ay; a quarter from the Mountain of Reims; a quarter from the slopes around Epernay; a quarter from the white grapes around Avize. If it is a very hot year, which will make a rich full-bodied wine, one would have to add to the amount of wines from the Mountain of Reims and those of the white grapes in order to make the wine lighter and to give it more bouquet; if on the other hand the wine is light and acid and lacking in body, because the summer has been cold and rainy, one would augment the amount of wines from Ay and Bouzy to give it the vigour it lacks.'

It is at the time of the *cuvée* that the firms who make wine of a

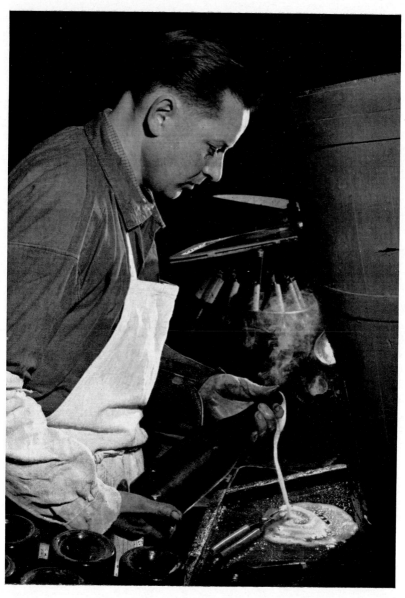

3 *Dégorgement*—blowing out the sediment

4 A view over the Côte des Blancs from the canteen of one of Lanson's *vendangeoirs*

traditional flavour and quality add a little old wine from a great vintage to compensate for any quality they think lacking in the new wine.

Bottling

After the wine is blended, it is left for some months to clear. It is bottled in the spring following the harvest and just before the second fermentation.

This is done on ground level, but immediately afterwards the bottles are taken down to deep cellars, where they stay for a legal minimum of one year after they have become sparkling. In the case of the best wines, they always stay three or four years.

We found that the English like their vintage champagne a year older than anyone else, and when we were there in 1957 we were drinking '52s that had not even been sent to the London agents.

Americans are the despair of the French wine industry, as they are so wedded to the hard drinks they take before a meal that they relatively seldom drink wine even in the luxury hotels.

M. Buddin told me sadly that on his last trip to the States he saw lounges full of women and men drinking several cocktails before meals, but never saw more than a couple of tables with a bottle of wine on them, most having merely iced water. 'No wonder', he said, 'that they have stomach ulcers!'

As between English and Americans, they say that an average Englishman remembers champagne, but not its maker nor its vintage, whereas an American vaguely remembers drinking a rather cute little sparkling wine somewhere in France.

The Remuage

During the second fermentation the wine throws a small deposit. This is got rid of first by shaking the bottles from time to time; then by putting them on racks called *pupitres* which are slanting and adjustable, the slope of which is gradually made more acute until finally the bottles are standing on their heads. During this time they are slightly shaken and sharply twisted each day in a way that will gradually bring the deposit down to the neck of the bottle.

This highly skilled work is done in a dim light—for the sake of the wine—and to the tune of some thirty to forty thousand bottles per man each day.

C

When the *remuage* is finished, the bottles are left in darkness for some years until required for despatch.

The Dégorgement

Then comes the most spectacular operation—*dégorgement* or the blowing out of the sediment. The *dégorgeur*, wearing leather hand guards and apron, prises open the cork with his hand; the sediment is blown out from the neck of the bottle; the thumb immediately covers the cavity; a quick glance shows there is no sediment left in the bottle; an even quicker sniff, that the wine is in no way corked. It then passes to its next stage, which is the *dosage*, which means adding sufficient liquor to make the different qualities and clear wine to make up for the loss in the *dégorgement*. If the wine is for a country with a predominantly sweet palate like Latin America, up to 15 per cent of the added wine will consist of a liquor made from cane sugar; for a *demi sec*, up to 10 per cent; for a *sec*, up to 6 per cent; for an extra dry, up to 2 per cent, and for a *brut*, up to ½ per cent. The amount may in each instance be less than these amounts, depending on the type of wine of the year's harvest. All my advisers confirmed time and again that the driest champagne, the English *brut*, is the best, as it is impossible to hide defects in dry wines by smothering them with sugar.

Thereafter the bottle is usually put under observation for several months whilst the *dosage* blends with the older wine, until finally it is taken out of stock, cleaned, labelled by hand, and packed to all parts of the world, where it will ultimately emerge golden and bubbling with pride.

There are a number of good hotels in Reims and Epernay, but for quiet and excellent cuisine we would recommend the *Cheval Blanc* at Sept Saulx, 14 miles from Reims, under the management of Lefèvre Chauffert. It has only fourteen bedrooms, so it is necessary to book in advance. It has a richly deserved star in the Michelin guide, and its specialities are *Pâté de pigeon*, *Écrevisses* and *Poulet à l'estragon*, all of which we had the extreme pleasure of eating with Etienne Lanson, accompanied by some of his firm's '47 and '49, each exceptional; the '47 rather more full-bodied, the '49 particularly delicate and beautifully balanced.

The only unsuccessful element in the meal was the écrevisses, which I asked to see. Along came a live much-shelled creature with black, bulging eyes and restless limbs, looking as pathetic as those tiny short-haired dogs beloved by luxury flat-dwellers in England and the 'ladies' known as *poules-de-luxe* in France.

Etienne and his uncle were determined to make us eat them, so we tried to forget the eyes and toyed with small snippets of flesh we were able to extract from the ultimately motionless claws. It was good, except that the brown streak going through the centre of the body was off-putting. The juice was superb— we discovered that it was in fact still champagne in which the wretched creatures had been boiled alive.

The *pâté de pigeon* was magnificent, and the recipe is given in Appendix III.

Tarragon is not much used in English cooking, and more is the pity, as it blends perfectly with many dishes, particularly, as we found at the *Cheval Blanc*, with chicken.

Their recipe for *poulet à l'estragon* is also given in Appendix III.

One evening we had dinner at a restaurant very popular with the Remois—*Les Chaumières*, about 2 miles out from the centre of Reims on the right of the road to Epernay, a hundred yards past the hospital. Their specialities are *Jambon en croûte*—we saw a complete one in the shape of a pig's head. It was carved for a wedding party a few yards away from us and they, seeing our interest in this light pink-fleshed meat, asked us to have some of theirs, which we happily did. The Remois are particularly fond of this way of cooking ham, as all the juices are preserved within the crust. It was very good, as was another of the restaurant's specialities, *Coq au Champagne*.

Another restaurant that we went to several times and can thoroughly recommend is the Auberge *La Garenne*, on the edge of the motor race-track, but avoid race days unless you really love a noise and a crowd!

III

Alsace

THE ROAD from Reims and Epernay to Châlons and on to Nancy and Strasbourg is an easy one. The country is very open and friendly. There is little traffic, and a lovely church just outside Châlons. Then, turning right for Bar-le-Duc, a straight, rather indifferent road is bordered by an attractive wooded country. In places the road undulates like the country-side.

One sees on the side of the road, as in so many parts of France, women gathering fuel in sacks, or knitting whilst cows graze, or picking herbs. Everywhere one finds women working. It always seems that the oldest women with the most bowed backs are doing the near-to-the-earth work—hoeing between rows in the vineyards, and things like that. Maybe they are closest to it. And even on a Bank Holiday—we were going along in this district on May 8, which is observed in France as a holiday, for the signing of the Armistice of the 1939-45 war—there is practically no traffic on that 200 miles of road from Epernay to Barr in Alsace. From Ligny the road becomes mountainous—it is a road lined with silver birch and many other trees—a very beautiful road. On through Luneville, wooded slopes, easy road, gracious trees, and the old Alsatian-cum-Lorraine muck heaps outside the homes, as well as great piles of wood awaiting sale or their turn as winter fuel.

I always find Alsace so very different from the Marne. In the Marne life is more consciously cultivated. It is big business. One finds it in all the people around—at least amongst the people whom tourists meet. They speak English, and are very proud of their smiling land and their sparkling wine. They like to show it and themselves off. But when you get to Alsace the countryside absolutely embraces you. You have mile after mile of vineyards facing the sun, you have the magnificent Route du Vin from which one can look down on the towns of Strasbourg and Colmar with their heritage of sadness. From the vineyard one sees the ant-like traffic racing from place to place, but around one is the sleepy

36

civilization which has endured many occupations, great travail, and which still is happy.

It is very much a patriarchal, family world with the one or two big houses all grouped round the industry, usually wine, which has made them prosperous.

In the caves that I visited this family atmosphere persists—life is much more leisurely than in the big Champagne firms. There it is fast-moving, people move bottles to containers, containers to cases. Much of the work is done at enormous speed—time and motion study personified. In Alsace Lorraine a little family is grouped round a machine. They work as fast as they want to— no faster, I'm certain. They laugh, they talk, and they smile, and I have seen this not just once but half a dozen times, and their faces are so nice, so friendly, so homely. They take you to their house and to their hearts, and within no time at all you are one of the family; you have met the son, the daughter-in-law, the little babies—there are always lots of little babies in these homes, sometimes children, sometimes grandchildren—you have met the dog. You find that the grandson, the son, the daughter-in-law and the grandchildren live absolutely next door. They have their meal, they walk over for their liqueur or their coffee with their parents.

It is a patriarchal life. The richest man is still as often as not the mayor of the village. He is the man whom they all love, and he continues to hold office for many, many years.

I found too, even in bigger towns like Colmar, a much more intimate atmosphere than one finds in Metropolitan France— not that I have found it unfriendly anywhere. Yet what a job these vintners have. One day I counted thirty-five walls on one slope alone. I asked M. Michel Brion of Les Domaines Viticoles Schlumberger, who was driving me in a rickety 2 h.p. Citroen around the paths outside the walls (they are not roads)—I asked him if they lose a lot of earth through heavy rains. 'Yes,' he said, 'every year some gets washed over every wall right down to road level. We don't throw it back again; we throw it one down, and so on all down the slope.' He went on to say, 'I suppose we should carry what is accumulating at the bottom up again, up the hill-side, and put it at the top to continue the process, but it's a very long trek up the hill and fortunately we own the forests at the back of the vineyards, so what we do is dig a little more earth out of the forests and scatter it on the top level, and the earth that was washed on to the roads gets taken away by motorists, so there is some virtue in motorists.'

On our first night in Alsace we stayed at the *Hotel du Parc* at Barr, which is very modest in price and friendly. It is on a corner, but the road is not very busy. It has a family atmosphere and is quiet and pleasant at the back of the hotel, and inexpensive. No luxury.

Barr is one of the larger and plainer of the Alsatian Bas Rhin wine towns, boasts several ancient houses, a twelfth-century clock on a Protestant church, and four fine wine makers, including Louis Klipfel, President of the Alsatian growers, and A. Willm, who combines the making of exquisite wines with a flourishing business as a wholesale snail merchant!

Young M. Willm imports a million snails at a time—five million a year. He imports them for canning; they come from Germany and Jugoslavia. There are only two ways of eating snails, which, incidentally, are starved by Willm for four to five weeks before they are served. This is about the time they hibernate, so it is no real cruelty to them. You either have them with a half-wine and half-butter sauce, which also contains garlic and parsley, salt, and butter; or, as in Burgundy, you have more garlic and no wine, therefore the sauce is very much stronger. The snails always taste the same, like sole leather of an indifferent tannage.

Monsieur Willm's *cave* at Barr is impeccable. They call it the library. The wine is perfectly set out in little sets of shelves—four thousand bottles each, instead of the vast *caves* of fifteen to twenty thousand bottles that one sees in other places. He gave us a dégustation. Sitting on miniature barrels in a little red brick cave, we tried all his 1955 Alsatian wines and several others. No spitting out here, this was wine for drinking! The library spread out around us—two hundred thousand 'books' full of liquid truth. The table was set with half a dozen bottles, several dozen inviting glasses, and a white cloth with gay red stripes. There were two other visitors and we were soon clicking our lips and talking. First the '55s, then Riesling '52—with a warm heart, body, bouquet, and *une belle couleur*. A Gewurtztraminer '53 was 'complete', the '52 was, surprisingly, not so good as the '53. The experts pointed out that the Gewurtztraminer '53 was so complete that its bouquet came to meet one 4 inches away from one's mouth. It certainly left a delicious impression on the palate for at least five minutes after being drunk.

Before leaving Barr we went to see Monsieur Klipfel, who has a fascinating house-cum-business premises round nearly four sides of a courtyard. You drive in under the middle, there is a house on the left-hand side, a lot of children about the place, and a happy atmosphere, and amongst it all are the cellars and the bottling plant. Some advice he gave me was, 'Don't drink Alsatian wines with rich sauces, if one has a "sensitive" stomach.' He told me that the Sylvaner is best at between one or two years, Traminer from two to ten years, Riesling two to five years, and Muscats two to four. The Traminer is at its peak between four and five years, Riesling three, Muscat two. We drank from many—it was good.

Sylvaner, the cheapest of the Alsatian wines, is light, dry, should be drunk early in the meal, and is best with fish. Personally, I find it rather feeble. Gewurtztraminer (or Traminer) has considerably more body—you taste the grape very much; there is a curious and quite delightful after taste. Riesling has less body than the Traminer, lots of character. A lovely drink, nice perfume, nice bouquet. The Muscat is much more grapey, it's a lovely wine with fruit—you can taste all the colours of the rainbow.

It was sad to leave M. Klipfel and the many wines he had organized for me to taste. Fortunately he had allowed me to *cracher* (spit). It had been a trifle embarrassing, as the President of the Alsatian vine growers had arranged the *dégustation* just for the two of us—my wife was packing—at the side of a room where a team of four cheerful-looking women were gossiping as they bottled and labelled the wine.

In the champagne area I had obviously not spat out at all—champagne is not that kind of wine. You either drink it or leave it alone. It does that to you. It elevates you above your normal social environment or income level.

So this, my early morning visit to M. Klipfel, was something of a social occasion! I had been told that all the professional wine tasters spat out and had steeled myself to it, but it was as strange as a new school.

Fortunately M. Klipfel waited hardly a moment. First he threw back his head, then he masticated the wine and then out it came as easily and perfunctorily as Bernini's fountain in the Piazza Navona. He hardly opened his lips; he just pursed them like a pouting prude and lo! the wine was spreading the dust three or four yards away.

Thus encouraged, my life as a *dégustateur* was begun and for the next three-quarters of an hour I tasted and spat; sometimes as part of a duet, at others on my own as the President was called to innumerable telephone calls or crises. It was fun. When finally I left with a sample of his fine wines in my car, a blend on my palate and a nip of genuine *eau de vie framboise* in a flask, I found the sun shining.

Fixing five suitcases on top of the luggage boot of our T.R.2 sent the sun in a bit but amused the locals. Poor car! It had three very large suitcases on its tail; two normal expanders on top of them, and within the boot a Dictaphone which has made this book a pleasure instead of a chore. There was also the typewriter which links you and me at this moment, and some forty books of reference none of which was even opened in the four thousand miles of our journey.

All the same we were soon away for Mittelbergheim, a distance of about 6 miles on the well-signposted route du vin d'Alsace. Mittelbergheim is a fascinating example of a typical Lower Rhine Alsatian village. Its 680 inhabitants nearly all work on the land or in supplying those who do. It is dominated in the classical tradition by a ruin—the Château d'Andlau—and Renaissance houses huddle around the Town Hall, which is classified as an historic monument and surmounted by a stork's nest.

M. Boeckel, the Mayor and many times President of the Wine Growers and Merchants of Alsace, is sad about the stork's nest, as it is empty, and his friends chide and blame him for it. The reason? M. Boeckel is a bachelor and what self-respecting stork, traditional harbinger of fecundity, would settle in a nest provided and paid for by a society led by so irresponsible a person?

'It is very sad,' says M. Boeckel unconvincingly. 'Of course I wanted to get married, but first I had to establish myself—or so my father said—then came the first World War. After it I was too busy helping to build up the good name of our wines again. Then, before there was a moment to look round, the Germans were back again; there was the second occupation, and now I'm too old.'

His widowed sister, the lady of the house, who treats him with all the indulgence usually reserved for favourite grandchildren, chips in sternly, 'And so, despite our beautiful nest, we poor citizens of Mittelbergheim have no stork.'

There are fewer storks in Alsace now than there used to be—

probably because the plain is very much drier than it was, through modern irrigation, and because the climate has become drier through the centuries. This in turn means fewer frogs and fewer small fish, so father stork has had to work far harder than he likes. They say in Alsace that the storks announce the spring. In a cold spring they arrive late and in an early spring they arrive in February. The young storks emerge from their nests late in May or the beginning of June, and can fly well enough in August to depart with their parents probably to the source of the Nile. No one in these parts seems to know definitely where they do go.

Before lunch we had a local sherry-type wine which left me uninterested, but the meal was accompanied with much laughter and some of M. Boeckel's own wines. Mittelbergheim is particularly renowned for its Sylvaners, and the example we had with the hors d'oeuvres was certainly very good of its kind and finely green; the Gewurtztraminer '52 was almost insolently fruity, yet, like the nose of one who has had the privilege of living too well, it had behind it a dry, companionable personality.

French wine men think Belgium and England the two most wine cultivated countries in the world, and it was interesting to learn from M. Boeckel that the older Traminers are to Belgians what Château d'Yquem is to the rest of the world. They are also less than half the price. Also, that the oldest record he has of sales to England is dated 1327.

With the sweet course we drank a Muscat '53—a rich green drink that I find delicious not only with the *entremets* but also with fish. As with all the fruitier Alsatian wines, it has a distinct dryness underneath its opulent outer face. It is a late maturing wine with a very different bouquet from the sweet Muscats of Southern France. It is difficult to grow and unfortunately is seldom shipped overseas, though it travels well.

By the end of this friendly, happy, well-wined meal I was beginning to appreciate why the sales abroad of Alsatian wines are increasing faster than those of any other district.

After lunch, sitting in brilliant sunshine on a verandah on the second-floor level, surrounded by other members of the family from adjoining houses, and with a fairy-tale view over the roofs of Mittelbergheim towards the vine-filled plain and the Vosges mountains beyond, I was to learn more.

Vines in Alsace are as old as recorded time. The Roman Emperor Domitian had all the vines of Champagne and Alsace destroyed in the year 91 and the more popular Emperor Probus allowed his legions to help replant them two centuries later. The vine in Alsace was cultivated even in Herucles' day, for it is also recorded that one day, when employed in adding to the already considerable size of the Roman Empire, the great warrior Herucles pulled in at an auberge near to the eventual site of present-day Colmar. He supped, started on his way, but was persuaded to drink a goblet of local wine which he found refreshing and pleasing to the palate. He called for more and more and more until finally falling asleep. Later that evening he awoke. The sun had slipped in the heavens and was about to tuck up for the night behind the distant Vosges, and more still, his army was out of sight. He dashed off in such haste that he forgot his battle-axe, which was treasured for many generations by the descendants of the innkeeper before being finally presented to the armoury at Colmar—and if you do not believe me, go and ask the Archivist of Colmar to show it to you, because the story is his!

In the olden days the wines of Alsace were often red and were usually sold under the names of the vineyard villages, though as far back as 1552 there is mention of Muscat wine. Today, Alsatian wines are sold under the name of the grape from which they have come. This is a result of the German occupation from 1870 until 1918, when Alsatian wine was seldom sold under its own name except very locally. Instead it was shipped to Germany and used there to 'stretch' German Rhineland wines. Naturally enough, as they were being exploited, the Alsatian growers concentrated upon quantity rather than quality.

This, however, left a difficult problem when the days of German occupation ended. Should they continue with the common big-yielding plants, or grub them up and plant fresh plants from finer stocks? Fortunately for wine lovers the Alsatian growers, led then as now by a Boeckel, decided to grub up all their old stock and wait until the new plants were yielding sufficiently high-quality grapes before exporting their fruits to other parts of France or abroad.

Amongst the vines predominantly chosen were the Chasselas blanc and the Chasselas rosé, which are both excellent table grapes and give a wine much appreciated locally as a *vin du pays*— an everyday wine which is seldom exported.

Then comes Sylvaner, which is remarkable for its vivid green, its slight sparkle, and its freshness. It is the wine for high days and holidays, fresh and not too alcoholic.

The Muscat, very much drier than its namesake of Southern France, is dry but strongly perfumed. It matures slowly, needs the finest slopes and is, consequently, apt to be a pricey wine. It is very green, its flavour is unique and distinctive.

Traminer and Gerwurtztraminer are one and the same thing, except that the Gerwurtz is usually made from selections of the best of the grapes. According to year the wine ranges from being somewhat sweet to being only a little less dry than a Riesling. Its bouquet is so pronounced, so insolent, that it is one of the easiest wines to recognize. It is popular in Paris and amongst women. The Alsatians say that it is the Don Juan of wines—young and attractive, strong, heady and bold. A wine for indiscretions and follies. A wine to remember.

There are two varieties of Pinot. The Blanc, which is the same stock as that which produces the great wines of Burgundy, Champagne, and Bordeaux. In Alsace it produces an amiable wine which is often chosen to accompany the fish course at great banquets. It is to Alsace what Beaujolais is to Burgundy—a wine for gulping, not sipping. Joseph Dreyer sums them up well in *Saisons d'Alsace* as 'comfortable wines, very solid, perfectly balanced but without any special character. Resembling in fact the qualities sought in a husband for a "marriage of reason"'.

The grey Pinot is also called Tokay as it is thought to have been imported from Hungary. It is the more delicate of the two but needs a lot of attention for a relatively small return.

Like Tokay, the Riesling is quantitatively unrewarding, but its quality is so much greater that it brings a worthwhile yield. It can be somewhat astringent in a bad year, but normally it is delicate, has a delightful bouquet, and is a very complete wine. A few minutes before writing these words we drank a bottle of Schlumberger's 53, a wine that we had fallen in love with long before meeting the gracious lady and good friend of England who is the *Patronne* of the Domaines. I had brought it from a cellar at 62 degrees and put it on the lowest shelf of our refrigerator for about an hour. It was a hot day and we wanted a cool drink.

When I took it out the shelf temperature was 44 degrees (or so it was when I checked it later) and it had entirely killed the wine, which for five minutes after being poured out had lost all its bouquet. Suddenly back it came—marvellously fruity, proud, dry and distinctive.

Wines that are too cold lose nearly all their bouquet but can quickly be brought back into 'condition' by the warmth of the hand round the glass. Throwing the wine around the glass also helps considerably.

Finally, in Alsace but practically never exported is a small number of vines which make unimportant wines. The Muller-Thurgau, a light musky wine; a Gold Riesling which the Alsatians like greatly; a dry wine called Knipperle and an even drier one, Le Burger, which has been usurped as the plain man's drink by Sylvaner. As a postscript, M. Boeckel explained that one has to learn that a Zwicker is a blend of a high-grade stock with a lesser one and an Edelzwicker is a blend of two wines of fine quality.

The wines of Alsace do not as yet come fully within the control of the *appellation d'origine* laws, though the Alsatians have made many Regional laws to ensure a high standard of quality in the wines they export. These include fixing an annual minimum degree of alcohol necessary in wines that are to be allowed to call themselves 'Alsatian'. This can never be less than 8 degrees of alcohol and in a good year is between 9 and 9½ degrees. When under 8 degrees it is never allowed to be drunk as wine and can only be used for distillation. When the degree minimum has been fixed at over 8 degrees any wines that have an alcoholic content between 8 degrees and the degree minimum for the year may only be sold as *vin de consommation*, i.e. as local wine without the right to call itself Alsatian. Anything over the degree minimum for the year will be allowed to call itself Alsatian wine.

Alsatians are quite certain about which of their wines should accompany the different courses. They say:

'First of all remember that a light wine should always be served before a heavier, fuller, richer one. This is true of all wines. It is as universally true that dry wines are best with the early courses of a normal meal and sweeter or more fruity ones with the sweets or dessert.

'With hors d'oeuvres or fish a dry white wine—Sylvaner, Knipperle or Chasselas. There are those, however, who swear by a Riesling or Pinot to accompany oysters and cold fish; and an Edelzwicker with all fish.

'With the main course of roasts, game or poultry, Riesling, Muscat Traminer, or Pinot.

'With cheese, any Alsatian wine (this is always the best course to accompany the choicest wine of the evening).'

Three hours earlier we had driven under the archway of the Boeckels' outer bastions, passed the firm's offices set in a tiny peaceful courtyard, and again passed under an arch—this time the passage which joined one of the three buildings of the courtyard with another. We entered an unknown, friendly and very beautiful world. We immediately made friends. This was Alsace.

It was sad to leave and particularly so to be going to a town —Colmar, the commerical capital of the Alsatian wine industry. We had avoided Strasbourg as we know it well through my having gone there just before the first meeting of the Council of Europe to organize and be Chairman of the first international Town Forum ever to be broadcast from one country to another.

We loved its bridges, its roofs, and its old houses. We had been immensely impressed by its Cathedral and laughed at its private vulgarity; thought little of its clock; much of its *foie gras*; had the good fortune to eat at the Maison Kammerzell; had given press conferences and interviews and started something for the Americans and others to copy. We had baked in its warm May weather and wondered how politicians would stand it in August. We had been back several times and always loved it.

Colmar was different. A new town and a small town. What had it to offer?

We took the clearly marked route du vin from Mittelbergheim to Colmar. Through Andlau with its seventeenth- and eighteenth-century houses, its twelfth-century parish church with the massive rectangular porch, to Itterswiller, near whose church is one of the most wonderful of all this hill-side's views of the plain and the forests beyond; on, almost in a breath, to the Renaissance fountains of Nothalten, through Blienschwiller which is tiny, to Dambach which calls itself a town—probably because it is so pleased with its medieval ramparts and its baroque high altar which is certainly worth seeing even if you hate pretentious magnificence.

Every few kilometres along this wine road you can take a tributary down to the main Strasbourg to Colmar road. You can join people to whom time means nothing—they go too fast—or you can remain in these almost make-believe villages and townlets.

Most of them were badly damaged by the retreating Germans

in the last war; some of them had only a house or two left standing, but all of them were immediately, feverishly, rebuilt in the
traditional Alsatian style and are already again looking like an
integral part of this happy countryside.

Colmar has forty-six thousand inhabitants and adds the obvious
life and virility of a country town to the capital of a province.
It lives by wine, tourism and commerce. Georges Duhamel has
called it 'the most beautiful town in the world', but it is not easy
to find the evidence for so eulogistic a statement nor to go far
with him in this respect. It certainly has many attractive houses,
but to me it lacks character and grace. We went there for two
reasons: to meet some of the commerical leaders of the Alsatian
wine trade, and to see Grünewald's Issenheim retable in the
Unterlinden museum.

Calm, harmonious Gothic cloisters of an old Dominican convent lead to the museum and to one of the starkest, most terrible
and realistic paintings of all times. On the cross one sees too clearly
the agony and suffering that Christ was bearing for so many. It is
a face that one cannot easily forget and which one should, perhaps,
always seek to remember. The genius of the mind behind the
paintings is seen in the contrast with the triumphant, ethereal
figure of the risen Christ ascending triumphant from the sepulchre.

We stayed at the Hotel Majestic, which at that time was so
new that it had not found its way into the Guide Michelin. It is
near the station, was only opened in February 1957, and is flanked
on two sides by main streets. We were on the side overlooking a
courtyard at the back and found it quiet and well appointed.
Its restaurant was adequate.

On our way to Guebwiller, where we were to visit the Domaines
of Schlumberger and see some of their many vineyards, we went
back on the route du vin and continued our fairyland journey.
The sun shone; our little T.R.2 was open to the mountains, the
heavens, and the song of birds. We saw unlikely villages, some
perched high and bare, others half hidden by a fold in the hill-
side. Some with rivers, others with storks—all with a quiet, good
beauty emphasized by their half-timbered houses, their sense of
proportion, their dominant churches, their comparative emptiness
by day, the cheerful faces of their inhabitants, and the feeling of
communal effort.

It was as if the long period of occupation between 1870 and
1918 had given these people an even greater affection for the

land around them than one finds in other rural areas. Whereas most Frenchmen look upon Paris with the kind of personal nostalgia that one could appreciate a distant Roman legionnaire feeling for Rome, here it is the very land they tread, the house they live in, which is their centre, which to them is all of France. In all other parts we found that a large percentage of the wives of the wealthy were spending the early summer in Paris. Here, except that just a few went there to cheer a Queen of England who had become their queen for a day, we hardly found Paris mentioned.

We had lunch at the little agricultural town of Rouffach—you turn left at the traffic lights at RN.83. We admired the magnificent church of St Arbogast—obviously inspired by Strasbourg Cathedral and the old houses opposite. We found small boys who spoke only German admiring our car. We had a delightful meal at the Hotel Central—the menu was only 425 francs and consisted of potage maison, artichokes, sauce vinaigre, boiled egg and onions (sounds awful!), boiled ham with chips, haricots, sauce picot. Cheese and dessert was not included.

It was at Rouffach that the American Twelfth Division joined up with the French Fourth Moroccan Division to cut in two the 'Colmar pocket'. Happily the old town suffered surprisingly little in the process.

Before leaving Colmar and the Lower Rhine we went to see the Director of the Syndicat d'Initiative, who assured us that visitors are always welcomed by four firms without prior notice and at a number more if intending visitors first make arrangements through him. The four firms are the Cave Co-operative at Bennwihr and also at Sigolsheim, the Cave Kuehn at Ammerschwihr, and the Cave Hugel at Riquewihr. The first three of these villages were completely destroyed during the war—at Sigolsheim the convent was taken and retaken no less than seventeen times in two months with such appalling casualties that it was nicknamed 'the blood bath'. Now they are rebuilt in traditional Alsatian style but with a rather more modern layout and the lightest of schools and churches.

Riquewihr, the pearl of Alsace, was spared the ravages of the battle of the gap. Here one walks straight back into the past. Wine growers then; wine growers now. Living in the same houses as their sixteenth-century ancestors; seeing the same clematis, geraniums and flowering laurels sprawling over the same fortified walls; looking up to the same thirteenth-century beffroi; the same harmony of wall and tile; the same loving labour tending the vines. They return this love by bringing to thirsty, but very sympathetic, palates, Riesling wine as light, as full scented, and as fresh as any their fathers had before them.

Who leaves Riquewihr to 'better himself' is mad.

Leaving Colmar we immediately got off the main road and on to the route du vin. We were to stay at Murbach for three days going round their own and their neighbours' vineyards with M. Brion and M. Stoeckel of Les Domaines Schlumberger.

Murbach is a fascinating, delightful place on a steep road high up above the vineyards of Guebwiller. Thick woods and mountains enclose three sides of the Hotel St Barnabé where we stayed. The only noise was the tinkle of bells on the mountain sheep and the fall of water outside, but not too far outside, our bedroom window. The double beds are rather small, otherwise everything is exceedingly pleasant, though I suspect that the hotel may be rather too popular on summer Sundays, as it boasts a rather ominous looking miniature golf course. When we were there in the early summer of 1957 a double room cost less than a pound and meals were both reasonable in price and exceedingly good in quality.

The dining-room is embellished by murals painted in the off season by the patron—M. Kœnig—a young man with a charming family. He is also the chef. When you become friends of M. Kœnig he will show you his paintings, though he is a modest man.

You may well be relieved to find that he paints in the classical tradition. His views are recognizable and livable with; his nudes could be, too.

You may wonder for a moment why all his landscapes are wintry ones—a man cannot be cold to whom women give such expressions—one like the portrait of Lady Hamilton in the Army and Navy Club, another that can only reflect the apotheosis of a total satisfaction. Suddenly you realize why the trees look barren and the nudes do not. Poor man, he is the patron and the chef. No summer painting for him till the tourists have gone!

Up the hill to the simple grandeur of Murbach Abbey, whose monks brought cultivation of the vine to the slopes below. Down the hill to Guebwiller and Madame Schlumberger, the warmest hearted, most welcoming lady we were to meet in four thousand miles.

Monsieur Brion, her nephew by marriage, manages the

Domaine—the biggest wine producers in the High Rhine, the Region said to make the best Alsatian wines, though this is a fact hotly denied in many a wine town and village of the Lower Rhine. She loves the English but is one of the few women who temper love with abstinence, as although she used to visit England each year—from the nearby airfield it takes her barely two hours—she will never stay more than nine days and she always goes to the same friends.

Most Alsatian vineyards are small and cover only a few acres at the most. The Domaine Schlumberger is a giant by comparison, cultivating 265 acres on a south and south-east slope of the mountain of Unterlinger, extending for 2½ miles and rising from a height of 750 feet at the very back doors of Guebwiller to some 1,400 feet before meeting the pine and chestnuts of the forest. In the old days the area comprised 2,500 separately owned vineyards; gradually four generations of Schlumbergers have bought every property that has come up for sale and now there are only a handful of other properties within the great vineyard known as Schimberg. You can easily recognize these as the vines are always planted in the traditional way in rows running up and down the slope, while those of the Domaine run in the opposite direction to help prevent the soil from being washed over the containing walls or out of the vineyard altogether. These walls cover an area of some one hundred thousand square yards and divide the whole vineyard up into *parcelles* of 7 to 12 acres devoted each to a single stock, those in the most favourable position being planted with Traminer, Pinot Gris and Riesling, those in the middle range with Sylvaner and Knipperle, and the remainder with Meunier and Chasselas.

Outside the retaining walls are wide paths from which giant sprays can cover the whole vineyard area and along which motor tractors bring supplies to the plants and which enable the harvest to be taken back quickly to the wine presses. M. Brion, a lean knickerbockered enthusiast who changes quickly from the appearance of peasant farmer to aristocrat at the fall of day and with the addition of an evening cloak, told me that he is experimenting this year with spraying from the air.

Much of the work, like tying the vines on to wires at the comparatively low height for Alsace of 3 feet, and the hoeing, is done by bands of women who pass through each parcel at least five times a year.

D

Harvesting starts amongst the less important grapes and ends, sometimes, with snow on the ground with the Traminer and Pinot Gris in the middle of the Schimberg. Here—almost exclusively in these northern vineyards—the *pourriture noble* is sought. This is a method of vine husbandry practised in particular in the Sauternes area of Bordeaux. It means that the harvest is delayed until the grapes have begun to shrivel on the vine, losing much of their juice in the process. This produces a kind of fermentation and gives the wine a greater, fuller sweetness as well as a very much higher alcoholic content than it would have had if it had been harvested earlier. It also means a much slower and therefore more costly harvest, as the pickers take only the grapes on which the *pourriture noble* has set in, and this will mean going over each bunch a number of times as the grapes ripen gradually according to the amount of sun and shade that they receive.

Anyone interested in an outstanding example of the application of modern methods together with the retention of the old craftsmanship and principles should visit the Domaines Schlumberger, where M. Brion has promised that my readers will have a very special welcome. In addition to this fascinating example of big-scale viticulture he will see fine hydraulic presses which press gently but fast; vast glass-lined reservoirs of wine; the latest principles in refrigeration; and all this alongside some eighty modern houses built to accommodate the workers; farms housing the cows and horses whose manure is needed for the land, and forests from which come the stakes that stand tall and gaunt in the winter months or lie hidden in green or golden foliage as sun ripens one of God's greatest gifts to man.

From Murbach or Guebwiller one should go up into the wooded mountains behind Schweighouse on to D.40. There is a superb and woody mountain road banked by little black cherry trees, which make the good Kirsch liqueur. The Alsatians love liqueurs, but the genuine framboise made from wild mountain raspberries is getting very rare and exorbitantly expensive. Raspberry pickers used to be like hop pickers, and came with their children for great parties and a good time, but now they are no more.

The forests belong half to the State and half to the local authority, although the bottom part of the woods, those parts which adjoin the vineyards, nearly always belongs to the vineyards leading up to them. After the vineyards end it is their bit of wood for some distance, and it is there they get all the stakes for their vines.

Every now and again you come across large restaurants with clearings around them about the size of five or six tennis courts, otherwise thick wood. On a Sunday you find lots of Alsatians up here singing, dancing, eating, drinking, and being happy.

If anyone abuses the strong wine and drinks so much that he gets *une chaude tête*—'warm head'—you will notice him go off wine and drink a glass of Vichy water which, they say, is an absolutely perfect cure. I cannot vouch for this as I did not drink too much, though I drank a lot.

D.40 goes on to Osenbach, a very good surface all the way, and then on to D.1 towards Epernay. In the course of motoring some 10 miles along it I saw only one country bus and two bullocks drawing manure carts. We came to Gueberschwihr— at least we were half a mile away from it by road and about 500 feet above it, the signpost D.1 pointing to St Marc. There they lost about 100 per cent of their vines this spring, but from that position on the road you get one of the most superb panoramas I have ever seen. On the left the ancient village of Hattstatt, on the right walled Pfaffenheim with its giant church and Rouffach enclosed in streams and poplars. We were there on Sunday and the church bells mingled their messages in our ears. Vines and wooden houses everywhere. The superb roofs of Gueberschwihr, its lovely church steeple—relic of an ancient Roman church—and the luscious green valley stretching for mile upon mile upon mile. In the plain some vineyards and many woods. The lower vine-yards consist of mixed vine stocks for local consumption, and then towering forests in the distance.

The plain that we looked across behind Gueberschwihr is 18 miles wide as the stork flies. I notice that here the workers in the fields nod their heads in greeting to you as you pass, just as in Rutland. They work Saturday mornings, and indeed do in most parts of France, but the children that work on Saturday mornings do not work at all on Thursday.

We went on to a very fascinating little village, Les Trois Epis, which rests just behind stork-nested Turckheim, where the Queen of Holland used to spend her holidays between the wars. It has one of the most wonderful views in Europe, and is where the rich men of Colmar live. There are also some good hotels there. Again on the route du vins to Kaysersberg, where a stone sentry box on the bridge is a picturesque reminder that this happy-looking, higgledy-piggledy town has endured many wars as well as an intense bombardment in 1944. Unhappily, Kaysersberg went modern in the early nineteenth century and pulled down the ancient church steeple which old prints show emerging harmoniously from the narrow unchanged streets which today are so delightful to the eye but tortuous to the traffic. Even Hansi who loved his Alsace with all the devotion of a poet whose land endures foreign occupation, says that the 'new' town is 'without character and without elegance'. He has only one excuse, 'Its warm orange colour makes a pretty spot in the green valley.'

We dropped down on to the plain at Guémar to lunch at the Brickerd restaurant, where we learnt that Traminer is the drink Alsatians take with their foie gras and where just for fun we drank both a Klipfel and a Hugel Grand Cru Riesling '53, with the *poularde de Bresse*. We all felt that the Hugel won handsomely.

Our afternoon was spent tasting, viewing, and much motoring, during which we twice passed through Ostheim. These villages tumble haphazardly about the mountain sides. All are poems in their own right. A curiosity is Ostheim, which was entirely destroyed in the war. It has been completely rebuilt except for one fragment of the wall of a church. 'Why?' you ask. Because that crumbling wall is surmounted by a stork's nest and storks bring luck. I saw her twice. First sitting upright and proud and secondly huddled with her crown just showing as she sought both to keep her brood dry and escape herself from the slanting rain.

In the evening we returned to Guebwiller to collect Madame Schlumberger and set out again to the other side of Colmar to try out a restaurant which she had heard much of but never visited. It was L'Auberge de Ill at Illhausern, a new inn in a village completely destroyed in the war. The village was, as ever, rebuilt in the traditional Alsatian timbered way except for the church, which is completely modern in style with a fascinating light wooden door and a stork's nest, though as yet no stork, on the lean curving roof.

The restaurant turned out to be one of the finest in France and is under the direction of M. Haeberlin, who had recently received the Diploma of Honour of French Gastronomy for a dinner he had served at the Grand Palais des Champs Elysées. A dish he is particularly proud of is *La Ballottine de Pigeon Prince Rainier*. On the face of it, it seemed no great compliment to the Prince to call a pigeon dish after him, nor in a land of superlative food did it sound particularly attractive to eat. However, I was persuaded— I usually am when harassed by an enthusiastic gourmet—and I shall never regret the choice. The pigeon turned out to be the least important part of the dish. To start with, every single bone had been removed from the body without appreciably cutting it. I gathered that they had mostly been pulled out and that the process takes a considerable time. Anyhow the carcass certainly maintained its usual shape, but what came out of its middle was unbelievable and ethereal: rare and very rich. It certainly contained foie gras. It was a dish to dream of and, I should think, often to make one dream, though in our case it did not. In case you think of going to visit M. Haeberlin, consult the current Michelin guide and then relate the cost of this glimpse of gastronomic heaven with the size of your purse. The table d'hôte menu this night was, I think, about thirty shillings. The *Ballottine de Pigeon* cost a pound a portion and some succulent trout braised in Riesling hardly less. Our dinner was certainly not dear at the price, but the price was certainly high!

It was sad to leave next morning after these happy days of meeting new friends; of tasting and wining and dining. We had motored several hundred miles in our week in Alsace and our abiding impression was that here is a land that one could happily come back to time and time again. All wine people have their roots in the soil—these were especially deep ones, as for forty-eight long years the people had been stateless. They never acknowledged the German occupation of 1870 but they were entirely severed from the land of France. And so they turned to the land and the buildings on it with a kind of passionate devotion that still courses in their veins. This was their little France; their happy land.

IV

Burgundy

THE VOSGES on one side, Swiss mountains on the other, and in between a plain containing two rather sad and apprehensive people in an open T.R.2. Sad because we were leaving new friends whom we had found delightful, apprehensive because we were going into one of the most sophisticated vineyard regions in the world—somewhat awe inspiring for two incompletely equipped amateurs.

The road from Alsace to Beaune is a pleasant one, particularly around Belfort. Sudden bends bring sudden views; thick woods enclose lush meadows; this is ideal picnicking country but there were no cars with G.B. on the back drawn up according to temperament in the shadows of a copse or the glare of a 'lay-by' nor were there any of the expensive-looking restaurants which attract Belgian and American-owned cars like moths to a chrome-mounted candle. This is off-the-beat-land.

A French friend had told us that if you see two or more lorries pulled up outside the doorway of a clean-looking *routier* it means that the food is good value for a steak and chips and some cheap wine and cheese. We thought we would try it and had a chance at Clerval where there is a gay looking *routier* just over the bridge. There were no lorries parked outside but there were two cars and it was Sunday so we could not expect many lorries anyway!

The dining room was charming but the menu was 14/- and very recherché—soup, duck, salad, fruit or cheese, coffee and a quarter of a bottle of Côtes du Rhône wine per person all included. The patrône was welcoming; her daughter nimble-fingered; the tables gay and the flowers plentiful. Unfortunately the food was ill-prepared and we left disappointed, in spite of the crowd admiring the T.R.2 with its gross overload of suitcases.

It was mid-May burning sunshine that afternoon and as we approached Beaune my excitement mounted as it does before returning to almost any of my adolescent haunts.

It is curious how the old emotions stay with us throughout our lives. How much easier life would be if any of us really grew up or even if the young realised that older generations share their same longings and fears and emotions—age brings restraint but little else except regrets.

I had lived for a year in Lyons, the commercial capital of mid-France. Had been more than happy there; worked a little; lived a lot. Played a season of Rugger for one of the great sides of France; gradually learnt how to drink Beaujolais for Beaujolais with them; gone back a dozen or more times; felt vicariously what occupation had meant to them and seen the spot where the Germans had murdered four boys in the Place Bellecour.

I had drunk many 'pots' of Beaujolais—especially at the Brasserie des Archers which was the headquarters of the Football Club de Lyon and I had been invited soon after the war to the banquet of the Wine Fair held at Mâcon.

This, though, was different. I was coming to Beaune, the capital of the wine district I believed to be the greatest in the world, with introductions to its peers—Louis Jadot, Louis Latour, Pierre Poupon, François Bouchard, Pierre Forgeot, Pierre Ponnelle, Jean Mommessin, J. Bichot—these and other great ones were to be my guides for a fortnight in the small, clearly defined district wherein a large percentage of the finest and most sought-after wines in the world is made.

My ever-obliging nervous system pumped an extra supply of adrenalin into my veins; my face reddened; my pulse quickened, and there we were in Beaune and receiving a most unwelcoming reception from an elderly maid at an hotel where we shall never stay again. She really was a *very* unwelcoming old lady, though she got slightly better during the week. First she looked at our luggage and said she presumed that we would not want it all in our bedroom; then she asked us to be in the hotel by 9 p.m., as there were no other guests—it is a commercial hotel with a Monday to Friday trade. Next morning she complained when we arrived down to breakfast at nine. On the other hand, the sister hotel which is under the same family management has an excellent table. Its restaurant is always full—weekends with Beaunois; weekdays with commercial travellers, despite the fact that it is neither the cheapest nor most comfortable restaurant in Beaune. Its speciality is value for money, and as if to accentuate this you get something as near to vinegar as I have ever drunk out of a wine bottle if you order the cheapest wine, though if you cast higher up the wide and fairly priced choice on the card you can get a first-class wine more cheaply than almost anywhere for miles. A curious pair of hotels with, they tell me, an interesting story behind them.

Some day, someone will write the great story of a small hotel —not the Grand Babylon type with the heroine cupping her small, lovely, mirrored breast in her hand, but a tale of struggle and sweat; of ever-changing direction always on the make; of the fears and worries of the staff; of high life below stairs and low life above; of cooking and cuddling; of love freely given and jobs dearly bought. A tale of cellars filled with fine wines lovingly cared and fairly sold. Of others in which dark things happen and whence quick profits are made from non-returning guests; of floods and follies; dirt and desire; of work well done and scuffled over; of creatures of all colours, creeds, and make-believe who for one day and age can call that place their home.

Most people approach Beaune from the Dijon-Lyons road. We had hit it from the side via Besançon and Dôle. Our first job, then, was to take the long road out towards the north and Chablis. This area, where the wine is the perfect accompaniment to the oyster, is easily reached by anyone taking N.6 for the south and sunshine. If you are wise you will have stopped at Saulieu for a meal or to stay the night either at the Poste, which has the grander bedrooms, or at the Côte d'Or, which is one of the eleven restaurants in the whole of France to which the Michelin guide has given its highest ranking of three stars.

We always stay and eat at the Poste, because we happened to have the most memorable meal of our life there when passing along this much travelled highway almost immediately after the war when on our way to write and take part in a programme called 'Lyon Revisited'—I, the re-visitor; Ted Livesey, the writer.

We went in tired, hungry and meat-starved. The meal we had was more gourmand than gourmet, but that was not M. Bonneau's fault. First an enormous hors d'oeuvre and then, after sharing a leg of lamb and a bottle of Bonnes Mares, a sumptuous *Gougère* (a cheese brioche); we thought we should never feel starved again. My only advice is to go there for dinner rather than lunch—and to follow Jorrocks's maxim—'Where I eats I sleeps.'

The drive from Saulieu to Chablis via Auxerre is easy and the total detour from N.6 to Chablis, Dijon and Beaune, which means in effect driving through the whole 120 mile length of the

Burgundy wine district, is only about 50 miles of a road which is far less crowded than N.6.

The vineyards of Burgundy are subject—like all those of France except Alsace—to very rigid control laws passed in the 1930s and called *Appellations d'origine*, or *Appellation contrôlée*.

This control is severe and covers all sides of wine making and its sale by wholesalers and retailers. Like all laws made on a National basis but controlling a Regional product, it is much criticized and sometimes rightly. It does, however, ensure that only wines grown from the stock that time has proved to be the most suitable will henceforth be grown in any area; that vines are only planted on the best sites—or else they have a minor title or are not entitled at all to the words *appellation contrôlée* on their labels; that they are planted at so many to the acre and are allowed to produce only so much wine. They even go into such details as the height to which the vines are allowed to grow and—very important this—the minimum degree of alcohol in the wine.

To benefit, at the receiving end, from the 109 wines of Burgundy entitled to an appellation it is important to know what they are and that they are not by any means of equal importance.

First of all we have to remember that the appellations fall into four classifications.

1. GENERIC APPELLATIONS

There are seven generic classifications which merely assure that the wine comes from within the territory of Burgundy as defined as a wine district. This means that they will be little wines usually coming from the plains (*i.e.* the vineyards with the least good orientation); they are also allowed to be planted more closely together than the more important classifications; their degree of alcohol is lower and their stock is not necessarily of the greatest. These will come to you with just a label containing one of the following names:

Bourgogne or Burgundy; Bourgogne Passe Tout Grains; Bourgogne Aligoté; Bourgogne Ordinaire; Bourgogne Grand Ordinaire or Bourgogne Clairet or Bourgogne Rosé if it is a Rosé wine. It will have the words *appellation contrôlée* printed on the label—as all the following and more important wines will have.

This will at least be some guarantee that the wine is an honest wine from the country and district it purports to come from—

though, unfortunately, it is comparatively easy for dishonest shippers in other countries, but more difficult in France, to mix inferior wines with the better ones.

It is of paramount importance therefore, if you enjoy wine, to deal with very reputable wine merchants, of whom fortunately there are many.

2. VILLAGE APPELLATIONS

A very large number of villages are entitled to produce wine called under the name of the village. These include:

Moulin à Vent, Fleurie, etc., in the Beaujolais; Mâcon, Pouilly Fuissé, etc., in the Mâconnais; Beaune, Volnay, Nuits Saint Georges, Meursault, etc., in the Côte d'Or; Chablis in the Yonne.

3. THE PREMIERS CRUS OR FIRST GROWTHS

In each village the vineyards are divided into *climats*; the best situated should produce the best wines and are allowed to add the name of the *climat* to that of the village. For example, in Vosne Romanée ten *climats* or vineyards can call themselves Vosne Romanée *premier cru*, or instead of the words *premier cru* can give their name—Les Beaux Monts, Les Suchots, etc.

4. LES GRANDS CRUS

Finally there are the great growths which by their position on the slopes, by the comparatively small quantity allowed to be harvested to the acre, and by the traditional high quality of their output, are allowed just to call themselves by the single name of the vineyard: Chambertin, Musigny, Corton, Richebourg, Clos de Vougeot, Montrachet, etc. Even then there may be, and is, a difference in quality in wines bearing the same name and appellation. This is well instanced with Clos de Vougeot, which is the *grand cru* of the commune of Vougeot, but which has sixty-five proprietors within the 226 acres of its great vineyard.

If you cannot find accommodation in small Saulieu all is not lost: all you will have to do is journey on a further 25 miles to Auxerre, capital of the department of the Yonne and a town whose considerable beauty is enhanced by the perspective given it by the two hillocks on which it perches. Its Cathedral at St Etienne was founded in the fourth century and has become one of the world's most perfect examples of thirteenth- and fourteenth-century

Gothic architecture with a striking resemblance to some of the Gothic architecture of the Champagne country. It was probably here that a church synod in 581 included amongst many others a law which forbade 'anyone to disguise himself at the New Year as a cow or a stag nor give himself up to excessive eating and drinking'. This seems to show a latent fear on the part of the Church that its Gallic adherents might revert to the paganism and water-worshipping that they practised before the coming of Christianity and the wine that Jesus blessed and the Church traded. It also seems to establish that the vine was not producing fine wines at that time, because ever since the Burgundians have become to a notable degree wine worshippers, though always recognizing that wine is one of God's greatest gifts which, like the love of a woman, can lead to perpetual misery if abused.

Chablis has been associated with oysters for many hundreds of years. Just as oysters need the acidity of lemon so can they equally be the perfect compliment, or vice versa of this driest of wines of which, according to Monseigneur Le Vin and my amateur translation, the Chevalier de Piis who presided at the Restoration dinner of the Epicureans said:

> *Qui pourrait mettre en oublie*
> *Le limpide et sec Chablis*
> *Qui joint, à tant d'autres titres*
> *L'art de faire aimer les huitres.*[1]

Chablis is one of those little wine towns which seems to live only for its vines and their wine. Picturesquely dressed M. Bergerand keeps a magnificent table and twelve rooms at *L'Etoile* and has given me some of his most famous recipes. But this is no tourist resort. If one comes here it must be because of the wine of Chablis.

In the old days Chablis was an exceedingly important wine production area producing a third of the total output of Burgundy. Then, between France's saddest year (1870) and 1900, came eight years when frost almost entirely destroyed the wine harvest, including one when the frost came in September. Two harvests

---

[1] 'Who can forget,
Limpid and dry Chablis,
Which to many another virtue adds
Enrichment to the oyster.'

were also ruined by mildew, and then came complete destruction of the grape roots by phylloxera, the louse—which was accidentally brought from America by some get-rich-quick French vintner who imported American vine stocks experimentally and thereby ruined hundreds of thousands of his fellow countrymen.

Fortunately it was soon found that the American root was immune to the disease and gradually all the old French varieties of grape were grafted on to American roots.

These bad years followed swiftly by complete destruction left only the richest in a position to replant—others had to go over to cereal farming, and as a result the only vineyards replanted after the scourge of phylloxera were in the region of the *grands crus*, though many small holdings continued to provide wine for the family, except in a bad farming year when they were forced to sell some.

M. Poupon, who was our guide to Chablis, explained why the Chablis region is a hard one. The vineyards are too near the northern limit for easy propagation of the vine; the vineyards are lower in the valley than in Champagne, and are much more vulnerable to spring frosts. Like Champagne, too, the vine roots are bedded in a subsoil of chalk or bituminous clay which gives the wine its clean, flinty and delicate taste.

Today the Chablis region is small—there are seven vineyards entitled to call themselves Chablis Grand Crus and some twenty can be called Chablis followed by the words *premier cru* or the name of their commune. Apart from these there is only a very large number of smallholders each making a tiny amount of wine and in many cases selling only their surplus to the merchant. Like all wine growers, they love their wine and therefore a surplus comes only in a very abundant year or when their other crops have done so badly that they are forced to cut down on their personal consumption of wine.

World demand for Chablis being far ahead of supply, it is always relatively expensive, and frequently the equivalent of the whole harvest is sold in France alone. In *The Wines of France* Alexis Lichine quotes M. Michel, one of the best of the seventy-seven growers of Chablis, as saying, 'I would say that less than a quarter of all the Chablis drunk every year is genuine. Maybe less than ten per cent.' Whilst Maurice Healey goes as far as saying, 'As French law does not run in England, the bottle of Chablis you get in a little Soho restaurant may not even be Gamay

Chablis' (a true Chablis comes from the Pinot, but in the plain, where the risks of frost are greatest, the hardier Gamay is often planted—this is not illegal as French law says only that the wine must be white), and goes on, 'It may come from one of the devil's cauldrons where they make the wine that ignorant people drink to their harm.' How then to recognize your genuine Chablis? First of all confine your purchases to a firm you know to have been reputably in business for some time or, if a newcomer, with the very, very highest credentials. Then, buy only a *Grand Cru* or a bottle with the words *premier cru* and *Appellation contrôlée* on the label or with the name of one of the communes given later. If you buy a bottle of what the French call Petit Chablis it will probably come from a Chardonnay grape; will possibly have the name Chablis on the bottle and a date. Neither is any guarantee of anything except that you can get a far better dry wine to accompany your oysters at less money and from a good vineyard in other parts of Burgundy, or, indeed, from the Loire or Alsace. Here is a list of the lawful designations of Chablis wine.

THE CHABLIS GRANDS CRUS

Vaudésir, Preuses, Les Clos, Grenouilles, Bougros, Valmur, and Blanchots.

Many reference books give La Moutonne as a Chablis *grands crus*. In fact, it is and it is not. Moutonne is a registered trading name of a merchant, Long Dupaquit, whose wine comes from the Vaudesir vineyard. Vaudesir is a *grand cru* by law. The name Moutonne is not, though it hides one!

CHABLIS PREMIERS CRUS

On the right bank of the Serein—Montée de Tonnerre, Châpelot, Pied d'Aloup, Mont-de-Milieu, Vaucoupin, Vaulorent, Fourchaume, Côte-de-Fontenay, Vaupulent. On the left bank of the Serein—Beaurroy, Troêne, Côte-de-Léchet, Les Lys, Séche, Chatain, Vaillon, Beugnon, Melinots, Butteaux, Les Forêts, Montmain, Vosgros, Vaugiraud, Roncières.

Dr. Guyot gives this appreciation: 'The wines of Chablis occupy one of the highest places in the ranks of French wines. Sprituous without seeming so, with body, finesse, and a charming perfume, their whiteness and clearness are remarkable. Despite their great and enduring reputation, their value is higher than their renown.'

For ourselves we delighted in the wine and think its steel-hard dryness and its green flecked colour well worth the longish journey from Beaune.

After the sound and fury of N.6 the quiet adequacy of N.5 takes one easily along the 70 miles to Dijon, the ancient capital of Burgundy.

It is certainly worth a stay during any visit to the Burgundy vineyards, as, though it is very much at the northern end except for isolated Chablis, one can easily do the journey into Beaune in half an hour.

François Ière, who was apt to see his land through spectacles of purest rose, paused at Talant on his way south to win the battle of Marignan. Looking down on the city, his well-travelled eye approved its fine buildings enclosed with massive walls; its imposing houses and picturesque squibbling streets; its mass of towers and spires—all a vast, living tribute to the wealth and energy of the ruling family, all subordinate to the massive structure of Louis XI's immense château, itself dominated by a huge watch tower whose 360 steps must have contributed considerably to the physical fitness of the guard.

François, his horse pulled up, sat quietly regarding the city for some minutes and then remarked, or so the oldest inhabitants tell you 'What a city of gracious spires.'

Like Oxford, though not yet known as 'city of screaming tyres', it is certainly a busy town today. If you are particularly interested in food and wine, take an autumn holiday there and visit it during its Food and Wine fortnight at the beginning of November: the weather is usually good. Try jugged hare with Pommard; carp with wine sauce; Pauchouse, which is a wine stew; capon with a Chambertin, or chicken fried in Volnay. Try a hundred *dégustations* (tastings).

You will be struck by the liveliness and vigour of the inhabitants; by their readiness to help you on your way; by the finest museum in France apart from the Louvre; by the grandeur of the great Palais and the line of the buildings facing it; by the view of its many ornate roofs—some like Northern Italy, others more friendly like Bruges—that you can look down upon after struggling up the gradually narrowing stairs of the tower of Philippe Le Bon.

From there you get, too, a superb panoramic view over to the rolling hills of the Côte d'Or and the Côte de Nuits with Dijon itself round and flat and embanked rather like the bottom of a dripping pan. You are allowed up the Tower at 10.30, 14.00, 15.00 and 16.00 hours and it cost us 10 francs.

You may find the Cathedral rather vast and unfriendly, but you will almost certainly be delighted by the church of Nôtre Dame built by the people of Dijon between 1230 and 1251. It quickly became the church of the people, though, in fact, it was also the church beloved by the Dukes of Burgundy. It is a most beautiful example of thirteenth-century Gothic and seems, somehow, to have acquired a special unity and grace—possibly because of its uninterrupted construction during such a remarkably short time.

We went into its light, happy, reverent atmosphere at about eleven in the morning. A constant stream of women shoppers came in quietly to pray or to enter the confessionals from which the lower half of their legs stuck out incongruously beneath the enveloping tapestry. Outside all was heat and hurry and the mundane, ant-like inconsistencies which total LIFE. Here was quiet and peace and GOD.

A few yards away from the Church the streets are closed to traffic and are a mass of jostling shoppers and stall-holders. We were immensely impressed by the picturesqueness of these streets in the old quarter, especially the Rue Musette and Place Grangier, where the housewife goes into action with her hair down and with no quarter given or asked.

The journey from Dijon to Beaune can be done at speed or slowly and reflectively—in keeping with the solemnity of a journey along *la route des grands crus*.

One soon realizes that the slopes on the right are almost covered with vines and that where they occur on the left the low-lying vines must inevitably get less sun and more frost than their aristocratic neighbours on the other side of the main road.

If you like wine the signposts will send you or your thoughts coursing off to the right; to Fixin with its deep red wines, its unexpected museum to Napoleon—a curious place to find tributes to the man who is alleged to have favoured Chambertin and Champagne above all other wines; to Gevry Chambertin, where the *Route des Grand Crus* actually starts and which boasts two of the most renowned vineyards in the world—Chambertin and Chambertin-Clos-de-Beze.

The vine road goes on to Morey St Denis, which produces

excellent wines little known either in France or outside, because for many years until the passing of the laws of *appellation contrôlée* they were sold as wines of Nuits St George. Many people think them the best value of any of the great wines today. I was particularly impressed by the colour and bouquet of a bottle of '49 Clos de Tart, one of the three outstanding vineyards of Morey, which I drank at dinner with M. Jean Mommessin one hot summer evening in his charming country house on the edge of Mâcon.

Quietly, vinously, the road curls on to velvety Musigny, which is intensely proud of its village church as well as its great vineyards.

Then on to the tiny town of Vougeot with its vineyard of just under 126 acres enclosed by a vast wall built by the Cistercians who owned the vineyard. It is now divided between many owners, though only a century ago it all belonged to one man, for France, too, has her problems of death duties. It is said of Vougeot that its fame is such that Napoleon ordered that all French military units should present arms as they marched past it. The story is also told of Colonel Bisson.[1]

The road goes on to Vosne Romanée, which commences a few yards past the south-western side of the Vougeot vineyard, producing, many think, the finest red wine in the world. One of its many outstanding vineyards, Romanée Conti, is known as the queen of wines, the wine said to have cured Louis XIV, thrilled Louis XV, and made Madame de Pompadour gastronomically covetous. It is only some 4½ acres large, but has been granted its own *appellation contrôlée*. There is a charming, gay-umbrella'd café on the main road just outside Vosne Romanée; I found it very expensive.

The last of the great wine communes on the Dijon-Beaune road is the one most easily pronounced by Anglo-Saxons and therefore very popular with them—Nuits St Georges. It is traversed by electric pylons and is scarred by the quarrying at Comblanchien, from which the Law Courts of Brussells were built, and the indignity of a television mast on the slopes of its share of the Mountain of Beaune—a mere slope of some 550 feet. It is a large area covering nearly 950 acres and is said to have the best weather of any in the Côte des Nuits. Its wine is full and dark but matures more quickly than those of Gevrey Chambertin.

[1] See Stendhal, *Mémoires d'un Touriste*.

Then come some lesser vineyards on the plain, and finally the prosperous and surprisingly small city of Beaune, in olden days often the home of the Dukes of Burgundy. Now, except for its commerce and wine, as aloof from the battle of life as Bruges.

Before and after going to Beaune I heard critical stories about dark deeds in its cellars.

The complaint is that the wine is 'stretched'—that large amounts of cheaper wine from the Côtes du Rhône, Provence, and Algeria are added to the Burgundy from the great communes. Many consider this proved by the fact that sales of wine to Beaune from these other sources are considerably greater when Burgundy has had a poor year in either quantity or quality. Is this necessarily cause and effect?

Before condemning the Beaune merchants out of hand one must remember that in the plains many smaller wines, like those of the *vins fin de la Côte de Nuits*, and all those cultivated by their peasant owners as a spare-time occupation, will suffer the most, because of their lower elevation, from any spring frosts. This was particularly obvious in the early summer of 1957, when most of the tiny vineyards growing wine for personal consumption were wiped out.

Now, these thousands who cultivate their vines simply for their families' own pleasure are amongst the greatest wine drinkers in France. They are mostly men and women who work long hot summer hours in the intense heat; who take a couple of bottles or so out with them to the fields, and who expect as their right a bottle or two in the evenings and more on the fête days with which their calendar is liberally embellished.

Quite obviously they are not going in a time of shortage to buy the already overpriced great Burgundy wines, for which world demand is at least double the potential supply. So, according to pocket, they buy the wines of Provence or Algeria, whilst their slightly more affluent fellows who normally buy the recognized wines of the plain, turn to the Côtes du Rhône when the plain wines are in short supply and priced up because of scarcity. An ingenious theory and my own!

All the same it is unpleasantly obvious that many of the wines which are sold in other countries as Mâcon, Beaujolais, or Chablis, to mention three of the most 'stretched', are not from the districts where these delightful wines are grown. Fraud probably exists in Beaune—it exists in all communities—but

E

far worse wine frauds occur in the importing countries, where it is equally easy to mix cheaper wines with better ones and where the French laws of *appellation contrôlée* do not run.

The French are making constant and largely successful efforts to ensure the honest shipping of wine. Those who criticize them seldom make any at all. In England we have many thousands of shippers and merchants whose businesses have been built up during centuries of honest trading and whose names stand high. Unfortunately there are others who are in business for quick profits. It is not difficult to find out which are the good firms and to deal with one of them.

Like many a provincial town, Beaune has an appearance of quiet friendliness enlivened by a large number of pleasantly noisy children. The Place Carnot is quite delightful with cafés on two sides, a number of streets running away from it, and the towering spectacular roofs of the Hospices just behind.

Its principal and unique glory, the Hospice de Beaune, was built between 1443 and 1451 as a gift to the poor by Nicholas Rollin, Chancellor for sixty years to John the Fearless and the great Philippe the Good, Dukes of Burgundy. Louis XI was uncharitable enough to remark that 'It is only right that Rollin, having impoverished so many people, should build a hospital to accommodate them.' It is more likely that his charming wife, Guigone de Salin, persuaded him to embark upon this glorious tribute to his own success and the God who made it possible. In fact, Rollin's own character was fine and fearless. René Hervouin has said of him, 'He had enemies but overthrew them; he wore great responsibility with Christian solicitude and eventually decided to build and found L'Hostel Dieu de Beaune in recognition "of the great gifts that God, source of all goodness, has brought me in abundance".'

It is a sobering thought that of all the tremendous and magnificent state buildings built under his orders for the Dukes of Burgundy, all except this gift of charity have perished by war or through the dust of time.

Its art treasures and this 'infirmary for poor sick people who are in danger of death' make Beaune worth a visit quite apart from the many wines which lie waiting in the depths of its cellars or beneath old encircling walls and bastions.

A short passage leads from a typical small town street to another world. First one sees a superb courtyard, where the annual wine sales of the Hospice occur nearly every November, except when, as in 1956, the vintage is only thought good enough to be sold as Burgundy without the names of the famous vineyards that have been bequeathed to the Hospice during the centuries.

These sales are bustling, important affairs and are the first indication of international buyers' appreciation of the recent vintage which they have had an opportunity of tasting only the evening before.

For two reasons prices are apt to be on the high side—firstly, the wines have an international reputation, and secondly, because the receipts go to charity.

The Flemish-like courtyard is enclosed with graceful, timbered buildings, the grey and golden sloping roofs of the one opposite the entrance taking the eye upwards to the skies as if to underline how close in spirit these noble buildings are to the infinite above them.

Visitors (every forty-five minutes) are shown a vast kitchen with, on one side, a magnificent turnspit which turns any of three spits gently for hours. The steelwork of the spit and the old utensils gleam and glitter in the afternoon sun from the courtyard outside; opposite is a modern cooking range with vast electric and gas ovens. The menu is an attractive one and with a great variety of choice.

Nuns dressed in blue-and-white medieval robes, their serious faces crowned with large pointed cowls, fetch and carry, quietly and efficiently. Here one is mixing medicines in the dispensary; there through a half-open doorway is another stooping so compassionately, so gently, over a frail white figure; and nearby another looking at samples displayed by a travelling salesman. This is love, not work. All is repose, silence and gentleness.

Visitors are allowed to see the old chapel whose long walls are lined with little cubicles laid out now as they were at the time when they were peopled by the aged sick. In each a bed clothed in white sheets and bright red blankets. Deep white curtains enabled each inmate to achieve some measure of privacy; a thick hemp bell cord hung within easy reach and so did a bottle of wine, a pewter mug and a pair of gay, blue slippers. The daily wine ration was stopped some years ago.

As they lay there, the sick faced the altar and could join in the services. By their side a crucifix and the figure of the One who showed the way that was soon to be theirs. Around them goodness and grace.

The Hospital's museum contains some lovely tapestries and pictures, including Van der Weyden's world-famous 'Resurrection'. The guide will produce a magnifying glass and show you otherwise invisible hairs painted on a soldier's chin.

A former residence of the Dukes of Burgundy and the Kings of France is now the Burgundy wine museum. It is well worth a visit. The whole process of Burgundian wine making is displayed both photographically and through implements, barrels, measures, deeds, manuscripts and paintings. New and old, valuable and mundane.

There are a number of lovely examples of beautiful shallow silver bowls with charming curved handles called 'Coupe de Mariage'. They hold about half a pint of liquid and in olden days were drunk by the bride in the porch of the church before walking in for the ceremony. The custom is now dead, but the cups are handed down from generation to generation and can often be seen in use as a flower bowl.

The oldest mention of wine in Burgundy is in a manuscript written by Eumène, a Professor of Autun, to the Emperor Constantine at the beginning of the fourth century. 'These vines are much admired by those who know nothing better, but are so old they are hardly worth cultivating; the roots of unknown age have intermingled a thousand times, which stops them growing deep enough, and the subsoil is too exposed through rain and sun having forced the top soil down the slopes.' This loss of top soil is still a problem sixteen hundred years later!

The vines soon improved, and Gregory of Tours acclaimed their virtues as long ago as the sixth century when he said, 'On the west are very fertile mountains covered with vines which provide a noble nectar described as Wines of Chalon'; one finds that a *pièce* (228 litres in Burgundy) cost 165 francs in 1803. Now it costs at least 160,000 francs. The Clos de Tarts—a wine we drank subsequently with M. Mommessin, was the most expensive wine quoted on a long invoice, and in those days cost 450 francs for a piece—at least 200 times less than it costs today!

THE WINES OF THE CÔTE D'OR

The Côte D'Or is by far the most important vineyard area in Burgundy and, to many, the most important in the world. It

contains the Communes of Fixin; Gevrey Chambertin; Morey
St. Denis; Chambolle Musigny; Vougeot and Nuits St. George.
Additionally a number of vineyards situated in the communes of
Fixin; Brochon; Prissey; Comblanchien and Corgoloin can claim
the generic title of Vins Fins de la Côte de Nuits. These are vine-
yards of lesser quality than the great ones which carry the com-
mune name but are more important than the remainder of the
wines of burgundy which carry the generic title of Bourgogne or
Bourgogne Passe Tout Grains; Bourgogne Aligoté or Bourgogne
Ordinaire or Bourgogne Grand Ordinaire.

FIXIN

Leaving Dijon by Route Nationale 74 the first wine commune
is Fixin whose wines according to Danguy and Aubertin have
'spirituosity', a colour and a bouquet which develops with age
and which keep a long time. There are no 'Royal' wines in this
commune but there are many good ones.

In the old days three vineyards were considered outstanding.
Today these and three others are all entitled to carry the name
Premier Cru after the name Fixin. Or, if they prefer, to carry
simply the name of the vineyard. They are:

La Perrière, Le Clos du Chapitre, Les Herbelets, Les Maix Bas,
Haut Cheusots and Les Arvelets.

Their colour is always red though there is no legal reason why
they should not be white.

GEVREY CHAMBERTIN

Adjoining Fixin and some 7 miles from Dijon, the Route des
Grands Crus begins and it begins, very properly, with Chambertin, known as 'the wine of kings and the king of wines'.

At one time the Chambertin vineyard was entirely owned by
the Abbey de Beze; then part was sold to the chapter of the
Cathedral at Langres, who tended it for many, many years before
leasing it first to a family called Jomard and then to one Jobert,
whom they took to court for not looking after the vineyard
sufficiently well. They lost the case, but it is interesting that
already in the Middle Ages a strict attempt was being made to
maintain the quality of the great vineyards.

There is no doubt whatsoever that Chambertin was Napoleon

I's favourite wine, and there is a story that he took the wine with him to each of his great battles—except Waterloo.

The stories about Chambertin are legion, but the one I like best was told me by Macdonald Hastings, writer, wine lover, and member of the famous Saintsbury Club. It concerns Hilaire Belloc and is almost certainly apocryphal.

Towards the end of his life the great Hilaire Belloc was being entertained, and that of course meant that his fellow diners called upon him for a speech. He spoke well but somewhat sadly. Towards the end of his speech he turned to his listeners and said, 'You know, I'm getting a very old man and I shall probably meet Peter before I meet many of you again. And Peter will look down on me and he will say, "What is your name?" Mind you, he will know, but it's a matter of form. And I will reply, "Hilaire Belloc". And Peter will say, "What kind of life did you lead down below there, Belloc?" (as if he didn't know). And I will say, "Terrible, Sir. Some of it has been scarlet. There was one occasion . . . Oh, I am getting old . . . I forget the name of the village . . . I even forget the name of the girl, but the wine, yes, the wine—it was Chambertin." '

Chambertin is not a wine the 'little' man drinks. The whole amount comes from two vineyards only 70 acres large and it is in such demand, is so exquisitely husbanded, that its price when it still is in barrel in the cellars of Beaune is the equivalent of about fifteen shillings a bottle. Thereafter it has to be bottled; pay shipment charges; customs duties of differing amounts in different countries; and remain either in your cellar or someone else's for three to eight years before it reaches its apotheosis. If you add the very high overheads that a hotel which is prepared to stock many wines of the highest class must have you can easily see why it is that Chambertin costs from between £3 and £6 a bottle on the wine list of the best hotels.

We drank our first Chambertin in Louis Jadot's cellars. Louis Jadot is one of Beaune's great citizens. He additionally owns several famous 'parcels' particularly of Corton. He is one of the most delightfully forthright men in Burgundy and as a result has a number of unimportant enemies and many real friends.

M. Jadot has very definite, staccato, opinions on wines. He thinks (in 1958) that 'the '50s should now be drunk—a very early wine, the whites magnificent now. The '52s and '53s very good now and will keep for some years. The '53s better now, but the

'52s will be better in a year. The '54s likely to last less long than the '52s or '53s, but very good. '55 will be very good, particularly the red. '56 like'54, but there isn't much of it.'

I asked him how the distant buyer could be sure of getting a good wine. 'If a wine comes with a vintage date and from a good shipper and has an *appellation d'origine* it will be good. But mistrust the label that just says "Burgundy 195-". That means nothing. It certainly doesn't mean it is a vintage year or that the wine has any quality. You must have the name of the shipper and the name of the commune, and it must, must, must have an *appellation d'origine*.' (That means the words *appellation contrôlée* on the label.) We drank many wines with M. Jadot, some in 'piece', the normal Burgundy barrel which contains 228 litres, and some from bottles which it seemed very sad just to open, try, and leave.

The Chambertin was a '55 which M. Jadot drew off from the barrel in a long glass tube called a pipette. In its early life the barrel is only made airtight by a glass stopper which rests on what, in beer, would be called the bung-hole. A certain amount of wine always seeps out of this temporary stopper—it is meant to—and drops to the floor, making even lines on each side of the barrel, so that barrels containing red wine look as if they are painted with a streak of red paint. For tasting, the stopper is moved and the pipette inserted. It fills itself in a few seconds and is then withdrawn with a thumb held over the open top to prevent the wine falling out. Then your glass is reverently, but only partly, filled.

Our Chambertin was about twenty months old and due to stay in wood for another year or so. It was in fact far too young for drinking, but like the thoroughbred it was it already showed its breeding. It was *corsé* (full bodied), fine and, as the French say 'full of promise'.

Louis Jadot calls the keys of the cellar 'the keys of paradise', and says that the cellar stairs are the shortest road to Heaven; for good wine breeds good humour, good humour begets good actions, and good actions lead straight to Heaven.

He also thinks that the culture of the vine is *ingrat*, ungrateful, because of the many totally fortuitous difficulties. Difficulties like the spring frosts—in 1957 some 20 per cent of all the vines of Burgundy were lost with a preponderance among the vines in the plain—the vines of the poorer people and the peasant cultivators who have smallholdings as well as those little vineyards which they cultivate primarily for their own wine. Also a ten-minute hail storm in summer can ruin a complete vineyard. Then there are years that are too wet or too dry or which have too little sun or which are so abundant that there is over-production. Taken all in all, I was surprised to find him so cheerful!

In English we say, after over-indulgence, having 'a hair of the dog'. In French it is charmingly put:

> *Si pour avoir trop bu la veille*
> *Tu te sentais mal le lendemain*
> *Consulte à nouveau la bouteille*
> *Il n'y à pas de meilleur médecin.*

> If after having drunk too much
> You feel bad the next day,
> Consult the bottle again,
> There is no better doctor.

And another from the Jadot anthology:

> *Où l'on verse du bon vin*
> *Volontiers je fais longue pause*
> *Comme les fleurs de mon jardin*
> *Je prends racine ou l'on m'arrose.*

> Where one pours out good wine
> Voluntarily there I stay.
> Like the flowers in my garden
> I take roots where I am watered.

Back to Chambertin and the *Appellations Contrôlées* of:

GEVREY CHAMBERTIN

1. The two great wines are Chambertin and Chambertin-Clos-de-Beze. The latter can be called simply Chambertin, but the contrary is not permitted.

These wines, which are the outstanding vineyards of the large commune of Gevrey Chambertin, are always red. They come from an area of 70 acres owned by twenty-two proprietors and are described by the unparalleled French wine writer Gaston Roupnel as 'mingling grace and vigour and associating firmness and strength to finesse and delicatesse. All these contrary qualities composing an admirable synthesis of an unique generosity and a complete virtue. It is solely in this wine that every virtue of Burgundy is found.'

Then come six further red wines which comprise the *premières cuvées*. These have to have the same degree of alcohol—11·5— as Chambertin, but are allowed to be harvested at about 6 per cent more densely; nor are they gathered from slopes which have quite the same superlative position and soil structure.

2. They are: Charmes-Chambertin; Chapelle-Chambertin; Griotte-Chambertin; Latricières-Chambertin; Mazis-Chambertin; and Ruchottes-Chambertin.

Of them Gaston Roupnel says, 'These six vineyards have the right to add the name "Chambertin" to their own and nothing is more legitimate than this old custom. Between Chambertin on the one part and Latricières and Charmes on the other, there is a difference in the vigour and robustness which even in good years is compensated by an easy finesse, that is to say more marked and more refined.'

Finally come the wines which most of us have always thought to be Chambertin but which are the King's very much rougher and poorer relations. They are the wines entitled to the name Gevrey Chambertin, and this may lawfully be followed by the name of the actual vineyard in the following cases: Les Veroilles; Le Clos Saint-Jacques; Aux Combottes; Bel-Air; Cazetiers; Combe-aux-Moines; Estournelles; Lavaut; Poissenot; Champeaux; Les Goulots; Issarts; Les Corbeaus; Les Gemeaux; Cherbaudes; La Perrière; Clos Prieur (only a part) Le Fonteny; Champonnets; Au Closeau; Craipillot; Champitonnois called 'Petite Chapelle'; Ergots and three vineyards in Clos-du-Chapitre.

The probability is that if the wine is marked simply Gevrey Chambertin and is not followed by any of the above names the wine will come from less favoured slopes.

The wine of Gevrey Chambertin is always red and Gaston Roupnel describes it as being 'firm (that is to say having body and strength) and coloured, with a full and savoury body'.

MOREY-SAINT-DENIS

The great vineyards surrounding the charming little Gallic Roman village of Morey are hardly known outside France and are not even recognized for their worth in their own land. This is largely because a variation in slope and soil makes them very different in character from the wines of their great neighbours Gevrey Chambertin and Chambolle Musigny. Perhaps the nuns of the Clos de Tart bequeathed—no doubt vicariously—a streak of laziness or maidenly modesty to their character which left them content that most of their wine should be marketed as Nuits St Georges or as other great wines, until the laws of origin came along and left them possessors of a great but almost entirely unknown title.

Whatever the cause there is no doubting the quality of their wines, particularly the four great ones.

The one we got to know best was the Clos de Tart, which is entirely owned by one firm—that of J. Mommessin of comparatively distant Mâcon. M. Jean Mommessin was our host both for two meals at his delightful parkland home on the borders of this cheerful city on the Sâone and for the Banquet of the Wine Fair of France held in Mâcon each May. He loves to tell of the days when the nuns of the twelfth-century Abbey of Tart decided to cultivate the vine and so show that they were in no way inferior to their brothers in Christ of the monasteries of neighbouring Beze and Vougeot.

Many English and Americans are so absorbed in the progression of their careers that they can talk nothing but 'shop' and can dream only of greater and greater responsibilities until laid low by their occupational disease—stomach ulcers. Not so the thousands of Frenchmen like M. Mommessin who work wholeheartedly for the cause or profession they serve but who additionally lead the complete life. A life in which domesticity, political interest, artistic expression and gastronomic experience make a natural backcloth to a mind which is measured and orderly, which thinks logically and clearly, is averse to extremes and sets family life as the core and *raison d'être* of himself as an individual.

M. Mommessin is intensely interested in politics, in his family, in the art of living, and particularly in the wine which makes it possible for him and through which he makes it possible for so many tens of thousands of others.

He has also made an intensive study of the origins of French wines and took this as his subject when on November 4, 1954, he read a thesis upon being made a member of the Senate of the ancient and distinguished University of Mâcon.

I proudly possess a copy of this thesis on which is written—

'*À M. Denis Morris en hommage à sa brillante érudition vinicole et à son amitié pour la France.*' This, the kind of 'blague' beloved of the French, means no more than that he is delighted that I am keenly interested in French wines and that I love France.

In his long, interesting, and erudite thesis M. Mommessin talks of the old Greek legend which tells of how Bacchus found, one day, a young delicate vine plant whose fruit he thought delightful. He slipped it for safety inside a fossilized bird's leg but the plant developed so quickly that he soon had to replant it in a lion's leg bone and finally transplant this vine again into an ass's bone before finally being able to plant it in his native soil. These bones are said to symbolize the trilogy of wine—gaiety, strength and stupidity— and to emphasize that wine which has the gift of making people joyous and robust can also strike down those who abuse it.

Searching in history for genuine proof of the wine in Burgundy, his first unassailable documentation came from a paper written in the thirteenth century by Henri d'Andeli, who records a contemporary poem which enumerates twenty-five different major wine districts, including many of Burgundy. A century later Eustache Deschamps, a Champenoise, writes of the 'wines of Beauneys, Masconnais and Tournos' as well as in an earlier different poem of those of 'Auxerre, Bourgoyne, Gascony, Chablis, Givry and Vertus (champagne)', whilst Rabelais talked of an almost forgotten wine, St Pourcain, as being one of the greatest wines of his day.

M. Mommessin is convinced that the vine came to Burgundy from the west and not from the south as is popularly supposed, and brings in as powerful support the Discours d'Autun (mentioned on p. 68) which clearly states that vines, though bad ones, are found abundantly in and around Autun.

Then he turns to negative evidence by reminding us that Julius Caesar, that early war reporter, does not once mention wine in his *Gallic Wars* though, as was proved in the battle between Marius and the Teutons and again at the battle of the Marne, vineyards play a great part in the fighting of wars and frequently embarrass the Commander-in-Chief. As M. Roger Dion says in another context, 'It is impossible to ignore the difficulties that vines would impose on the movements of cavalry and one can only suppose that as Caesar did not mention them they did not exist.'

One thing is certain and that is that the Gaullois have loved wine ever since they first had it, and that much of it was exported from Italy to France in the first century after Christ. The profitability of this great overseas market led to tremendous overproduction in Italy and spelt ruin when the vine was imported into Gaul and was found to flourish there to such an extent that it not only satisfied the needs of the Gaullois but was exported to Rome, whose citizens preferred it to their own wines—as many of them still do!

It was this that led the Emperor Domitian first to forbid the planting of any new vineyards in Italy and then later to plough up half the vineyards. Even this was not successful and eventually, though ten years later, he ordered the same act to be carried out in occupied Gaul. French history books are at pains to point out that the Emperor Domitian had all the French vines grubbed up —they omit to say that he subjected his native land to the same treatment ten years earlier.

In concluding his address M. Mommessin says, 'No, Gentlemen, the vineyards of Burgundy don't go back into antiquity . . . and we can hope to have re-established truth by advancing this theory that their furthest origins were towards the end of the second century, there being absolutely no evidence to suggest that they existed before then.'

According to Dr Ramain the great wines of Morey are 'powerful nectars, well furnished, full of body, with a strong bouquet, with a very special flavour and a perfume of strawberries or violets'.

All I can say is that I did not notice the strawberries or violets either in the old vintages we drank in M. Mommessin's house nor in the younger ones in the *cave*. On the other hand, I found the older wine—a '43 Clos de Tart that we enjoyed with cheese from Citeaux—exciting and particularly agreeable to the nose.

The great wines of Morey-Saint-Denis are: Bonnes-Mares (of which only a seventh is in Morey-Saint-Denis, the remainder being in the neighbouring commune of Chambolle Musigny); Clos-St-Denis; Clos-de-la-Roche and Clos-de-Tart.

Wines entitled to call themselves Morey-Saint-Denis followed by the words *premier cru* or, alternatively, the name of their vineyard are: Les Ruchots, Les Sorbes, Les Clos Sorbes, Les Millandes, Le Clos-des-Ormes (parts of only), Meix Rentiers, Monts Luisants, Les Bouchots, Clos Bussière, Aux Charmes, Les Charrières, Côte Rôtie (which must not be confused with the wine of the same name from the Côtes du Rhône).

There are in addition twenty-five vineyards allowed to call themselves *premier cru* or to add the name of the vineyard. These slightly lesser wines of Morey are all red wines (though they could be white) and are described by Danguy and Aubertin as having 'a beautiful colour, a bouquet which develops with age, lots of body, of vinosité and a great capacity for remaining at their best for a long period'.

CHAMBOLLE MUSIGNY

Quietly the vineyard road curls on to Musigny, which shares its pride between its attractive village church and its wines. Musigny, one of the Princesses of the Royal Blood of Burgundy, is the softest, most velvety of wines. It gives to the palate something of the smoothness that flighty old men yearn for as they compare the cheek of a young girl with the time-coarsened skins of their own contemporaries. And like rougher, ruder wines it sends its strength coursing through veins be they old or young.

It is a curiously feminine wine for this country of masculine vigour. It has serenity and elegance and a delicate savour in keeping with its graceful names—Les Bonnes Mares, Les Amoureuses, Les Charmes. They tell you locally that the vineyard is called Amoureuses because it needs only the men to have drunk some of its wine for the women to be amorously contented.

Like Fixin and Morey-Saint-Denis, the wines of Chambolle Musigny are relatively underpriced, though many will agree that all the great Burgundies are today far more expensive than they should be or than is healthy for the trade of Beaune which is, we found, very worried lest wine lovers turn to the lesser but still very agreeable wines of the Côte du Rhône or even further afield to Provence or Algeria.

Gaston Roupnel calls Musigny 'the wine of silk and lace whose supreme delicacy is guiltless of anything violent and which knows how to conceal its vigour', whilst Alexis Lichine in *Wines of France* goes so far as to say that 'it is one of the finest of Burgundies, still unknown and little appreciated, it overshadows all the wines of the other Côte, that of Beaune, with the exception of Corton'.

Two of its many vineyards—Musigny and Bonnes Mares—share the honour of an *appellation contrôlée* on their own. They make a red wine with just a very small amount of white. Of these Les Bonnes-Mares, Les Amoureuses, and Les Charmes are the best known in England and America. There are a further seven-

teen vineyards entitled to call themselves *premier cru* or by their
vineyard name. They are: Les Cras, Les Borniques, Les Baudes,
Les Plantes, Les Hauts-Doix, Les Chatelots, Les Gruenchers,
Les Groseilles, les Fuées, Les Lavrottes, Derrière-la-Grange, Les
Noirots, Les Sentiers, Les Fousselottes, aux Beaux-Bruns, Les
Combottes, aux Combottes.

CLOS DE VOUGEOT

Before we went to Clos de Vougeot we had the very great pleasure
of lunching with Monsieur and Madame Louis Latour at their
home. M. Latour, who is considered by many to be the greatest
shipper of burgundy in the world, owns some of the finest and
most carefully cultivated vineyards in Burgundy, including vineyards in Chambertin, Romanée St Vivant, Corton and Chevalier
Montrachet. They had gone out of their way to give us typical
Burgundian foods—pâté de canard, jambon en croûte, and poulet
de Bresse—and we had the great honour of drinking accompanying wines from their vineyards in Beaune, Romanée St Vivant and
Corton.

It was in a very contented mood that we went first to visit
M. Latour's vineyards in Chambertin and Chevalier Montrachet
and his immaculate cuverie at Château Corton-Grancey in Aloxe-
Corton, where the wine is hand-pressed among gleaming brass
and copper and perfect order; a condition with which one
immediately associates M. Latour.

After this we went on to Nôtre Dame de Cîteaux. Cîteaux had
always fascinated me, not least because the monks and cellarers
had done so much for the cultivation of the vine. Twenty-two
set out to conquer a marsh, nearly failed, and then achieved all
their hopes through the courage, energy and godliness of one man,
St Bernard.

The Cistercians soon encircled the world with monasteries and
monks, and conserved for two centuries their virtues of simplicity
and godliness until the wealth their diligence had earned corrupted
their leaders. The revolutionaries confiscated the land and dis-
persed the monks; the monastery was sold, the buildings pulled
down and even the stones removed—only the ancient library
remained.

The arteries of the Cistercians continued to beat throughout
the world, but their heart was destroyed. Finally Trappists
returned to Cîteaux and today eighty-four Fathers and Brothers

live a life there dedicated to the praise of God, to manual work, and to study and reflection.

Their days start at two in the morning with the psalmodie; mass follows at four, and then come six more services interwoven with spells of manual work and study until, after meals of a frugality that only just raises them above starvation level but embellished with the wine of the country, they retire for a very few hours.

Apart from their responses, prayers, psalms, and the grave and simple melodies of the Gregorian chant, they maintain complete silence, except for one Father who shows visitors like ourselves round the solemn, beautiful place.

To me it all seems terribly sad. These men with their gifts of endurance and piety have surely more to give to their fellows than prayers and continual silence, but they do not think so and they certainly look happy, though somewhat incongruous, with their heavy cloaks and cowls, their shaven heads and tired faces, as they set about mundane tasks as carpenters, labourers, stone masons and cooks. Their world is heavily weighted with silence and prayer.

It was logical to go from Cîteaux to the greatest of the many vineyards these diligent monks acquired or brought into being. It appears that St Bernard of Cîteaux took over a defunct monastery of the order of St Benoit near to Vougeot. The first working task he set his monks was to farm the waste lands. The vines flourished exceedingly and produced a wine of ever-increasing renown; more and more of the area was made into vineyards and finally a huge enclosing wall was built around it. Today it is one of the most famous vineyards in the world—the Clos (enclosure) de Vougeot.

We were welcomed by a flash of forked lightning and a crash of thunder loud enough to shiver the centuries old timber in the two largest wooden presses we were to see in the whole of our visit. They were installed in the great hall by the Chevaliers du Tastevin, a Bacchanalian confrérie formed twenty-four years ago to publicise the merits of the great Burgundy wines.

The Confrérie first bought and restored the great Château and then furnished it in a way fitting for their renowned wine-tasting sessions and the enthronements of new Chevaliers, which involves a special ritual accompanied by the songs of the Cadets de Bourgogne. At the end of the ceremony the newly elected

Chevaliers—Statesmen, Ambassadors, writers and others—are presented with a purple and gold sash and a silver tasting cup known as a Tastevin.

Eight years ago the Confrèrie formed an annual 'Tastevinage' to which sixty leading wine merchants, vineyard owners, brokers, consumers, restaurateurs and wine writers were invited as a jury to judge the qualities of unidentified samples. From the many wines submitted this élite jury selects a number which they find worthy of the official 'Tastevinage' seal. I notice that each year a few more of these are being offered for sale in overseas countries, and have myself found some excellent examples of Volnay and Clos de Vougeot '47 in the cellars of Smith and Hoey of London. They are very, very fine wines but they are for the connoisseur—they are not cheap. The Confrèrie has its banquets in a vast hall whose stone pillars, garnished with coats of arms, rest on beams as huge as those that are used as levers in the presses in the outer hall. The *Grands Crus* entitled to be called Clos de Vougeot have all to be red in colour and of 11·5 degrees of alcohol. Dr Morelot says of them that 'with La Romanée, Le Chambertin and several others they are in the first rank of all wines of the Côte d'Or and perhaps even in all France'.

Four adjacent vineyards have the right to call themselves *premier cru* or to add their vineyard name to that of Vougeot. These are Le Clos-Blanc (which makes white wine), Les Petits-Vougeot, Les Cras (parts), and Clos-de-la-Perrière (which makes red wine).

VOSNE-ROMANÉE

I had never thought that wine was a simple subject. Burgundy soon showed its infinite complexities. Wine snobs speak knowingly of the merits of a 'Burgundy 1952' or a Beaujolais '53 as if merits were common to all the wines bearing a similar name. How few appreciate that there are several thousand different parts of vineyards entitled to claim an *appellation d'origine*, plus thousands more making wine either for personal consumption or for sale as wine of the Region in Burgundy alone. And that though all these wines will share a communal quality they will all have it to a different degree.

A casual remark M. Bichot threw out in his deep and extensive cellars was illuminating. Pointing to a huge pile of barrels he said, 'Last year we bought about five hundred hogsheads of Pommard '55—do you realize that it meant making seventy-five different purchases?' Words that make one realize how very small the vineyards are and how easy it is for two bottles of apparently the same wine bought at the same time and part of the same dozen to vary, let alone two bottles bought at different times and from different shippers, though in fact each wine may have the same name and vintage on the bottle.

As in Chablis, we learnt that most of the small vineyard owners in Pommard sell when they need the money. We learnt, too, that Bichot bought only 1,000 pieces of wine in 1956 as they thought the wine was too costly and of poor value (a piece holds 300 bottles or 228 litres).

We saw here, too, a vast vat of Beaujolais with fifty thousand litres in it. It was glass lined and was being kept for a customer in England who liked buying 'vintage' Beaujolais only. The English merchant was not all that wrong, as everyone knows that English and Americans each love buying wines with a vintage date on the bottle. But economically he was fooling himself, as the wine will not improve after about three years. The French drink by far the greater part of their Beaujolais in the year after it is harvested, but then they take it in large gulps as befits this great thirst-quenching wine—the carafe wine of France—whereas we drink it in refined little sips as if it were something much more precious than it is.

For lunch young M. Bichot took us out to the Restaurant des Gourmets at Marsannay-La Côte, a few hundred yards off the main Beaune-Dijon road about 5 miles out of Dijon on the right-hand side. Les Gourmets is a Michelin 'one star' and well deserves it—not that I have ever found any below standard.

For the menu at 1,000 francs we chose snails (eight of them of the usually leathery substance but flavoured with magnificent sauce—that is, if you like garlic!). After this, turbot; then poulet à la crème, which was quite delicious and of which we give the recipe in Appendix III; then cheese and finally strawberries and ice-cream. For wine we drank a Corton blanc and a Marsannay which is the speciality of the restaurant and good it was, though very little known.

We were in receptive mood as we went to the vineyard which was to be the highest of many highlights—La Domaine de la Romanée Conti, which produces the whole of La Romanée, the whole of La Tâche, three-quarters of Richebourg, and a large proportion of Romanée Conti and Romanée St Vivant.

F

M. Bichot's large, gleaming white car seemed strangely out of place as we pulled into what looked to be a small, somewhat impoverished smallholding with its buildings on all sides of a very ordinary looking farmyard. This was the Domaine which controls probably the greatest and certainly the most expensive red wine in the world!

We were welcomed by Madame Clin who acts as *régisseur* and M. Noblet, the *Chef du Cave*. M. Noblet, an enormous man of 6 feet 6 inches, was wearing a short pullover, an open-necked blue-and-white shirt, blue jeans, wellingtons, and one of the cheerfullest smiles I have ever had the pleasure of meeting. He looked just like the village fast bowler dressed for a day's gardening.

There was a grin on his deep-browny-red, almost brick-red, face as he told me that during the occupation they did all their black listening—to the B.B.C. French Service—on a wireless set hidden inside a large wine press.

The *cave* is quite astonishing. Somehow, when thinking of this superb wine with its deep red labels and the bottle number on each one, you expect to see something quite extraordinary in the way of a cellar. Not a bit of it. Here there is no need for 'bull'— the only worry is that the superlative quality of the wine shall be maintained each year.

The cellar door is a very ordinary one; the lighting adequate— no more—and the total length of the cellar that contains all the newer wines in wood is only that of a cricket pitch and 7 yards wide.

1956 was a shocking year for Burgundy, and in any case the wines of Vosne Romanée are at their best at between eight and ten years old. Yet the wines we tasted, which had only been harvested eight months earlier, had already a quite astonishing quality.

M. Noblet told me that so far as possible they still make wine by the ancient methods. It is still fined with white of egg and only bottled when the moon is in a certain quarter. They keep sheep to secure the manure for the vineyards and they make a special compost which includes sheep manure and the marc from the end of the previous year's wine making.

They harvest as late as possible, usually in October, and every drop of their wine is bottled in the domaine, a practice which is little, though increasingly, employed in Burgundy compared with Bordeaux, largely because the individual holdings are so small in Burgundy.

After the wine is bottled it is stored in the ancient cellars that were built, inevitably enough, by the monks of Cîteaux when they tended these vineyards. The establishments to which the cellars were attached were destroyed in the religious wars, but the Huguenots left the cellars intact.

The two little cellars where the older wines are stored are much more exciting than the other. Here are little piles of great vintages, most of them being kept for world-famous restaurants and hotels —I saw thirty magnums of 1953 (the last of the stock) earmarked for one London restaurant. Those sold to the great wine merchants leave the cellars as soon as bottled. I noticed that a high proportion of the bottles were magnums and was told that this was because wine is at its best in a bottle this size and that the wealthy who buy this wine can afford it so. In a good year with no frost some six thousand bottles of Romanée Conti are produced—a tiny output for a large world—and as a result a bottle of Romanée Conti costs about £2 at its youngest, which shows why, in a restaurant in another country, the wine must cost from £6 a bottle after it has been kept for its potential customer for eight years or so.

Incidentally, I noticed a very young Romanée Conti and a La Tâche listed at £3 in a restaurant within 2 miles of the vineyard.

In their excellent book *Les Vins de Bourgogne* Pierre Poupon and Pierre Forgeot quote Dr Ramain as saying of La Romanée Conti, 'A magnificent wine with a powerful bouquet of violets mingled with a scent of cherries, as radiant as rubies and exceptionally smooth'; whilst of Richebourg Camille Rodier says, 'This splendid vineyard, which possesses an incomparable richness of bouquet, is one of the most sumptuous of Burgundies.' The pity is that so few of us can ever taste it.

In addition to La Romanée Conti and Richebourg, which each have their own *appellation d'origine*, the one covering an area of only 4¾ acres and the other 20, there are five other outstanding vineyards: Romanée, La Tâche, Romanée-Saint Vivant, Grands Echezeaux and Echezeaux. The two latter are sometimes omitted from lists of Vosne Romanée wines, but this is wrong, as the laws of *appellation d'origine* firmly place them within the greater area of Vosne Romanée.

In addition to the *Grands Crus* there are ten vineyards which are

allowed to call themselves *premier cru* or to use their vineyard
name in addition to that of Vosne Romanée. They are Aux
Malconsorts, Les Beaux-Monts, Les Suchots, La-Grande-Rue, Les
Gaudichots, Aux Brulées, Les Chaumes, Les Reignots, Le Clos-
des-Réas and Les Petits-Monts. Like the Grands Crus their colour
is always red.

NUITS-SAINT-GEORGES

The last town of the Côte de Nuits is the one which gave its
name and which is its capital. Nuits-Saint-Georges is a busy,
thriving little town which must have been much more attractive
before the invention of the infernal combustion engine.

There was a time when it was simply called Nuits, but its
inhabitants were so proud of the wine made in the Clos-Saint-
Georges that they sought permission to add the name Saint-
Georges to that of the village. As a result the greatest vineyard
—Les Saint-Georges—has lost the identity which made it famous
earlier in the century.

I have never much liked the sparkling burgundy of which the
town pretends to be so proud, and am happy to find the opinion
is not only shared by the majority of Burgundian winemen but is
attributable—as with so many of the sparkling wines obtainable
at a low price in France—to the fact that it is usually made of low-
quality wines which the sparkle slightly but insufficiently, dis-
guises.

The *premiers crus* of Nuits-Saint-Georges are, according to a
great authority upon them, Dr Lavalle—'In general less firm,
less hard than the wines of Gevrey and are ready sooner; they
have more body and colour than those of Chambolle Musigny.'

For myself I had drunk so many unpleasant bitter wines in
darkest Soho masquerading under the name of Nuits-Saint-
Georges that I was astonished to find how pleasant they can be
on the occasions that we sampled them in the cellars of Louis
Latour, Louis Jadot, Calvet, Bouchard, Bichot, and others. I feel
that by fraud a good many people have done the fine wines of
Nuits a great disservice so far as the English market is concerned.

The outstanding vineyards of Nuits-Saint-Georges are Les
Saint-Georges, Les Vaucrains and Les Cailles. These together with
those from Nuits-Saint-Georges and Premeaux whose names
follow are entitled by the law to the words premier cru or to use
the name of their vineyard. They are:

Sur Nuits

Les Porets, Les Pruliers, Les Hauts-Pruliers (part), Aux Murgers, La Richemone, Les Chaboeufs, La Perrière, La Roncière, Les Procès, Rue-de-Chaux, Aux Badots, Aux Cras, Aux Chaignots, Aux Thorey (part), Aux Vignes-Rondes, Aux Bousselots, Les Poulettes, Aux Crots (part), Les Vallerots (part), Aux Champs-Perdrix (part), Perrière-Noblet (part), Aux Damodes (part), Les Argillats (part), En la-Chaîne-Carteau (part), Aux Argillats (part).

Sur Premeaux

Clos-de-la-Maréchale, Clos-Arlots, Clos-des-Argillières, Clos-des-Grandes-Vignes, Clos-des-Corvées, Clos-des-Forêts, Les Didiers, Aux Perdrix, Les Corvées-Paget, Le Clos-Saint-Marc.

LA CÔTE DE BEAUNE

Our visits to the Côte de Beaune were in the company of M. Louis Jadot, his nephew M. Andrew Gagey, M. Louis Latour and M. Poupon of Messrs J. Calvet. A great company!

One of the first things M. Jadot give us was a lesson in *dégustation*. Whether at home or deliberately tasting in a cellar, where you do not swallow the wine, you should use a tulip-shaped glass so that the bouquet will come to you through a comparatively small channel.

Never more than half fill the glass, as you will need to throw the wine about in it with a circular motion which will send it wallowing round. This is easiest if you keep the base of the glass on the table. It is not necessary in fine old wines, but is essential in new ones where the bouquet is rather hidden.

Having tumbled the wine about, take a little in your mouth, throw it around inside, chew it and make it gurgle in the front of your mouth by holding it around your front teeth whilst drawing in air. Then, if you are going to try a lot of wine, spit it out. If you are practised you will spit several feet and in a long stream —like a Spaniard proving he is not frightened when in danger. Then taste again two or three times, always spitting out, and finally just flick what is left in the glass on to the cellar floor. Then you are ready for the next go.

When sampling or drinking with a meal always go from a lesser to a greater wine. No wine must kill another in advance.

The art of wine drinking is an art in comparisons of pleasure. One must have a starting-point, a wine of lesser degree which will point the way, clear the palate and put one's olfactory senses in a state of excitement and expectancy. To start a dinner with a Romanée would be an error, as without having started with a good modest wine one might miss something of the mellowness, vigour and delicateness and the subtle bouquet—different in all wines—that makes the synthesis and symphony that is a great wine.

In England we are far too content to choose a meal and then serve a wine—and one only—with it. In putting the emphasis on food rather than wine I am sure that Brillat-Savarin was wrong. The wines should be chosen first and then dishes thought of that will be their perfect complement.

In France and to a lesser degree in England the demand is growing for half bottles, particularly amongst young couples. This is so that even dining *à deux* one can have the opportunity of trying two wines, or alternatively so as to precede a great wine with a lesser one. The thing to do, of course, is to have a white wine like an Alsatian Sylvaner or Riesling, white Burgundy or Graves or an Entre deux Mers with the fish and then go on to a red wine with the meat or cheese. Alternatively, one can start with an inexpensive wine like an ordinary Beaujolais with the meat and have half a bottle of one of the Burgundy *grands crus* or a great Bordeaux château of the Médoc, St Emilion or Pomerol with the cheese.

In France connoisseurs always drink their great wines with the cheese, by which time most English diners have finished their wine.

Having chosen the wine and the food, how does one start enjoying it? First, I suggest by talking and thinking about it and by making comparisons. You must learn some of the accepted wine words—and what grand words they are too—*corsé*, which means full-bodied; *fruité*, full of fruit and with a bouquet of flowers; *dûr*, rough or not ready; *enstrangent*, tardy, late and probably with too much tannin in it; *fin*, delicate or light; *delicat*, more distinguished than *fin*.

Having learnt these and a few more, try to make an assessment of each and every wine you drink. If they have a real character you will find them each different—you will even find that bottles of the same year and vineyard have a slight difference in taste,

which is why wine men like drinking magnums if there is a small
party of them, as then there will be practically no difference in
the wine that any one of them drinks.

Our first visit in the Côte de Beaune was with M. Jadot to
Aloxe Corton, where he and M. Latour own two of the greatest
vineyards. They are next to each other facing south-east and on
the higher slope of the hills, superbly placed to get the sun from
the first to the last of the day.

From them you can look right-handed with Beaune in front
of you, to Chagny in the near distance in a fold of the hills; then
the slopes of Mâcon and the Beaujolais; and going further eastwards on a very clear day, to Mont Blanc.

In between, a vast fertile plain with, everywhere in May, the
reddish earth just touched with the green of the young vines.
On one or two of the slopes some of the *pièces* were planted in
wheat or some spring or summer vegetables. These were vineyards
that had been grubbed up. The vines in this part have a life of
about thirty-five or forty years, at the end of which time they
must go. There is nothing else for it. The vineyards are let rest
for three or four years after being grubbed up, so, to use Monsieur
Jadot's expression, 'that the earth can lose its taste of wine'.
They also like to get some frost in the earth and to get some new
elements. The Corton slopes are very, very small *pièces*. There is
no question of spraying from the air here as in Alsace.

Monsieur Jadot then took us down the slope to Pernand
Vergilesses, where a separate *appellation contrôlée* is allowed. They
make a high quality wine, better than the lowest on the Corton
slopes, but not as fine as those on the summit, though with
similar characteristics and which keeps well.

And then to Savigny, which gives a wine which is not full
bodied but supple and delicate and rich in bouquet. It was very
interesting to see that the vines here had already been sprayed
with sulphur. They had had the great frost of May 8 in these
parts. They did not suffer very badly, not as badly as Reims and
Epernay, but they did lose some, and Monsieur Jadot, as an
experiment, sprayed those of his vines that had just been touched
the day after the frost, in the hope that it would harden them.
There is one vineyard in Savigny which so often gets frozen
that they say here that it freezes itself with fright!

M. Jadot took us to his *cuverie* where I found that the 'serious'
firms do not use vast glass-lined vats to store their great reds,

but that the wine is put into new barrels which yield a certain amount of tannin which is good for the wine. Before that, for the fermentation, the wine goes into very old barrels which are not finally washed out until the next harvest.

Dangerous gases are thrown off during the fermentation, which lasts from five to fourteen days according to the temperature, during which time the skins and pips rise to the top but are pushed back into the wine again. Incidentally these new barrels cost £10 each and an average sized merchant will need a thousand at least.

After about four to six days the wine is drawn off and separated from the marc (the skins, pips, etc.). This will produce between 80 and 90 per cent of the total volume of wine. The rest is called the *vin de goutte* or the drop wine which is obtained by pressing the marc gradually but firmly. As with champagne, the great firms never mix the first pressing with the second, but of course many firms do.

M. Jadot thinks that the mixture of wine from vines ten, twenty and thirty years old produces a better, more complete wine than juice from vines of any one year. He also stressed, time and time again, the importance of the luminosity of the air, and we noticed throughout our trip that the better the vine district the better it was for photography.

He also says that stones are one of the most important things that one can have in any vineyard as they keep the vines warm at night, a belief that was later warmly endorsed by Baron Le Roy at Châteauneuf-du-Pape.

After lunch, in which great vintages of Corton figured large, we went to the wine museum at Beaune with M. Gagey, and there saw something of the antiquity of the vine—right back to Gregory of Tours in the sixth century.

After this post-prandial relaxation M. Gagey took us to do some serious tasting. On the way he passed on a lot of wine lore.

Red burgundy is at its best at from four to thirty years of age depending upon the year and the vineyard. He deplored the present high prices of burgundy—the price is too high and the demand too great, he thinks.

We asked him why it is that we always found the *caves* dirty in Burgundy and got the answer we expected—'Because a little dirt and damp is good for the wine.'

He went on to tell us how difficult business is for wine merchants in Beaune (like farmers, they are always in great difficulties but usually manage to convey an atmosphere of considerable well-being.)

They always have to carry a stock of several years of some eighty-four different *crus*, which is why one always sees so many small barrels in Burgundy as compared with Alsace. Of course there are great barrels—immense ones only a little smaller than the giants of Vougeot—but they are only used for the first few weeks before the wine is racked, drawn off, and put into small new barrels holding only 228 litres.

As we walked into the cellars M. Gagey mentioned non-chalantly that he proposed to give us a *dégustation* of some twenty wines. This seemed quite a lot!

In passing he told us that when you have wines at home in your own cellar, be it large or small, you should always have the label on top, as this will correspond to the position that it had in the cave, and so any deposit that may form after you have received the wine will be in the same position that it was earlier in the wine's life.

With him we sampled Pouilly Fuissé, Chablis Fourchaume, Meursault, a Puligny Montrachet 'Les Combiettes', a Meursault Genevrières, and a Corton Charlemagne. Those are of course all white wines, they were all 1955, and they, like the reds which we went on to, were in an ascending order of merit.

In Rouges we started off with an ordinary Bourgogne, a Côte de Beaune village, then a Beaune, a Pommard, a Beaune Têurons, which is a wine I personally liked very much indeed, Nuits-Saint-Georges, a Gevrey Chambertin, Charmes Chambertin, a Beaune Clos des Ursules, a Corton Pougets, a Bonnes Mares, and a Chambertin.

He told us that there are four things that one must do when try-ing wine. First look at it and say 'What a lovely colour'; second, smell it and say 'What a beautiful bouquet'; third, drink it and say 'What a good wine'; and fourth, look at your glass and say 'What a pity that it's empty.'

ALOXE-CORTON, LADOIX-SERRIGNY AND
PERNAND-VEREGELESSES

There are three *grands crus* in Aloxe-Corton—they are Corton, Corton-Charlemagne, and Charlemagne. The Corton is red or white, but only some 10 per cent is white; the other two white only. The two appreciations which M. Poupon and M. Fourgeot think most exact are by Dr Lavalle, who says, 'Cortons of good years are perfect wines worthy of the most exalted gourmets and the most solemn occasions'; and Camille Rodier, whose opinion of Corton Charlemagne is, 'A white wine of great allure; rich in alcohol [it has to have a minimum of 12 degrees], strong, golden, full of sap with a bouquet of cinammon, a taste of gunpowder.'

The latter is a description which very exactly fits the bottle of 1952 Corton Charlemagne shipped by Louis Jadot which I bought many months before I met M. Jadot, but which has been by my side in diminishing volume whilst I have been writing this chapter.

Additionally certain vineyards in Ladoix-Serrigny and Aloxe-Corton have the right to call themselves *premier cru* or to use their vineyard name. They are, in Ladoix-Serrigny: La Maréchaude, La Toppe-au-Vert, La Coutière, Les Grandes-Lolières, Les Petites-Lolières, Basses-Mourettes. And in Aloxe-Corton they are: Les Valozières (part), Les Chaillots (part), Les Meix (part), Les Fournières, Les Maréchaudes (part), En Pauland (part), Les Vercots, Les Guérets.

There is a story about Corton that one meets on all sides. It concerns the Emperor Charlemagne, who was devoted to Corton rouge but found it embarrassing to drink in public because it stained his white beard. Regretfully he instructed the court cellarer to obtain a white wine from the same slopes so that his affection for wine would not become too obvious on ceremonial occasions. The white wine was duly produced by substituting the Chardonnay grape for the Pinot, and the Emperor approved it. Thenceforth he always drank it in public though returning to his favourite red in private.

PERNAND VERGELESSES

Some of the *grands crus* of Corton, Corton Charlemagne, and Charlemagne are in the commune of Pernand Vergelesses.

Four vineyards have the right to the words *premier cru* or the vineyard name. They are Les Basses-Vergelesses, Creux-de-la-Net (part), Les Fichots and En Caradeux. They are most attractive wines—reds and whites—and they keep well.

We found that the consensus of opinion about Corton Charlemagne is that it is usually at its best after three years and seldom after seven or eight years, though the '28s are still great wines.

SAVIGNY-LES-BEAUNES

A number of vineyards in this little-known commune are allowed
to call themselves *premier cru* or carry the vineyard name. They
are:
*Aux Vergelesses, Aux Vergelesses Dit Bataillière, Les Marconnets,
La Dominode, Les Jarrons*
Basses-Vergelesses, Les Lavières, Aux Gravains, Les Peuillets
(part), Aux Guettes (part), Les Talmettes, Les Charnières, Aux
Fourneaux (part), Aux Clous (part), Aux Serpentières (part), Les
Narbantons, Les Hauts-Marconnets, Les Hauts-Jarrons, Redres-
cuts (part), Aux Grands-Liards (part), Aux Petits-Liards (part),
Les Rouvrettes (part), Petits-Godeaux (part).

BEAUNE

Beaune was once a walled city and the caves of three of the
largest merchants are built into the ancient bastions.

In many places the width of the wall is at least 30 feet. At
Calvet's one sees a little oval of wood and this is the entrance to a
culvert where the protecting cannon used to be mounted. The
culverts are so narrow that tiny little pockets were scooped out
by the side of the cannon so that the soldiers could avoid the
cannon's recoil.

All the merchants told me that caves are best slightly damp and
that we should keep our own cellars moist if we are keeping wine
in them for a long time, as otherwise the corks will be attacked
by microbes which let air in and thus will eventually cause damage
to the wine.

M. Poupon of Messrs Calvet not only took us to the vineyards
south of Beaune—he took us to one of the most delightful hotels
we met in the course of our visit.

This was the Hostellerie Bourguignonne at the charming village of Verdun-sur-le-Doubs. It is perfectly placed for those
wanting to visit the whole region of the Burgundy vineyards,
as it is 36 miles from Dijon, 13 from Beaune—M. Poupon made
the journey sitting on the folded hood of the T.R.2!—and 13 from
Chalon. The restaurant is full value for its Michelin star and lower
priced than most. Meals can be taken out of doors in the open or
in the shade of trees, or in a most attractive restaurant which has
a glass wall dividing it from the kitchen so that one can follow
the cooking of one's meal.

There are only fourteen bedrooms—another fourteen are to be added during 1958—and they are exceedingly comfortable and well furnished. The only snag is that the place is too popular at the weekends, particularly Sundays. Otherwise it is very quiet.

There is a magnificent menu at 1,000 francs. We particularly enjoyed the *Pâté de Caneton*, which was a cold pie of young duck. Then we had a pauchouse verdunoise—two fish of a *maigre*-type, i.e. thin and dry in texture, in this case first *brochet* (pike) and *perche* (perch) plus two *gras* fish (oily or fat), and one of them called *la tanche* and the other an eel. They were served in a sauce or white wine, with fried bread rubbed in garlic. We had a bottle of Pouilly Vinzelles, a white Mâcon of 1955, and then ham grilled in cinders, with mushrooms and a cream sauce made with sherry, vol au vent and mushrooms. It is absolutely delightful and presumably 'comparatively' easy to make. The sherry sauce had in it cheese as well as cream. With that we drank some '49 Nuits-Saint-Georges bottled by Calvet.

If you spend time in Burgundy or have business to do in Beaune the journey to Verdun will be very worthwhile. We very much wish we had found it earlier in our stay. Incidentally it would be fun for walking, too, as the River Doubs is only some 40 yards from the hotel and the Sâone a few hundred.

It was from M. Poupon that we learnt, amongst much else, about V.S.R.—a mark we had already seen once or twice on wine lists in Burgundy but had never come across in England. It stands for 'Very Special Reserve'. It is a non-vintage wine and is usually a mixture of two years, each of which has complementary deficiencies or virtues. Recent examples of V.S.R. mixtures are the '53s and '54s and the '50s and '51s. In '52, which was an exceptionally abundant and excellent year, there was of course no need to mix anything.

I asked M. Poupon about the drift from the country to the towns in these parts. He said: 'It hardly exists as the vineyards are becoming more and more mechanized and this attracts the younger generation. After the war the young men left the towns where there was little food or work and went to the villages to stay with relatives. Some of them were ex-Army men, of course, and were mechanically minded. They found lots of ex-Army motors about. In their spare time they experimented with motor hoes. They made them high so that they could sit well above the vines on each side as they hoed between the rows with these very amateur machines. They found it worked, and as a result modern vineyards mostly are running up and down the slopes, because, if sideways, the motor hoes would topple. So if you see vineyards running sideways you will know that it is probably a very small property, and that the owner is cultivating the vines and doing all the hoeing by hand. If they are up and down you can almost bet your bottom dollar that they've been motorized.'

Next day we went a tour of the Beaune vineyards. First to those of the commune of Beaune whose outstanding wines are so highly priced but whose *premiers crus* have a softness and lightness that is most endearing. The vineyards that may call themselves *premier cru* or use the name of the vineyard are:

Les Marconnets, Les Fèves, Les Bressandes, Les Grèves, Les Teurons, Le Clos-des-Mouches, Champs-Pimont, Clos-du-Roi (part), Aux Coucherias (part), En l'Orme, En Genêt, Les Perrières, A l'Ecu, Les Cent-Vignes, Les Toussaints, Sur-les-Grèves, Aux Cras, Le Clos-de-la-Mousse, Les Chouacheux, Les Boucherottes, Les Vignes-Franches, Les Aigrots, Pertuisots, Tiélandry ou Clos-Landry, Les Sisies, Les Avaux, Les Reversées, Le Basdes-Teurons, Les Seurey, La Mignotte, Montée-Rouge (part), Les Montreve-nots (part), Les Blanches-Fleurs (part), Les Épenottes (part).

The wines are about 97 per cent red.

The other day I met a man who, like his father and grandfather before him, had been a wine merchant all his life. He said to me, 'You know, there's no doubt at all that the merchants of Beaune stretch their wine. Why, I buy myself the equivalent of about a twentieth of the whole amount of Burgundy put up for sale at the Hospices de Beaune and I am only a comparatively small wine merchant.' This very charming and knowledgeable man was absolutely astonished to learn that the total sales of the wine at the Hospices de Beaune was only about one-half per cent of the total amount harvested in a normal year and that the sales at the Hospices are only of wines from vineyards which have been bequeathed to the charity during the years.

POMMARD

Before going to Pommard and Volnay we had a most exquisite lunch with M. and Mme François Bouchard. The menu, by my side as I write, teases my palate. It reads:

MENU

Chablis ıer *Cru* *Fourchaume* 1950	*Gougères chaudes*
—	—
Montrachet 1945	*Brochet du Doubs* *Sauce Mousseline*
—	—
Volnay-Caillerets *Ancienne Cuvée Carnot* 1889	*Filet de boeuf* *printannier*
—	—
Romanée 1865	*Fromages*
—	—
Château-Coutet 1943	*Tarte aux fraises* *patissière*
—	—

We had had the usual aperitif of rich Frenchmen—champagne. M. Bouchard was somewhat apologetic. 'I could', he said, 'have given you more excellent wines than the Volnay and the Romanée. They are too old and have lost some of their warmth, their body, their vigour. They are very tired. But I thought you would like to be able to say that you had drunk two of our greatest wines made from French roots before phylloxera ultimately destroyed them.'

Needless to say the great wines had lost something of their colour and quality, but they were still superb, and I can only think that M. Bouchard's cellarman must have opened many bottles before he found any so good.

The wines of Pommard keep well, but they differ a good deal in quality and body, especially in England, where wines are often sold under the name which bear little resemblance to the full, firm wines that Henri IV loved so well and which are so popular in the Netherlands.

There are a number of *premiers crus*:

Les Rugiens-Bas Les Rugiens-Hauts (part), *Les Epenots*
Les Petits-Epenots (part), Clos-de-la-Commaraine, Clos-Blanc, Les Arvelets, Es-Charmots, Les Argillières, Les Péze-rolles, Les

Boucherottes, Les Saussilles, Les Croix-Noires, Les Chaponières, Les Fremiers, Les Bertins, Les Garollières, Les Poutures, Le Clos-Micot, La Refene, Clos-du-Verger, Derrière-Saint-Jean, La Platière (part), Les Chanlins-Bas (part), Les Combes-Dessus (part), La Chanière (part).

MEURSAULT

Apart from telling you of the Hostellerie du Chevreuil, which is excellent, and that there is a *syndicat d'initiative* in the Town Hall, the Guide Bleu merely dismisses Meursault, one of the most charming towns of the côte, with the words, 'renowned for the quality of its wines'—as if this white wine with its dry steely taste needs any bush! Next to Montrachet and Corton, the wines of Meursault are thought by many to be the greatest dry whites in the world—a view not shared in Bordeaux!

We found on the many occasions that we were able to try them that they seemed more than any other to combine a dry flavour with a degree of body that one seldom 'feels' in a white wine except the more heavy vinous wines of Sauternes.

Camille Rodier describes them as being 'rich in alcohol, of a beautiful colour of greenish gold, clear and brilliant, very refreshing to drink with an aroma of ripe grapes and a suspicion of nuttiness'. He has said all!

The vineyards entitled to call themselves *premier cru* or to use their own name are:

Aux Perrières, Les Perrières-Dessus, Les Perrières-Dessous, Les Charmes-Dessus, Les Charmes-Dessous
Les Genevrières-Dessus (part), Les Genevrières-Dessous (part), Le Poruzot-Dessus, Le Poruzot (part), Les Boucheres, Les Santenots-Blancs, Les Santenots-du-Milieu, Les Caillerets, Les Petures, Les Cras, La Goutte-d'Or, La Jennelotte, La Pièce-sous-le Bois, Sous-le-Dos-d'Ane (part).

VOLNAY

Judging by the appreciation that the French and all wine lovers have always shown for Volnay it is a most heavenly wine! For many years there has been a catchphrase, 'Nul n'est gai, sans boire de Volnay', roughly meaning, 'One cannot be gay unless one drinks Volnay'.

De Moucheron, in a most charming book, *The Great Wines of Burgundy*, says that in the fifteenth century Volnay already had the reputation of being the most delicate and the most perfumed of the *crus* of the Côte de Beaune, and goes on to speak of them as producing the least full-bodied of the wine of the Côte.

Today they are wines of a smooth, balanced elegance which come to meet you if you draw the cork after they have taken on the temperature of the room. These are certainly wines for a great occasion.

The wines come from the commune of Meursault and include a number of vineyards entitled to the assuring words *premier cru* or to carry the name of their own vineyard. They are:

En Caillerets, Caillerets-Dessus, En Champans, En Chevret
Fremiets, Bousse-d'Or, La Barre ou Clos-de-la-Barre, Le Clos-des-Chênes (part), Les Angles, Pointe-d'Angles, Les Mitans, En l'Ormeau, Taille-Pieds, En Verseuil, Carelle-sous-la-Chapelle, Ronceret, Carelle-Dessous (part), Robardelle (part), Les Aussy (part), Les Brouillards (part), Le Clos-des-Ducs, Les Pitures-Dessus, Chanlin (part), Les Santenots (rouges), Les Petures (rouges), Village-de-Volnay (part).

THE COMMUNES OF MONTHÉLIE, AUXEY-DURESSES AND SAINT-ROMAIN

Many fine wines come from these three communes which we visited with M. Poupon, but they are little known in England. For many years they were sold under the names of their great neighbours—especially the wines of Auxey-Duresses and of Monthélie, which M. Poupon told us were usually sold as Volnay or Pommard.

Before going to Meursault and Puligny-Montrachet we spent a very interesting morning with M. Bouchard's son in the famous firm's cellars. We learnt that a great firm like theirs always has at least a million bottles in stock. We heard yet again about hailstorms and the worry that vintners have about them—which is why they may have as many as half a dozen different *pièces* scattered about within the same large vineyard. It is said that you can lose a year's income in ten minutes of midsummer madness. Having scattered vineyards is a considerable insurance against total loss, as the hailstorms are very localized, but it greatly adds to production costs.

PULIGNY-MONTRACHET

Our final visits to the Côte de Beaune—with M. Poupon—were to

5 The *cuverie* of Château Corton-Grancey at Aloxe-Corton, Burgundy

6 Tasting wine (M. Dubos)

7 Grape picking in the Marne

Puligny, Chassagne, Santenay, Saint-Aubin, and to the lesser wine districts of Cheilly, Dezize and Sampigny-les-Maranges.

Montrachet is a wine which has captured more imaginations than almost any other. Its perfume is variously described as 'divine' and to be 'of nuts'. Of grapes it is the grapiest; of honey the honeyest. It is said to have 'absorbed more sun than any other' and is acknowledged even in Bordeaux as being the equal, though, of course, a world apart in flavour, to Château d'Yquem.

The vineyard itself is small—only 20 acres, of which part is in the commune of Puligny and part a few hundred yards away over the main railway line.

It is not particularly impressive to see—my advice is not to spend time visiting any of these communes. Montrachet is very expensive and said to be much stretched. Alexis Lichine reckons in *Wines of France* that the total production of the outstanding *cru* of this great district was only 900 cases in 1949 and that some 400 of these cases were kept by the growers or sold by them to their friends. Five hundred cases is little for a vast world, hence the high price and the temptation to fraud. Mr Lichine has done a very useful job by listing in his book the proprietors of Montrachet and also the principal owners of another *premier cru*— Chevalier-Montrachet.

All the great wines of Puligny-Montrachet resemble closely the Montrachet which is the *Tête de Cuvée* (the outstanding vineyard). They are Chevalier-Montrachet, Bâtard-Montrachet, Bienvenues-Montrachet and Criots-Bâtard-Montrachet.

These, in their turn, are closely followed by:
Le Cailleret, Les Combettes
Les Pucelles, Les Folatières (part), Clavoillons, Le Champ-Canet, Les Chalumeaux, Les Referts, Sous-le-Puits, La Garenne, Hameau-de-Blagny.

CHASSAGNE-MONTRACHET

Apart from possessing a proportion of Montrachet, Bâtard-Montrachet, and Criots-Bâtard-Montrachet, the next-door commune has some magnificent reds as well as whites. The whites include some that are very different from those of Montrachet; they are not nearly so fulsome and have a very personal delicateness. The principal reds are:
Clos-Saint-Jean (part), Morgeot (part), Morgeot dit Abbaye-de-Morgeot (part), La Boudriotte (part)

La Maltroie (part), Les Chenevottes, Les Champs-Gain (part), Grandes-Ruchottes, La Romanée, Les Brussolles (part), Les Vergers, Les Macherelles, En Cailleret (part).

The whites are:

Morgeot (part), Morgeot dit Abbaye-de-Morgeot (part), La Boudriotte, La Maltroie, Clos-Saint-Jean, Les Chenevottes, Les Champs-Gain, Grandes-Ruchottes, La Romanée, Les Brussolles, Les Vergers, Les Macherelles, Chassagne ou Cailleret.

Camille Rodier thinks highly of the reds, which are little known, and to that extent very much better value than some of the great wines of the Côte de Nuits which they resemble.

MÂCON

On our way to Mâcon we made a short detour to the region of Mercurey, turning off N.6 at Chagny not far from the ruins of Cluny, which lie surrounded by vineyards. To think of the greatness which made Cluny 'shine on earth like a newly risen sun', to ponder on its influence on medieval society, think of its two thousand branches scattered throughout Europe and of its ten thousand monks, then to see these vine-enclosed ruins, makes one feel how very small a speck one is on the desert of time.

It is from this district of Rully, Mercurey, Givry, Montagny, Mâcon, Pouilly-Fuissé, Pouilly-Loché and Pouilly Vinzelles, plus that of Beaujolais, that most of the Burgundies come.

Until 1922 the wine of Rully was sold as Mercurey, and in fact the growers went to law—unsuccessfully—seeking to be allowed to continue the practice rather than fight their way on to the market with an unknown name. Luckily they were unsuccessful, as by efficient marketing and real quality of production they have since secured a good market both for their white still wines and for the sparkling champagne type wine which they originated, so far as the Burgundy district is concerned, way back in 1830. This wine is not made from Pinot noir but from a mixture of one-third Chardonnay and two-thirds Aligoté. Only if this is done and if natural fermentation occurs may the words 'Bourgogne Mousseux' be put on the label, if not it is only 'Vin Mousseux'.

There are five *premiers crus* in Mercurey. They are: Clos-du-Roi, Clos-Voyen or Les Voyens, Clos-Marcilly, Clos-des-Fourneaux, Clos-des-Montaigus.

The wines of Mercurey possess a reputation for consistent quality and we certainly found the examples that we drank uniform in their excellence.

It is a district which has resisted the pull of the big cities; its inhabitants are typical ruddy-faced Burgundians and the holdings from which they obtain their livelihood seem pathetically small. In the past there was a good deal of belt tightening and philosophical awaitment of better harvests or better prices—and how seldom these two come together! Today these very small growers have banded together and formed co-operatives which have effected considerable economies in buying sulphates and so on, as well as securing a steady market through modern publicity.

It was interesting to find that these French wine co-operatives have no political ambitions or life. One of the sturdy independent-looking vintners, telling me what a difference the co-operatives had made to him and his like, said, 'We French are great individualists—especially those of us who live by land and wine, but we have found that the only way to remain individualists is to co-operate, and we are very glad that we have!'

Givry is a much bigger—and more attractive—town than its near neighbours and makes a pleasant red wine much of which is said to be unlawfully mixed with better-known wines of the Côte de Beaune. Wine is by no means its only preoccupation, as it is the chief town of the Canton.

The indolent Saône laps gently along the quaysides of Mâcon carrying its oarsmen, some of its goods, and somehow setting the tempo of its corporate life. Its little narrow streets rise quickly and unevenly towards the vineyards with here and there wide squares or boulevards which show that its citizens were capable of town planning if they could be bothered, but in the main its rose-coloured houses and fine public buildings sprawl close to each other in a jumble of periods and patterns kaleidoscopically and comfortably.

It was exciting to be invited for a second time and after ten years as a guest to the wine fair of France, and with M. Pineau, then French Foreign Minister, as guest of honour.

Four hundred guests sat down. With the first course—*Jambon en croute Perigueux* (ham cooked in pastry and served with a cream sauce with wine and truffles)—we heard a mixed choir singing drinking songs and saw them in traditional dress. The first song was in honour of Lamartine, and I wondered if M. Pineau would not sooner leave this room as Lamartine had so often done, to journey back to the simple shooting lodge at Milly, 6 miles away, or to the embracing tranquillity of the poet's later home at St Point, which is now named Château Lamartine and where most of his relics are kept. It is surely one of the most peaceful places in Europe. Its trees and hill-side and spaciousness, its very air suggesting the possibility of quiet composition and considered thinking rather than the hurly-burly of trans-oceanic travel and the organized confusion that now passes for diplomacy.

The banquet consisted of six courses and the opportunity of trying thirty-one different wines! One did not, of course, but there they were and one knew that the vintners of France had vied for the honour of providing them. The easiest wine, the most 'cuddlesome' as a *chef du cave* described it to me when I lived in France as a young man, was a Beaujolais—Moulin à Vent 1955. The most exciting a Clos de Vougeot 1949 and a Clos de Tart 1950.

Then came the speeches and the man we had all been waiting to hear, M. Pineau. I was sitting five places away and had been quietly watching him.

A little man with a great sense of purpose and nervous energy. I have often seen his like come in to bat number eight in a village side and save the day. He had appeared relaxed as he studied the singers and dancers, but all the time his brows were furrowed and his knit hands twitched. When he came to speak it was to an audience in part critical of his policies but mellowed by good food and wine.

He spoke of many things—of trade, of wine, of fellowship and family life. But one thing he said cut right through politics and frontiers. Turning to the Mayor of Neustadt in Germany, he said—and everyone present knew that M. Pineau had spent seventeen months in one of the horror concentration camps— 'The most important thing our two countries have to achieve, Mr Mayor, is an understanding of each other so that we may never again take up arms against the other. Last week', he continued, 'I saw your countrymen play mine at basket-ball. This is the kind of rivalry that young men should engage in—never more should we older men send young men of twenty to fight each other.' The German Consul-General, who is one of the few still living who was associated with the plot to assassinate Hitler and whose face is scarred with the torturings he has received from the

Gestapo, bit his lips and nodded his head. The wine no longer made one think of happy things . . . this small man had made us all sad. . . .

During the five hours that the V.I.P.s—'the big vegetables' as they call them in France—had been banqueting, the Fair had been filling up, and I went to see what it was like when not kept clear for the privileged few. It was Sunday afternoon and it was chaotic . . . all the world, his wife and their children were there bent on much sampling and an afternoon out. So if you visit the Wine Fair of France at Mâcon—around May 20 each year—avoid Sundays. On other days I was assured it is not overcrowded.

Tasting a full glass costs between 9d. and 1s. 6d. according to the wine, and it is possible to share out portions between several people in a party. There are some hundred wine stalls and over five hundred wines from all over France are there to be tasted. Incidentally the wine fair forms part of a general fair, but this is of decreasing importance.

Before you leave the vineyards of Mâcon and Beaujolais—and they splash down to within a few hundred yards of the main road to the south—try to visit Milly, St Point, and the Château Monceau where Lamartine wrote *Les Jacobins*. The three visits demand only 20 miles motoring in all. Here you can see where Lamartine lived his active life as poet, writer, politician, and wine grower. The views all around you capture the poetry, the tranquillity, the repose, and the clarity of vision in this man's life. You can see the simplicity and beauty of his home; imagine the quiet reading aloud which so influenced the poet and which his father's sonorous voice gave each evening as a present and relaxation to the adored mother. You can see the study in which Lamartine worked from five o'clock each morning and the glorious unchanged hill-sides that were the inspiration to his older years as Grazziana was to his younger. You can see busts and paintings of this man who looked more noble than any Roman, see original letters to him from many of the great men of his world; and—looking out again over this scene of peace, of hill-sides covered with vines, with shrub, with stunted trees; with bright colours, giant crags and verdant green—can re-echo those words of Cowper's which Lamartine himself so often used, 'God made fields, men towns.'

Whilst we were at Mâcon we stayed at a little hotel, discovered in *Auberges de France*, called *Le Manoir* at Charnay-les-Mâcon, about 2 miles out of the town.

If you like sophistication, chromium plate, and cars which could also accommodate the family next door, avoid Le Manoir. It is unpretentious, inexpensive and simple. It is furnished like a prosperous Victorian home whose head inherited it in 1900 and decided it was to her taste. It is a higgledy-piggledy agglomeration of pictures, furniture and peeps into the past. It is clean, comfortable, enclosed by trees, and as quiet as any hotel I have ever known. Its food is good, its service excellent, its wine cheap. It is old-fashioned, and to me quite delightful.

Whilst we were there we spent a lot of time tasting and sightseeing with M. Jean Mommessin. M. Mommessin was President of the Wine Fair Committee and of the wine merchants and growers of High Burgundy. Officials and telephone calls broke in on him every few minutes and yet somehow he managed to spend the greater part of two days looking after my wife and me; showing us again around the Lamartine country; taking us to the rock of Solutré, where our prehistoric ancestors slaughtered forty thousand cattle for personal consumption by driving them to a drop of a thousand feet, at the bottom of which they were immediately carved up; giving us *dégustations*; taking us for two meals to his house and making us feel very much 'wanted' when we joined the celebrities of the French political and viticultural world at the Banquet. You have to be a very big man to be able to do all this when you have so many more important things on hand.

The red wine of Mâcon is honest-to-goodness won't-let-you-down-ever-as-long-as-I'm-not-diluted kind of wine. Not much bouquet, a pleasant fruity taste—a good accompaniment to a sandwich at the club, a lunch with a cousin, or a first step towards an appreciation of wine by the younger members of the family.

In Mâcon a hogshead is called *Foudre* instead of *Fut* as in Beaune and the wine is stored for two to three months in glass vats and then drawn off and filtered. It is interesting to see one great vat above another so that they can be filtered without outside air getting at the wine. The sequence is one year in *foudre* and one year in a *pièce* of 215 litres (228 litres in Cote d'Or), but it should be put in bottle a maximum of two years after being put in *pièce*; Pouilly Fuissé after a year.

If the red wines of Mâcon are 'ordinary', the whites, on the other hand, are magnificent and are serious rivals of the over-priced wines of the Côte de Beaune.

The *premiers crus* of Pouilly-Fuissé, which like the wines of Pouilly-Vinzelles and Pouilly-Loché come from the Chardonnay grape, are Fuissé, Solutré, Pouilly, Vergisson and Chaintre. Their colour is a radiant gold tinted with green; their flavour an indefinite freshness with a suggestion of melon.

Graded after these superb white wines come those entitled to be called Mâcon superior or Mâcon followed by the names of any of seven villages—these are about equally white and red; then come the reds and whites grown from the Gamay or Pinot and which are sold under the name Mâcon or Pinot Chardonnay Mâcon if they are white. If your bottle just has the word Mâcon on it and no overprint saying *appellation contrôlée* it is likely to be a wine of less importance than any of these.

BEAUJOLAIS

We were so happy at Le Manoir and in Monsieur Mommessin's company that we were annoyed to find that Thoissey, where we had been booked in by Monsieur Geoffray, the President of the wine growers of the Beaujolais, was only 12 miles away. However, when we got to *Le Chapon Fin* at Thoissey we soon realized that we had come somewhere pretty good.

We arrived at about 4.30 to find a group of large cars outside the hotel and a luncheon of vine growers just breaking up. However hard times are the growers usually manage to keep a stiff upper lip—like stockbrokers and farmers who somehow thrive even if forced to eat their own stock.

So when you find ten or twelve of them (and we found half of these had been fellow guests at the Wine Fair banquet) spending four hours over lunch you can reckon that the table is very good. This was further borne out by Michelin, who gives the restaurant two stars, and by M. Blanc, whose menu was magnificent.

Getting to Thoissey taught us something that I had never learnt in all the times I had motored towards the French Riviera —that if you cross the Saône at Mâcon and proceed along the other side of the river to Lyons you only have to motor about 2 miles further and there is no traffic whatsoever until the last mile or two.

The only snag about the *Chapon Fin*, if you are prepared to pay the very much warranted price, is that the floors of the corridors creak in the way they do in some of the newer airport hotels in Germany. I talked about this to M. Blanc and he told me that this would be put right during 1958, in which case I would strongly advise staying as well as eating there.

Before dinner we went back across the river and climbed into the mountains first to see M. Geoffray and then to go on to Vaux, which is the original of Clochemerle.

M. Geoffray is a charming person. He lives in a little château, which gives the name to his wine, Château Thivin. His office and workroom, which is about the size of a large bathroom, has got seven guns hanging up on the wall—all guns that he is using. Vintners love *la chasse*.

If you go to Vaux during the daytime you will find it strangely deserted, but wait until the men come back from the fields; from Villefranche or St Georges. Go on a Sunday and you will find boule being played in the square; you will find business being done at the café and the tobacconist, in fact all the happy, care-free life of Clochemerle. The only sadness is that the heroines of the book, be they sharp-tongued or round-breasted, voluptuous or virginal, are much older than you will have pictured them.

Whilst we were in the Beaujolais we were told time and again how mad foreigners are who seek 'vintage' Beaujolais.

A Beaujolais can be drunk the year following the harvest and is best drunk at two to three years, though the *grands crus*— Brouilly, Côte-de-Brouilly, Chenas, Chiroubles, Fleurie, Juliénas, Morgon, Moulin-à-Vent, Saint-Amour—keep well up to five years. The next grades of wines are the Beaujolais-villages. They are: Juliénas, Jullié, Eme-ringes, Chénas, Fleurie, Chiroubles, Lancié, Villié-Morgon, Lantigné, Beaujeu, Régnié, Durette, Cercié, Quincié, Saint-Lages, Adenas, Charentay, Saint-Étienne-la-Varenne, Vaux, Le Perréon, Saint-Étienne-des-Ouillères, Blacé, Arbuissonnas, Salles, Saint-Juliè, Montmelas, Rivolet, in the Rhône. And: Leynes, Saint-Amour-Bellevue, La Chapelle-de-Guinchay, Romanèche, Pruzilly, Chânes, Saint-Verand, Saint-Symphorien d'Ancelles, in Saône-et-Loire.

Then come the Beaujolais Supérieur and the Beaujolais which are imported into England and America in the largest quantity. They are the élite of the carafe wines of France. They are the cuddlesome wines. Wines which the French think should be drunk in large quaffs and of which they say there is only one place to drink them—between the cellar and the top of the stairs (i.e. quickly).

A friend of my playing days with the Football Club de Lyon in the nearby city which consumes so much Beaujolais that it is said to be washed by three rivers—the Rhône, the Saône and the Beaujolais, once pushed his nose far into a glass of particularly succulent Beaujolais, kept it there for many a second, looked up dreamily and said, 'If only I could keep my nose *en pension* here for life!'

Having had a whole year to test out the Beaujolais I am prepared to be more dogmatic about it than about most French wines. To start with it is an honest wine, if allowed to be by the get-rich-quick boys. It has a magnificent ruby-like colour ('like rubies splashed on a Roman sunset' someone once said). It is inexpensive, as soft on the palate as easy on the eye and can be drunk *chambré* in cold weather, or slightly chilled in hot in much the same quantities as one would drink iced lager, and in the process only loses a little of its bouquet just as it quickly loses some of its colour if kept waiting too many years before joining forces with your palate. It is an impatient wine, and like many such, wants to give of its qualities immediately and without delay.

The actual *grands crus* vary greatly. Fleurie is the most even, at the same time carrying a slight taste of violets; Brouilly and Juliénas the deepest coloured and most fruity; Moulin à Vent the most distinguished, like the superb view from the side of its windmill—a view best photographed in the forenoon.

To get to Moulin à Vent you turn off the main village street and immediately pass a snug little *Dégustation* (all Beaujolais villages have them) in which are two attractive prizes won by Moulin à Vent wines—one a cup and one the green figure of a young man holding a cluster of grapes over his head. They were won in 1956 by the *commune*—one for being the best wine of its type in the world and the other for the best wine of the year containing not more than 11·5 degrees of alcohol. The prize was offered to encourage growers to produce a more delicate wine.

When you visit the Beaujolais—of which Villefranche is the commercial capital but St Georges des Rennes much the more typical—you will be struck by the cheerfulness and robustness of the people you meet; this they attribute to the fact that in their own district they drink no less than half of all the wine the abundant Gamay grape brings to them.

Usually when one sees people going out to work in the fields one sees that they have a small barrel called a *barlet* strung across their backs or on to their bicycle. It is of a convenient shape and holds between 2 and 4 pints of wine, which is considered a fair half-day's ration for an agricultural worker.

Incidentally if you have heard of the bad, common Gamay or remember reading about it in the chapter about Chablis, ignore all its shortcomings when thinking of it in the Beaujolais. Here it reaches its apotheosis, the soil and subsoil suiting it to perfection and producing a wine of infinitely greater character and distinction than in the plains of Chablis. The soil of Beaujolais is, in general, granitic and clayey without any limestone. It is hard and bare, yet the Gamay loves it!

Leon Foillard tells a charming story which illustrates the astonishing amounts of their wine that inhabitants of the Beaujolais drink. It is a custom in those parts to offer a glass of wine to anyone doing a job about the place. This well suited a Breton glass seller who, in the course of several dozen calls a day, consumed a number of *pots* of wine. By the end of the day he and his fragile load of glass could usually be seen careering zigzaggedly along the road to the accompaniment of a raucous call of '*Oh, le vitri, oh, le vitri!*'

On one such occasion a householder, thinking the Breton had had enough, only half filled the accustomed glass. The Breton looked at him in disgust and then without a word took his diamond out of his pocket, cut off the top of the glass, and explained to his outraged host that he never bothered with the empty part.

The Beaujolais are at pains to point out that the man was a Breton, if he had been one of them he would not have staggered!

Another story tells of the occasional years like 1956 when the grapes lack sun and the wine is feeble and green. It is said that three drinkers are then necessary—one to open the barrel, another to drink it, and a third to make a nasty grimace! They hasten to point out, though, that such years are rare!

There is no doubt that the Beaujolais love their wine almost more than any other possession. A last traditional story—they

come tumbling out of the racks of memory. A gay-looking trooper
turned up at a little vineyard; the husband was away but the
attractive young wife sought a sale and took the visitor down to
the cellars for a *dégustation*. The man knocked out the bung,
put his glass under the gurgling wine, turned to the hostess and
said, 'Put your finger in the hole.' She did; he drank. A minute
later he broached another barrel and again made as if the bung
was broken. 'Here,' he said to the lady, 'put another finger in
this whilst I go to fetch another cork.' She obliged and stood there
with arms outstretched, a finger of each hand holding back the
wine in the barrels. He regarded her quizzically for a few minutes
and she said, 'Hurry up, what are you thinking about.' His reply
was, 'I was thinking that I could do you a mischief—what do
you think about it?' The story has many endings—but in none of
them was it the wine that was lost.

Back at *Le Chapon Fin* at Thoissey we proceeded to one of the
richest and most beautifully served meals I have ever eaten. The
food cost thirty shillings a head and was the cheaper menu—
the *menu gastronomique* cost £2. From pâté with truffles we passed
to a choice of frogs, quenelles, poisson meunière, snails or chit-
terlings in wine sauce; then Capon of Bresse cooked in cream
sauce followed by Crêpes Parmentier of which M. Blanc gave
me the recipe, for you, and then a choice of cheeses, fruit melbas,
and so on. The cooking was superlative; the service faultless, and
the wine list admirable with the great classic wines there in plenty
but additionally—not tucked apologetically away in a corner as
if to say, 'I dare you,'—the Regional wines well displayed and
reasonably priced. We started off with an excellent half bottle of
the Pouilly Fuissé *maison* and then went on, for sentimental
reasons, to the Château Thivin which was quite first class—full
and aromatic despite the fact that it was less than two years old—
how mad our restaurateurs and wine merchants are to make us
drink old Beaujolais and pay more for the 'privilege'.

It was interesting when one thinks how many English and
Americans think they should get a bottle of good wine in a luxury
hotel like this for a very low price, to see a couple of Frenchmen
at the next table quite happily pay £3 for a bottle of Romanée
Conti '52. A high price? Yes! But an outstanding bargain at that
price for that quality.

This meal was our last, except for a frugal *café complet*, in
Burgundy on this trip. Tomorrow we were to lunch at *La Tante*

Alice in Lyons—a pilgrimage we always make if we are within a hundred miles of the great city which lies tranquilly, somewhat greedily, within the entwining limbs of its twin rivers Rhône and Saône—the city where many years earlier I had been young and very happy.

V

Lyons and the Côtes-du-Rhône

UNTIL THE time when it is over-populated with ghosts most people have a continuing affection for the places where they were young and happy. For that reason many roads lead me to Lyons.

I had first lived in Lyons when I was seventeen; had worked in the famous Tanneries Lyonnaises; played football for its premier club; learned a little about life, a lot about living. I had found how abundantly kind the French can be to the stranger within their gates; had come to appreciate their sense of humour; found them frighteningly uninhibited, intelligent; very conservative and not nearly so 'naughty' as English moralists made out.

At first it seemed odd that many of my contemporaries had mistresses whose existence was known to all members of their family and in fact subsidized by some and about whom they were teased, whereas their sisters were not allowed to dance—this was in the mid 1920s—more than two dances in an evening with the same man. I found it less odd when I witnessed the almost terrifyingly sincere affection these young people had for each other, the completeness of their 'fidelity' so long as the romance lasted—which was often for a very long period, sometimes running into years.

Few writers of historical or travel books have much first-hand knowledge about different *types* of people. Yet their trade demands that they should make judgements and assessments, and so they are apt to 'consult' others who have already written up the subject.

This is the reason, I believe, why all the books one has ever read about the people of Lyons make them out to be dull dogs—solid and stolid, rather like English food.

But they are not. How can they be? Firstly they are racially a mixed bag of Italians who brought the great silk industry, of Germans who introduced printing, and of many others fleeing from persecution in the Middle Ages. They gave birth to Laurent

Mourguet, inventor of the Guignol or Puppet Theatre. They have the greatest reputation in the world for gastronomy, and their restaurants are relatively finer than those of Paris, New York and London.

On my first day in Lyons the directors of the Tanneries Lyonnaises, who had agreed to be responsible for me during my year in France, took my father and me to one of the most famous of the many mothers and aunts of gastronomic Lyons; to *La Mère Fillioux* whose specialities were then and are now *quenelles de brochet* and *Volaille de Bresse demi-deuil* (chicken cooked in a skin and a casserole). These are also the speciality of my favourite Lyonnaise restaurant, *La Tante Alice* who has given me her recipe for quenelles, which is an ethereal-just-of-this-earth kind of dish vaguely associated with fish (perch has a place in it).

At that first luncheon I was told that the original Mère Fillioux had died a few years earlier and that no less than 500 carriages had followed her funeral cortège. There was a rather charming custom—which my socialist friends will deplore—of the rich sending just a carriage to pay tribute to those who were their friends, but of such a different social class that it would merely be an embarrassment if they had attended in person.

I also learned that my grandfather had given a party in the same restaurant some thirty years previously—gastronomic memories are long—and had ordered the brand and type of champagne that he thought the best, only to find that his guests quietly added soft sugar to bring the wine up from the very much drier English taste to the *demi sec* then beloved by the French. I was told that my grandfather would not usually have departed from the traditional Beaujolais Grand crus or Pouilly Fuissé, but that this was a very special occasion!

Lyons is subordinate to its rivers—slow, smug Saône and rushing Rhône—the river which Madame De Sevigné found both beautiful and terrifying; the river which 'fights against you, swallows you up, and throws you where it will': the river in which I once bathed with two others, one of whom had cramp and was dragged to his death. . . .

The two rivers merge just south of Lyons and are there so close that the whole city is one of quays and water fronts (15 miles of them); reflected lights, gracious bridges and clean hosepiped streets. There is no disguising the fact that Lyons is an industrial city but, like Nottingham, she is also a gracious one. Her streets are wide, the Place Bellecoeur, Sunday haunt of stamp swappers, one of the finest squares in Europe, its eighteenth-century houses and restaurants as easy on the eye as its food to the palate.

It was in Place Bellecoeur that the Germans shot three young Frenchmen during the occupation and left their bodies lying in the sun—as a warning to others. The Archbishop of Lyons telephoned the Military Governor and asked for the boys' bodies for Christian burial. His request was refused. He telephoned again and said that unless the bodies were reverently brought to him within an hour he would go down personally, dressed in his full regalia, and carry them back one by one, and that he would not be responsible for public reaction. The boys' bodies were brought.

If you visit Lyons go to the *syndicat d'initiatif* in the Place Bellecoeur and tell them what your interests are. These syndicates are usually very helpful and in Lyons particularly so. Get them to arrange a visit to one of the families or small groups—the *canuts*, who still make luscious silk fabrics by hand—the descendants of those who revolted when Jacquard invented his automatic loom. These *canuts* are immortalized in *Le Guignol Lyonnais*, which was created by Laurent Mourguet at the beginning of the nineteenth century, and which is the father and mother, or so the Lyonnais think, of all the wooden marionettes in the world.

There are constant showings of Le Guignol at a little theatre down by the Saône, but you will have had to live in working-class Lyons a long while before you understand much of what is said, as it is all in workers' slang. None the less, it is well worth a visit, as is also a summer season of open-air plays in the vast old Roman Forum discovered during the last war on the slopes towards Fourvière.

A very fine view of Lyons and the surrounding country from the heights of Fourvière can be obtained either by motoring through the steep and narrow streets of the old silk quarter or by a ride in the swinging funicular, not all of whose journey is perpendicular. It is said that one can see Mont Blanc from Fourvière and maybe one can, though personally this achievement has always eluded me.

If the astonishing gastronomic subtleties of Lyons' restaurateurs tempt you to prolong your stay you will find that a visit to the casino at Charbonnières, in a delightful setting only 6 miles away, will give you an opportunity of some modest gambling, a visit to the Guignol, and even a donkey ride.

We left Lyons, *La Tante Alice*, and two life-long friends with regret to stay at Condrieu, where we had chosen *Le Beau Rivage* as a hotel modest in price but with a Michelin star for cooking. The only Michelin that we could lay our hands on—ours was under a pile of luggage in the T.R.2—was a mid-1920 one which showed that whilst the amount of francs to the pound had gone up some twelve times, the price of a meal had risen forty times, which goes a long way to explaining why the English who used to find France a cheap place for holiday-making now find it so very expensive.

Our dip was a lucky one, as the *Beau Rivage* is a delightful and well run hotel on the opposite side of the Rhône from the main Lyons-Riviera road which one has the pleasure of leaving at Vienne—and which one can avoid on an almost trafficless and very attractive road for the whole 60 miles to Valence.

The view from the *Beau Rivage* is delightful; the swift-running Rhône laps the hotel; terraces have gay tables and shady trees and most of the bedrooms private balconies.

The one snag about the hotel is that it is only a hundred yards from a branch railway line and bedrooms on the side are therefore within easy hearing of the occasional goods train that chugs through. The main bedrooms facing on to the Rhône are much quieter. It is noisy and booked up at the weekends. The menu at 1,000 francs was outstandingly good value and the wine list contained a most wonderful and inexpensive wine—Château Grillon, which we visited the following day.

Our guide for all the vineyards of the Côte du Rhône except Château Neuf du Pape and Rasteau was M. Deschaux, Regional Controller of the office of the *Appellations Contrôlées*. First he took us to the Côte Rôtie, where we looked at the famous, immense and steep blonde and brown slopes before meeting M. Jasmin, the President of the Vignerons of the Côte Rôtie.

I asked him if it was true that an ancient landowner gave the two vineyards on these steep roasting slopes one each to his two daughters, one blonde and one brunette, and that the wine the vineyards produced came to resemble the characters of the two women. He said, 'Yes, it is certainly true that the one which matures quickly is said to have belonged to the daughter who was gay and beautiful when young but soured when old, and the other which matures much later to the one who came in time to be a wonderful old woman; but,' he said, shaking his head sadly,

8   Pouring grapes into the press

9 Pressing: this must be done very gently

'I'm afraid there's more to it than that—you see there's more iron in the earth of the brown slope; it has a better exposure and the wine it makes is *plus foncé* (darker). Also there are more white grapes in the blonde than in the brown.' The law says that the red wines of the Côte may be 100 per cent rouge and that they may not be less than 80 per cent from the Syrah grape.

M. Jasmin took us to his *cave* at Ampuis and opened a bottle of his own 1947—it was the colour of port. He said that it would be at its best in another three years and would keep for several more. He told me they keep their wines a minimum of three years and sometimes four in barrel and that the wine is very popular and is usually drunk too young.

We drank a number of other wines of the Côte Rôtie during our visit—some twenty years old, others younger. The younger wines were hard though full-bodied, the older had finesse and a distinct flavour, something between violets and raspberries. The principal vineyards are Pommière et Turque, Pavillon rouge, Le Moulin, Tharamont-de-Gron, La Landonne, La Grosse Roche, La Grande Plantée, Le Grand Clos, La Garenne.

I asked what *Vignerons* in Ampuis thought of the stories of their wine being used to stretch those of Burgundy, and everyone seemed convinced that this happened particularly when Burgundy had a lean year, as their Côte du Rhône wine is much more full-bodied and makes up the deficiencies. Proprietors here are much smaller than in the Côte d'Or. They nearly all also grow fruit and vegetables, and usually sell their grapes on the vines to merchants. Just occasionally, and only in a very good year, do they make the wine themselves.

The vineyards of Condrieu, Verin and St Michel are all included in the *appellation contrôlée* of Condrieu. Like those of the Côte Rotie, the vineyards rise steeply a few yards back from the banks of the Rhône. One result of the steep elevation is that the vines all get the maximum amount of sun; another, that they are very difficult to work as mechanization is impossible.

Experts are apt to dismiss the wines of Condrieu and Château Grillet as being fine local wines—I can only think that they have never tasted them, as these white wines are fit for kings and all discerning people. They have a taste all their own—an indefinable something coming from the soil and the seldom cultivated Viognier grape. It is significant that the famous restaurant *Pyramide* at Vienne, which, when M. Point was alive, was thought

H

by many to be the finest in the world, serves Condrieu wines as a speciality.

Few people know of Château Grillet, which is the smallest area—only 4 acres—to have its own *appellation contrôlée*. Many wines claim a taste of violets—Château Grillet has it and though it sounds quite filthy, it is not.

Château Grillet is a single property looked after by M. Besson, who combines the functions of *Régisseur* and *Maître du Cave* with being 50 per cent of the labour force and looking after the cherry trees which are at the side of the vineyard.

The day we were there the *mistral* was rushing down from the north—it has to. It is the only way the wind can escape from this long and wide Rhône gorge, so it blows and it blows and it blows. The *mistral* extends a little way along the Riviera but is less strong there, as the Rhône has several mouths through which it whistles. There is some relentless quality about it, and the hotter it is the worser, which shatters people's nerves, causes many a quarrel, and sometimes sends people mad—maybe Vincent Van Gogh in Provence was one of its victims.

There was no sign of *mistral* nerves about M. Besson as he descended the ladder from which he had been cherry picking. His first gift was one of luscious, dark cherries; his second of knowledge.

He took us to the tiny vineyard rising steeply behind the château—it seemed to me that at least a quarter of the area was taken up by the retaining walls of the terracing and the paths—at any rate it is certain that they produce far less wine than any other district which has its own *appellation contrôlée*.

He pointed out that there is practically no depth of soil. 'Pull gently at the roots of one of the vines.' I did so and nearly removed it. The few inches of soil is overlaid with large stones of granite flecked with gold quartz which keep the vines warm at night.

Then to the tiny *cave* where the *vendange* is brought and where we found an old press like the one at Clos Vougeot but smaller, with the date 1897 and the words 'American Press' carved on it—it is somehow curious to think of this ancient vineyard having one of its most vital parts made in the New World.

There are only four casks in this tiny *cave* where the new wine arrives and the whole area is less than the size of a squash racquets court.

M. Besson told me that they fine the wine five times before

putting it in bottle. They had only fourteen *futs* for the whole of their harvest of white wine for the 1955 harvest. The harvests differ tremendously. Fourteen *futs* in 1955, eight in '54, and '53, and fifteen in'51. In 1951, he said, they had a wonderful spring; the grapes were large; then they had lots of rain and little sun, and so although they had fifteen *futs* it was poor wine according to their standards. The wine stays one and a half years in *fut* and six months in bottle before they sell it.

It is all bottled on the Domaine like the Romanée wines and the greatest wines of Bordeaux, and it should be drunk when it is two to three years old, after which it will gain absolutely nothing. Practically none of the wine leaves the immediate district.

Whilst we were reverently drinking a bottle of '52 M. Besson told us that he tries to harvest as late as possible to get the sweetest grapes (do not think from this that his wine is sweet, as it is certainly not), but that he is thwarted because his neighbours all harvest early, with the result that all the local insects descend on the Château Grillet as they have nowhere else to feed. All the same, M. Besson reckons he can hang on for about a fortnight after everyone else has finished harvesting and that much of the superb quality of his wine comes from this calculated risk.

Vineyard by vineyard we moved down to Tournon, which is one side of the Rhône and Tain l'Hermitage which is the other and where we lunched at the *Chabert* restaurant, which is bang on N.7, where the menu was 800 francs and 1,000 francs. It is very well worth noting as a stopping place for those who want to relax for a while from the battle of N.7. We had the 800 menu, which included an hors d'oeuvres of eight dishes including ham and butter, sole delightfully served, then any kind of grill one cared to choose, and lastly the choice of many cheeses or a sweet. We found that many restaurants on N.7 are expensive and poor value—this is certainly the reverse. The wine they wish to serve is, of course, Tain, and mighty good it is.

The wines of Hermitage are about 80 per cent red and 20 white. The white should be drunk with the hors d'oeuvres and fish, the red with meat and cheese and especially with game and other highly-seasoned dishes. It is a very masculine wine that is apt to be astringent in its youth or if served too soon after the cork is drawn. Unlike nearly all other wines Hermitage should be allowed to breathe for twenty-four hours before being served—

put a piece of muslin over the neck and then leave it to take on the temperature of the room in which it will be drunk. Be careful not to serve the whites too cold—they lose all their bouquet if served at less than 50 degrees.

The reds have a brilliant colour and a very rich flavour due to the combination of the Syrah grape and the bright yellow sun which pours its golden rays on it. They keep for many years and are really only at their mellow best after eight to ten. The straw-coloured whites which come from Marsanne and Roussanne grapes are dry, have a most delicate bouquet and mature only slightly sooner than the reds.

The vineyards here are tiny and wine growers own many different plots called *quartiers*. They maintain, as do the champagne growers, that different *quartiers* bring different qualities and so they mix their wine, taking bouquet from vines from Greffieux, body from Meaux and finesse from Bessard.

I lunched at Le Chabert with Louis Bambert and his fellow directors. He had founded the co-operative movement in Hermitage, but takes no credit for it saying he merely copied the Burgundy co-operative. Behind his back I was told of the wonderful job he has, in fact, done to help bring prosperity to the small proprietors of this part of France.

It was interesting, after all the publicity I have read about plastic corks which cost 2 francs against genuine corks costing 5 francs, to hear that they thought the plastic corks were only suitable for vin ordinaire and that they were going to stop using them for their wines with an *Appellation Contrôlée*. Apparently it is thought that they do not let the wine breathe, rather like the difference between a plastic material for clothing, which makes one sweaty, as compared with wool which lets the air get through.

After lunch we went up the hill behind the river to the hermit's cave at the top. This is the cave with the date 1350 over the grilled door, from which the vineyards get their name and is said, according to Father Benedictus, once to have been inhabited by a persecuted Christian whom the beasts fed but who was very thirsty until God sent down some angels and wine growers (all of whom go to heaven) to plant heavenly vines which flowered overnight. On the other hand, James Joyce claims that the vines were planted by St Patrick, whilst Désaugiers supports the legend of a Crusader called Bacchus seduced both by a nymph who gave him grapes and by the beauty of the site, with the words:

'Ah,' said Bacchus, 'the end of my voyage,
Farewell, companions, good-bye,
Here I make my hermitage,
Here this hermit shall lie.'

We went hazardously as far as a car could and then had to walk for about twenty minutes up to the heights where the hermit's cave still exists. It is not in fact a cave, it is like a little church and is surmounted by a cross. However hot below, it is fresh and lovely here. The vines go tumbling down the steep hill-side and you can see the Rhône breaking through a line of mountains. They call it 'la trouée héroique du Rhône', because it actually broke through the granite mountains and divided them in two, leaving on one side Tain and on the other side Tournon. What a time that must have taken—thousands and thousands and tens of thousands of years—and, of course, it only got through because of some streak of impurity in the granite, and once having trickled through, then time did the rest.

They make only red wine on this mountain slope because of the granite. The white wine is made on another part of the mountain where there is limestone in the soil.

The principal vineyards are: Les Hermitages: La Sizeranne (red) and Chante-Alouette (white), La Chapelle (red and white), Maison-Blanche (white) and Rochefine (red), Marquise de la Tourette (red), Cuvée de Gallier (red and white), Cuvée Bergier, Cuvée Mure de Larnage (white), Hermitage Belleroche (red and white).

Next day we visited St Joseph, Cornas and St Peray, ending up at Châteauneuf-du-Pape for the night.

The *appellation* of St Joseph was only created in 1955; before that it was merely sold as Côte du Rhône, but the six communes making the wine constantly achieved such eminence that they were granted their own mark. They are therefore very little known in England or America, though like neighbouring St Peray they had a world-wide reputation in the fifteenth century, when they were a favourite wine in the court of the Czar of Russia.

Like Hermitage they make 80 per cent red and 20 white wine, but the wine is much less full bodied than any of its neighbours and with very flavoured meat is not so attractive as Château Neuf du Pape or Hermitage. There is a curious divergence in wine law here, as the whites keep better than the reds, which are at their best at five years against six to ten for the whites, after which they have a tendency to become yellow and ultimately to maderiase.

We tasted a number of wines, but it was a very hot day and very early in the morning and my palate did not do justice to the reputation that impartial M. Descaux said they have justly acquired, though I did enjoy a '54 we drank with two growers, M. Fern and M. Sauzon—a delightful pair in blue jeans and black velvet jackets who also grow cherries, apricots and pears and send them by plane to England each day. The wine certainly had a magnificent perfume and a slight after-taste of violets, a flavour I find less attractive in red wine than white.

The adjacent wine fields of Cornas and St Peray, a few miles on the other side of the river from Valence, make very different wines—Cornas comes from the Syrah and is always red, with much more body than its northern neighbour, St Joseph, probably due to a far greater amount of tannin in the grapes. Its principal vineyards are: Piedlavigne, Chambon, La Mure, Minangois, Le Gros, La Fontaine, La Côte, Septvaux.

The wine is kept three years in barrel and is at its prime in eight to ten years. The best recent years are '47 and '49, which will keep for twenty years, and—an exception to nearly all other French wines—1956 which is remarkably good. We drank a delightful '29 which still had a fine bouquet and perfume but which was 'over the hill'—much more yellow and less corsé than the younger wines.

St Peray, which used to make red, now only makes white wines from the Rousette—both still wines, and also sparkling, by the same method as champagne.

The wine of St Peray has been famous for centuries—Pliny and Plutarch remarked on its quality; Queen Victoria appreciated it; Lamartine, Dumas, Daudet, de Maupassant and Prévost wrote in praise of it, and Barbey d'Aurévilly, who preferred it to all other wines, wrote to a friend whom he wished to compliment very warmly, saying, 'You are the St Peray of my friends.'

The villagers of St Peray claim that their wine inspired Wagner when writing *Parsifal*, as a letter exists (in the museum of Tournon) dated December 2, 1877, in which he ordered 'another hundred bottles to be sent' to him at Bayreuth. As Wagner completed *Parsifal* in 1878 the villagers are perhaps justified in thinking that it was cause and effect!

Whatever the past, it seems tragic that these magnificent sparkling wines—and those of Vouvray—are hardly imported into England and America. I tasted a number of bottles of the very dry, dry and medium dry and found them excellent. Locally they claim that the wine is distinguishable from champagne as coming from a warmer climate; it is softer, since no sugar has been added to it as to champagne. For myself I would say that the flavour is so similar to champagne that not three in a hundred would know the difference though, in fact, it is less delicate and its bubbles a shade more boisterous.

Not long ago I attended a large reception at which the guests showed the warmest appreciation for the 'champagne' they were drinking; it was in fact a champagne type wine from the Loire, inferior to sparkling Vouvray or St Peray. Why should hosts to helots pay for champagne!

This fine sparkling wine costs about 8 shillings a bottle bought in St Peray, so it could be imported into England or America at a much cheaper price than champagne and would introduce this kind of wine to a public that cannot afford the world's most famous wine. It is a pity that no one takes up the challenge!

St Peray wines are sold direct to private customers, as they are boycotted by the trade—or vice versa—because of a quarrel they had some years ago when local merchants sold an inferior wine with the village name on it and so got the quality wines a bad name.

I suspect that one of the reasons that St Peray has not a greater export trade today is that many of the old smallholdings have been made over to the safer occupation of fruit trading, and that the quantity of wines that can be offered is comparatively small. There are, though, some very big firms, like Cotte Vergne, who have several times won the gold medal of France for their wines and who have an English trade mark, *Golden Hill*, dating back from the days when they did a big export trade.

On the other hand, there are little tiny firms like Leon Mathon where a team of three people, the proprietor, his brother, and a very elderly workmate, form the whole of the labour force for the dégorgement and labelling of the wines, of which there were only some two or three hundred bottles on the pupitres awaiting dégorgement compared with some million in a large champagne firm.

Whenever you are near enough, visit St Peray; call upon M.

Cotte Vergne, taste some of their wines; take some away with you, and be sure to climb the hill-side dominated by the ruins of the feudal château of Crussol and look across the village-filled valley to a vineyard with one of the finest aspects in France, but with only about 50 per cent now planted in vines owing to economic pressure.

VI

Châteauneuf-du-Pape and Tavel, Wine of the Sun

OPINIONS VARY as to when the South of France really starts. For some it is on the Channel boat or in an aeroplane; for others with the first whiff of a French cigarette or taste of a *vin du pays*. For me it is where the olive trees start in the Rhône valley, where the *mistral* tears furiously as a tantalized bull; where yellow sun showers gold on trees and vines and earth; where rocks tumble down the hills of history and where people talk for exercise.

Châteauneuf-du-Pape is such a place. Approaching along N.7 from the north one goes through the villages of Lapalaud, Mornas and Piolenc, gay with brightly coloured baskets, brooms and sun hats (buy yours there, not at home), and turns off at Orange; or one could go the whole distance on the other side of the Rhône on N.86—the same quiet road that runs parallel with the Rhône from Vienne, though this would have to be left at Bagnols sur Cèze.

We stayed at *La Mère Germaine* at Châteauneuf-du-Pape—one of two renowned restaurants in this little sleepy town whose inhabitants stroll about talking politics, rugby football, and wine. They are quite impervious to the hooting demands of traffic or the passage of cart or bicycle—they are talkers. *La Mère* has only four rooms and numbers five and six, the quiet ones, look far out over the vine-filled plain.

The dining-room is charming and there are shaded or sun-baked tables on terraces. The menu is 800 and very good value for its Michelin one star.

We had come here particularly to meet Baron Le Roy De Boiseaumarie. The Baron, one of the most venerated and respected men in France, has dedicated his life to his country, its vineyards and its wine. A pilot in the first World War, shot down and almost killed, he survived to found the *Institute National des Appellations d'Origine*, of which he is President. He is also President of the French Wine Growers Association and of the International Wine Committee, as well as being a keen sportsman and owner of many hundreds of acres in the primitive plains of the Camargue, home of wild bulls and splendid Arab horses.

We were just finishing dinner when the Baron arrived to tell us his plans for next day, which included about a hundred miles of motoring; visits to a number of vineyards, a look at Orange and Vaison-La-Romaine, and a ceremonial call on the Prefect in his lovely Governor's House at Avignon. The expression 'a ball of fire' is an overworked one, but here was a man who poured out nervous energy in restless waves. In no time he had made it abundantly clear that we were not to keep him waiting a minute when he called for us at 8.20 next morning. Time was the opportunity of service and, as such, precious.

Next day we first went to the summer palace of the Pope, from which the village gets its name. For long a crumbling ruin, its watch tower was destroyed by the Germans on their last day here. As Baron le Roy said, it was 'une belle bête', a beautiful beastliness. Till then there were steps up to the tower and you could see over to both sides of the plain, it was an astonishing view. Now it is lost for ever.

The vineyards here have had a varied history. When Phylloxera came in the latter part of the nineteenth century every vine was lost within a year and a half. The peasants could not afford to hang on until the American stock had begun to yield and so they planted the land with corn, but before they could begin they had to move all the stones—and there are stones everywhere. I have never seen such stones, they are the biggest stones on cultivated ground, I suppose, anywhere in Europe. The stones, in fact, are so bad that when, in April and May, the paths between the vines are being ploughed up, they have to change the leading tine on the plough twice a day—it just breaks to bits as it goes through them.

Baron Le Roy says the stones keep the heat in and warm the vines at night, and they also produce damp, humid subsoil because they shield the moisture at the time the sun is blazing above on to the vines.

In order to produce corn, the peasants had to move all these stones, and there you can see them—huge piles of enormous stones at the side of each little half-acre plot.

Now, whenever vineyards are replanted or when they grub up the old vine stocks and replant with young, they re-scatter the stones, and it is only in the very few vineyards which have continued all the time that you just have a steady carpet of stones.

There is a tremendous difference here between the appearance of the good and the bad vineyards, the stony and the non-stony. As Baron le Roy says, 'Il faut le voir pour le croire'—it is necessary to see them to believe them.

The wine of Châteauneuf-du-Pape is known all over the world. It is full-bodied, has a remarkable bouquet and a high degree of alcohol (the highest minimum for unfortified wine—12½ degrees—in France). Its great qualities are the result of a rigid campaign waged by Baron le Roy to eliminate the many hybrid vines that brought disrepute to the Region in the early 1920s and to depend on a blend of the thirteen varieties traditionally planted in the district. Through Baron le Roy's enthusiasm the wine growers of Châteauneuf had in fact agreed and made laws, rules and regulations in 1923 which anticipated by twelve years the national adoption of the laws of *applelation d'origine*.

The vines live for an average of forty years, though many that the Baron has are eighty years old.

Suddenly, 3 kilometres from Orange, the soil changes, it becomes browner with far fewer stones—that is the end of the region of *Appellations Contrôlées*. There are further vineyards, but they are nameless, they are Côte du Rhône, a wine of lesser quality. There are far more orchards and far more arable lands in the plain.

We went with the Baron to Orange to see the Roman Amphitheatre which Louis XIV described as 'le plus bel mur' in France. It is a staggering arena that holds some ten thousand people at a time. It has a great music and drama festival at the end of July. This year the Comedie Français played *Coriolanus*, and *The Damnation of Faust* was also given. There is practically no echo in the vast arena—just enough to be absorbed when the arena is filled, and speaking down from the stage one can be perfectly heard right up at the back, and vice versa almost as well.

In Roman times there was an awning over the whole of the arena and you can see outside where it was fastened down on pieces of stone jutting out the whole way round. There is a moat in front of the stage, and there are signs of the old marble facing on the stone, although most of it has gone, destroyed either by age or those who wanted stone for themselves.

Along Le Plain de Dieu, which contains very poor earth and suffered from a fierce mistral when we were there, the Baron hooted his way over cross-roads, always at about 120 kilometres an hour, with the spirit of an aviator making for home. We were not in the Côte du Rhône area here, but it recommences at the river Sablet at L'Ouvez, a sun-tanned village crowned with a cross. A village of very fine wines.

We went then towards Voisin, past Seguit nestling in the mountain-side. We were making for warm-roofed Vaison-La-Romaine, whose famous ruins, including the Maison de Messii, have been uncovered through the generosity of an Alsatian tobacco manufacturer.

The foundations are plainly visible, and as well as a number of the walls of an aristocratic dwelling of the Roman times one can see the kitchen and even the shape of the ovens. The basins in the ovens, incidentally, were hewn out from a piece of stone of impressive dimensions. I looked at the Baron, and could not help thinking that he was saying to himself, 'a stone like that would keep half a vineyard warm'.

Behind the huge house there is a Forum in fine condition, ten of its thirty-four pillars in perfect preservation. The Forum is backed by rose gardens, and back again behind this, cypresses and many, many other trees. Whilst we were walking in the gardens, I asked the Baron if he spoke English, and he said, 'No, a governess taught my children English, then when she'd finished with them she taught my wife, and then she wanted to teach me, but' he went on, 'I may be old and antique but I'm not for sale. And anyhow I know the essential words when I go to England—roast beef, wine and where is the water closet.'

We took a delightful road back from Vaison-La-Romaine to Orange—D.69—which runs along by the side of the river L'Aygues, which is, in the patois of Provence, the waterway.

We went to the Co-operative at Rasteau which makes very good wines; we called in there quite unexpectedly but, as the Baron said, it was impeccable. The *cave* was built in 1925 and has been three times enlarged since then. It makes a superb full dessert wine said to be first mentioned by Pliny in the first century, and also an apéritif wine which is rather sweet for English tastes. All this district lost a large part of its olive trees in the great frost of 1956, and you see them in the fields or by the side of the fields uprooted, absolutely destroyed, with others not uprooted but standing gaunt and naked.

At Sainte-Cecile-les-Vignes there are two most interesting things; one a modern Wine Co-operative, opened only in May 1957, where instead of excavating for their *caves* and putting their wine below earth, there are three enormous canisters like petrol containers, the kind of things which one sees in petroleum stores in America and England, and in which the wine is stored. The other is a statue of Baron le Roy, who is surely one of the few men (except conquerors) who have seen their statue unveiled in the prime of their life.

All this district is most fertile—where there are no vineyards there are truffles, wheat, olives, and cypresses. At Serignan we saw the garden where G. H. Fabre made his famous study of insects.

We went back to our hotel, the *Germaine*, at Châteauneuf-du-Pape for lunch, where amongst our hors d'oeuvres we had a *caviar provençal*, which you can make by pounding black olives and anchovies together and mixing with vinegar and a little onion, and where we learned that tomatoes are called 'apples of love' in Provence.

The patron saint of these parts is St Pierre de Luxembourg, who is the saint of the wine growers and also the boss of all thunder and lightning. He was a Cardinal of the Pope at the age of twenty, and was patron saint of Châteauneuf-du-Pape.

He is known as the Cardinal of the Liberation, because in the liberation the colonels and senior officers of the Maquis were only about twenty years old. Only a few years ago someone was sheltering under a balcony in a thunderstorm, it was struck by lightning but, it is said, because he was praying to St Pierre at the time, although everything around was destroyed and tons and tons of masonry fell, he was absolutely untouched.

The Patron Saint certainly does them well, as I learned that they have some fourteen good years for wine-making out of fifteen, compared with one bad, two medium and one good in the Côte d'Or.

The great *crus* of Châteauneuf-du-Pape are: Château Fortia, des Fines Roches, de la Gardine, Rayas, Vaudieu, Clos des Papes, Domaine de Beaucastel, de Mont-Redon, de la Chartreuse, Terre-Ferme et Cigales, La Bernardine, Saint-Patrice, Saint-

Préfert, Grande Gardiole, Princes d'Orange, Les Olivets, les Cailloux, Chante-Perdrix, Chante-Cigale, Domaine de Nalvs, le Vieux Moulin, Clos du Mont-Olivet, La Solitude, Les Cabannes, le Vieux Télégraphe.

The wines are so excellent in flavour and so constant in quality that I, who delight in them, always wonder why they are so considerably lower priced than the wines of Burgundy.

We left Baron le Roy most regretfully. He is a tremendously exciting, vital personality, who obviously overworks himself terribly, who ought to give up, but who cannot and just keeps doing far too much.

From Châteauneuf-du-Pape—also immortalized by Alphonse Daudet in the charming story of the Pope's mule—to Avignon is only 7 kilometres as the bird flies, but is 15 by road. From Châteauneuf the Pope's Palace at Avignon stands out like a torpedo boat sailing towards the east—a most remarkable silhouette. It is said that the two Palaces were in constant visual communication and formed part of the chain of fortification built to protect Avignon and the approaches to the Rhône valley.

We had spent so much time with M. Descaux and Baron le Roy that we were unable to go to Tavel, whose rosé wine along with that of the Loire we think amongst the most delightful of summer drinks. It varies little in quality and has been of the élite since 1304 when Philippe-le-Bel described it as 'the only wine'—an extravagant phrase from one who must have had access to the great *crus* of Burgundy.

Tavel is obtainable all over the world, its best crus being: Château-d'Aquéria, de Trinquevedel, le Domaine de Manissy, le Prieuré de Monté-zargues.

The wine is best chilled and goes with anything, though throwing a slightly gun-metal flavour with fish; is very supple and mellow and has a clear, slightly orange-tinted colour. If you do not know it 'go to' and quickly repair an oversight in your gastronomic education.

As ever, Avignon was very full—it suffers from N.7 which skirts around it—but the Pope's palace was as lonely and lovely as ever; the bridge not at all reminiscent of Madame de Sévigné's comment—'This Bridge of Avignon which is dangerous to pass even with the greatest care! A sudden gust flings you against an arch! It is a miracle that you were not drowned.'

For those who are fascinated as I am by Madame de Sévigné's

letters it is quite easy to make a little pilgrimage in honour of her pen and go to her daughter's house at Château Grignan. After a visit to Tavel cross the Rhône at Donzère—a total distance of about 15 miles. Otherwise just turn left off N.7 at Donzère and it is only about 10 miles before you come to the impressive ruins of her son-in-law's château-cum-palace with its spacious terraces and long compelling view. From the château it is only a short walk to the Grotte de Rochecourbière from which the amiable letter writer loved to address her lengthy epistles.

Her son-in-law must have been a constant worry to doting Madame de Sévigné—Violet Hammersley tells, in *Letters from Madame de Sévigné*, of how he 'threw himself into all manner of intrigues and dissipation,' of which his affair with Ninon de L'Enclos was perhaps the most innocuous. Ninon was also to be the mistress of his son, and most probably of his grandson, the young Marquis de Grignan. When she died at the age of eighty-five she was said to have lost few of her charms. On her tomb the following words were inscribed: 'Ci git le corps de Madame la Comtesse Ninon de l'Enclos qui mourut à l'âge de 85 ans. Elle fut renommée pour sa chasteté pendant les dernières années de sa vie.'[1]

It is by getting off the great trunk roads that the traveller can hope to assess something of the spirit and life of a foreign people, can appreciate, for example, in Provence, something of their deep traditions, their ancient tongue which they cling to as obstinately as the Afrikaner or Welshman; can begin to realize what a land of contrasts it is, deserts and lagoons; sun and searing wind; rocks and market gardens; vineyards and palm trees; mountain village and fertile plain; turbulent river and placid sea; ancient monument and chrome-plated café; vivid days and dark nights; bones of history and bodies of tourists.

From Avignon we went on to St Rémy to see with our own eyes some of the scenes which had flashed like truth across Van Gogh's intense perception.

In a cold, grey country like England, the glaring yellows, the orange, green, red and vermilions of the 'southern' paintings, his black cypresses, silver-grey olives and pink earth seem a million miles from truth. Come to Provence and you find him real, live, honest, observant. Here are leaning cypresses, rocked by

---

1 'Here lies the body of Madame la Comtesse Ninon de l'Enclos who died at the age of 85. She was renowned for her chastity during the last years of her life.'

the moaning mistral, rickety bamboo hedges, tiny fields and grotesque buildings.

Here are people with different faces, no longer the round ruddy faces of the Burgundians, instead the more aquiline descendants of earlier Romans and Greeks.

Through fertile land from St Rémy to Arles, with thoughts of Van Gogh and Cézanne in our minds and their inspirations before our eyes—cypress trees and vineyards, dark hills and sweet-smelling thyme, feeling the harder brilliance of the air, hearing the perpetual screeching of the cicadas, experiencing 'the simplicity, the gravity of great sunlight effect' as had Delacroix, Picasso, Gauguin and Van Gogh before us.

We went up to 'uninhabited' Les Baux, drank in its impressive starkness. In the great, long mountain road there were occasional fertile folds interspersed with dead olive trees. Everything was very sinister, dead life everywhere, some vines. At the mountain top we found the wind-whining village, less deserted than travel books make out, although I think it is only recently that the old houses have been remade in order to sell curios, paintings, textiles, wrought iron, everything you can think of for the tourist trade.

It must be bone-cold in winter, yet just below the actual village of Les Baux is a very fine restaurant which, believe it or not, has a large swimming pool attached to it for the tourist trade and for those that come up from the plains in the hottest part of the summer.

We left on the road to Arles, and at Fontveille on D.33 we came quite unexpectedly on Alphonse Daudet's Windmill looking very companionable about half a mile from the cheerful little village, though in somewhat bleak surroundings.

It's a charming little windmill—it should be with such a Patron. Now it is a bird sanctuary on top and a museum down below. It looks across on one side to Les Baux and on the other to the plain.

Coquettish Arles is worth either a detour or a real visit. Once a great Roman city and port (the Rhône is placid here), it is now possessor of many fine architectural monuments—the Roman theatre and arena, the cloisters of the Cathedral of St Trophime, thought to be the most beautiful Romanesque church in Provence, and many more.

It is impossible, too, to spend long in Arles without being impressed as Van Gogh was with the classical beauty—Greek rather than French—of many of the womenfolk, and with the colour of the fields and plain enclosing it.

To know Provence would be to know much of humanity and life, of sunshine and seaminess, and it would certainly include an appreciation of the happy wines of the ancient country—wines which contain some of the magic and much of the character of Provence—true *vins du soleil*.

VII

The Riviera and the Wines of Roussillon

W<small>E CUT</small> across from Arles to Montpelier, Béziers, and Collioure, to have a fortnight at the fascinating fishing port of Collioure.

This meant leaving the wines of the Riviera to memory—the fragrant rosé of Bellet, Bandol, and Cassis; the rough but very palatable vins ordinaire of these sun-baked slopes; the delightful red wine of the Isles de Pourquerolles which we once drank very chilled but still with a delightful bouquet at the Auberge de l'Arche de Noe—well worth the twenty-minute sail from the port of Hyères; and the full-bodied red wines of La Palette.

It meant, too, turning our backs on the expensive end of the Riviera—the hotels and restaurants of Nice and Cannes and the wealthy miles in between with Antibes as their luxuriating heart—where one woman in twenty knows she is rightly dressed and the other nineteen feel cheated by their fashion paper.

Nor, this trip, should we see the infinitely nicer stretch between Fréjus, where American troops fought so gallantly in the landings, and Hyères. Nicer because quieter, less obviously 'fashionable' and with practically no commercialized entertainment—of little appeal to the many-headed.

I must not leave you with the impression, though, that this stretch with Le Lavaundou as its most precious jewel is inexpensive—its best hotels, though small, are very good and appropriately costly, and its beach makes almost as costly a couch as any in the Côte d'Azur. When we were last there, in May 1956, a tiny hut—shoulder-width—a beach umbrella and a strip of matting to lie on cost about £7 a week and by August it would be double. True it is possible not to hire these amenities, but this means that you have to go several hundred yards away from the best beaches, as the hut men have a monopoly. This is a contingency that has to be considered all over the Riviera, though many hotels do have their own 'beaches'—mostly rocky.

The road from Arles to Collioure is rather dull. Around Montpelier, typical estuary country and very bad surface; then very scrubby with mountains on the right—often, as at Salses, surmounted with grim and formidable Moorish fortresses—vineyards on the plain and shallow water and islets on the seaside.

At Béziers, where we spent an uncomfortable night, one seems to walk from France into Spain, although the frontier is still 80 miles away. Restaurants are on each side of a long, rectangular, tree-lined promenade—rather like the famous Ramblas in Barcelona. Here young and old start their evening promenade at about nine o'clock and boy meets girl . . . families chatter, communal gossip is flayed.

There are vast wine districts in this part of France. Languedoc in the main produces coarse table wines and a very fruity bronze sweet wine, beloved by Rabelais and Voltaire, called Muscat de Frontignan, which I remember drinking with the dessert at the first postwar banquet of the Wine Fair of France. I well recall its bouquet, finesse and smoothness—all grape and goodliness. Like the dessert wines of neighbouring Roussillon, they have a very high alcoholic content, somewhere around 21·5 to 24·7 degrees, and so must be taken a good deal more carefully than the majority of British and American tourists realize!

At Collioure one drinks the wines of Roussillon, which are divided into five districts: Banyuls, which can be red, white, pink (called Granache), and rancio (old); it is sweet or dry, very cheap, undistinguished, and admirable for holiday drinking. The others, which all produce heavy sweet wines as well as table wines, are Maury, Rivesaltes, Côtes D'Agly and Côtes de Haut-Roussillon.

The French serve these sweet *vins doux naturels* as apéritifs, at teatime with sweet cakes, and also drink them with dessert. Local restaurants have a charming habit of passing round loving cups of the sweet dessert wines in glass containers with spouts similar to Spanish *porrons*. These are very hygienic loving cups as the spouts are held a few inches from the mouth by amateurs, a few feet away by experts, and heavy sweet liquid pours into open mouth or not according to skill or the 'state' of the consumer.

These vineyards are as old as civilization. The first vines were

planted in 217 B.C. by old sweats left behind in the swift advances
of Hannibal's army. Subsequently viticulture seemed to have been
little organized until Charlemagne brought the district under firm
government in A.D. 778. From then onwards one can see on old
maps and charts hill-sides covered with vines and olives, though,
as usual, they did not reach their highest state of cultivation until
the monks took over cultivation, nor did they escape the notice
of the elder Pliny, who in chapter six of his fourth book of natural
history warmly praises the muscat and sweet wines of the Region.

The vines of these parts seem to acquire something of the
warmth and welcome of the slopes they adorn; in the plains they
are cultivated by motor tractors, but on the steepest—and best—
slopes running down to the sea it is the mule and the human back
which aids the plough and the spraying.

We explored a number of seaside villages within a few miles
of the Spanish frontier before settling for Collioure. Port Vendres
we thought too commercial and spoilt by the docks; Banyuls had
its attractions—lots of life and gay-looking restaurants—but we
thought the public beach inadequate and found the private beach
proudly advertised as belonging to a leading hotel about the
size of a double bedroom—and dirty at that.

So we settled for Collioure, which turned out, despite atrocious
and unseasonable weather, to be a very attractive little fishing
village.

We stayed at the *Hostellerie des Templiers*, having our meals in
the main hotel near the harbour but sleeping in the quiet of an
annexe a few hundred yards up the hill.

Except in the last fortnight in July and during August it is
never advisable to book in advance on the French Riviera, as so
very many hotels are best seen first, as they have the main road
running within a few feet of the bedroom windows—this applies
equally to the Italian Riviera. At Collioure there are several hotels
with excellent restaurants, but they are intolerable unless you are
capable of sound sleep on a railway journey.

Collioure is very Spanish (or to be exact very much itself,
which is Catalan!). The *patois* is difficult to follow, soft and long
drawn out. Every fine night the whole town turns out for its
promenade, men in blue, women in black, much hand-shaking,
happy laughter, dancing of the Sardan (in late July and August).

The sea front consists of three little bays with a mole behind
one, the fishing port of the small town behind another, and the

ancient fort of Le Château Royal, once the residence of the Kings of Majorca, Queen Anne of Aragon and the Empress Marie of Austria.

At nightfall the fishing boats put out with lights like large Japanese lanterns in their bows to ring this happy place with bobbing jewels; the air is heavy with talk and warm scents and laziness seems an end in itself.

We were unlucky for two-thirds of our stay as the rain beat down, the river, which was dry when we arrived, became a threatening torrent, and the Catalans, who are vaguely jealous that they have not got one of their own, blamed the whole deluge as a manifestation of 'La bombe atomic'.

Very few of the hotels have their restaurants open until mid-June and make arrangements for 'pensionnaires' to eat at one or other of the several good restaurants in the place.

The *Templiers* restaurant is always open and is the centre of life in Collioure. There are never less, except on feast days and Sundays when they are excluded, than about twenty fishermen playing cards and chatting loudly and excitedly. The bar counter is in the form of a ship and the walls are covered with a fascinating collection of modern paintings all given to M. René Pous, the proprietor, in gratitude by the many painters he has befriended. There one can see a lovely ceramic bowl by Picasso, who lived here early in his career, an Henri Matisse in the form of an enormous and gay invitation card, works by Cavannay, Cosson, Pignon, Coutaud, a particularly delightful beach scene by Pignon, and a portrait of Jane Avril by Toulouse Lautrec.

It's great fun at the *Templiers*; all the family working—Madame Pous is a magnificent chef, her husband an attentive patron, and their children cheerful helpers. The food is excellent—as it was also at *La Balette*, *Le Frigate*, and *La Terrasse* (we thought the latter a particularly good hotel and that the bedrooms on the beach side would be quiet so long as there are no fishing boats putting in early, a factor we could not check).

In this part of France one is offered a preponderance of fish, and excellent most of it is. At the *Templiers* we had bouillabaisse every three days or so—a hot-pot of many fish which is one of the great delicacies of the Mediterranean. We also often had large sardines as a fish course and were soon shown that the best way of eating them is to hold head in one hand, tail in the other, and gnaw! Another of Madame Pous' specialities is *loup flambé*—the large fish first being grilled and then being covered in brandy and set fire to by your side (this, like *langouste*, is an extra if you are en pension, which cost us 22s. 6d. a day each with a private bathroom).

The beaches are delightful, though I should think the main bathing one would be pretty full in season.

There is one snag—which is often found on rocky Mediterranean shores and which I have come across at different places all the way from Spain to Capri—and that is that the foreshore harbours many *oursins* which are very prickly sea urchins. If you tread on one it breaks off leaving a number of little spikes in your feet. These are mildly poisonous and very annoying and have each to be levered out.

At the risk of being avuncular, may I implore you not to get too sunburned—remember that the sun's rays in the Mediterranean are at their most burning in early May to June, and that right through from April to October they can cause tremendous pain to the unwary in as little a time as twenty minutes if the anatomy portion is unused to sun and particularly if the subject is fair-haired.

Unable to keep entirely away from the vineyards, I spent two days with M. Toutchkov, the energetic and charming Regional Controller of the *Institut National d'Instituts d'Origine*.

The vines of this region are as mass produced as wine can be; every four lines or so of vines one sees a large path between the row, and this is left so that motor tractors can pass through spraying eight rows at a time.

Our first visit was to the *Cave Co-operative* at Trouillas—where about sixty thousand hectolitres of wine a year is made—five times as much red and rosé as white. The wine is full value and they have only one real regret, they say that all they see of British and Americans is the back of their cars, so do call. The enterprise is vast and interesting. To give you an idea of local values, their wine when we were there in 1957 cost, on the spot, about a shilling for a bottle of red, one shilling and twopence for the rosé, and five shillings for the sweet dessert wine.

It was stormy weather when we were there and stormy weather in the summer means much more sulphur spraying, otherwise the grapes are lost from disease. Our road was hedged in with vineyards—they make about a third of all the wines of France in the Midi, the wine of the carafe, though not so good as Beaujolais.

We went to vineyards in Millas and Estagel, which makes good white wine, and on to the co-operative at Maury who make sweet and table wines and would welcome visitors; then to the Gorge de Galamus high above Maury and well worth a visit. From the summit one can look down to where the river Agly has cut its way through the mountain or go to the three centuries old hermit's cave.

Near Maury we visited one of the finest vineyards of these parts—Le Mas Amiel where the vines grow to fifty to sixty years old and which makes some of the finest V.D.N. (*vins doux naturel*) in France.

Here, following a centuries old practice, they put some of the wine out in *bombonnes* made of glass—like large crocks, and the shape of a closed flattish brandy glass—containing about 30 litres of wine, and these they leave outside in the sun for five to ten years. This is to produce a further oxidization so that the wine becomes *très rancio*—that is, it becomes a sweet maderized wine which is added to the young wines to give it a special flavour. Incidentally a young wine in these parts is about five years old.

One notices many cypresses—planted for two reasons. One to shield the living vines and another to guard the dead in the vast mausoleums they have in the cemeteries here. The vines here need a lot of sheltering because there is a tearing north wind which accompanies the river Agly down the valley. It brings good weather, and, of course, you do not notice that it is cold in the summer because the sun is so hot, but in the winter it really is something in the way of a wind, and is called La Tramontane—Catalan for 'the hill wind'.

We saw many of the sixteen thousand *vignerons* in Monsieur Toutchkov's region and finally visited the Château de Vaulmy, which is very near to Argeles, and drank wine on the terrace there, a V.D.N., but much drier than any other we had had.

It is an astonishing view from the Château de Vaulmy—right across the bay on one side and backed by superb mountains with many valleys in them which are not discernible except just as little breaks in the pine trees which you can see in the background. The Château welcomes visitors and sells direct to the public.

One evening we went to Perpignan to see the Catalan dance, called the Sardan. We had a very good and reasonably priced meal at the *Brasserie Alsacienne*—to change from fishy foods—and then we went to a narrow street where I suppose there was only about 10 yards between the tall walls of an ancient building and the cafés and hotel entrances opposite, in one of which an eight piece band was playing. By these walls sat some five to eight hundred people at tables with a scattering of waiters dashing around serving them.

The band took quite a while tuning up and showed off rather noisily. Then the dance started. It was a very catchy kind of four-time and very soon a little group of about six people on our left joined hands in a circle and started. Then we noticed another group had started—a rather bigger one—and so it went on, people just getting up, and joining one group or another—like attracting like and frumps dancing together. For two or three minutes they danced rather slowly, just bobbing away in four-time.

Then the music made suddenly far more noise, got quicker, and everything got much gayer and much more exciting, but it was all in a way very decorous. They just changed position very, very slightly—5 or 10 yards left or right during the whole dance. Otherwise they were just doing these quite complicated steps to themselves and hardly looking at the people opposite to them on the other side of the circle. As the music got more excited they rose higher and higher on their toes and moved more quickly.

This goes on altogether for six or seven minutes; then it stops, a few quiet notes; then off again they go, first to a slow start, then more quickly, until the dance ends after about a quarter of an hour.

As the evening goes on more and more people start dancing, there is no ceremony. Newcomers break into any group, the watchers are intent; the waiters move about quickly under a blue-black sky, which accentuates the blaze of light from the cafés. What strikes a stranger is the complete absence of self-consciousness in the dancing, the simplicity of it. It is just something that happens every fine day from the beginning of summer to the middle of autumn in Perpignan and other Catalan towns.

In contrast to this charming and simple relaxation was a bull-fight we went to at Seret. It was loathsome.

It is a bestial, bloodthirsty sport and exists, I gather, only in Spain, parts of Latin America, and in Southern France where it is illegal but where a token fine is paid—in advance! The arena was comparatively small, holding perhaps five thousand people. It was a gay scene but one which soon became a dripping pan of fresh red blood and tender, still palpitating flesh set with a back-cloth of vivid blue sky and verdant mountain.

The audience consisted of family parties whose young mostly got whiter and whiter, whose Mums looked on with all the stoicism of women who have known personal pain, and whose Dads yelled themselves hoarse as the blood spurted and the matadors and toreadors pursued their sadistic trade, their personal bravery and the spectators' collective sadism finally reaching culmination in the death of a creature which a week before had been wild and happy in the open spaces of the Camargue.

Please believe me and do not go, even though here in France the horses are protected and seldom get killed, though one nearly did this deathly Whit Sunday. To say that it is skilful or requires brave men is no defence, it belongs to the dark ages of cruelty and black magic and pagan sacrifice.

Also, at small 'corrida' like the one at Seret it is exceedingly ill-done. The bullfighters were either fat old 'has-beens' or presumptuous 'want-to-be's'. Several times they even roused the anger of the crowd at the inept butchery with which they gouged great raw crimson holes in the back of the bulls' necks—and never were they very impressive, except one toreador who eventually got tossed by the bull, who, poor dying going-to-be-killed-for-fun animal, left the real enemy writhing on the ground and went after the billowing, annoying, highly-coloured, hated pieces of cloth which he had come to associate with the pain he was suffering.

Suddenly the dying rate accelerated, the great beast's tongue started lolloping out, the blood streamed, he started pawing the ground and he was dead. And Dad cheered. And Mum passed the cherries. And little Jeanne had colly-wobbles.

VIII

Armagnac

ARMAGNAC IS a brandy made in Gascony. It is deeper coloured, less delicate, than Cognac and has far more variations in quality as there are no great firms like the distillers of Cognac but, instead, hundreds of little ones.

It is usually sold in flat, round bottles and some, particularly the oldest Armagnac of the Marquis de Montesquiou, is in exquisite bottles that your wife eggs you on to finish as she covets them for lamp-holders. They are made by Baccarat and their vintage is 1893, so they are not inexpensive, though cheap for what they are.

The Marquis de Montesquiou is so anxious to help anyone who wants to learn about this relatively lesser known brandy that he flew down from Paris to entertain us at the Château de Marsan, a long, lovely building built gracefully in several centuries and belonging to the family for over a thousand years. It is set in 400 acres of vineyard and farmland, much of it modernized to include co-operative ventures which he has set up for his neighbours and villagers to share.

I asked him how it was that the Château was neither destroyed nor confiscated during the Revolution, and he replied, 'Well we had several other castles and they took them; but they left us this one as they were rather fond of us'—an affection one can understand if the Marquis's ancestors were as interested in the well-being of the community as he is.

There is no doubt that he is devoted to the exploitation of Armagnac. He thinks it the world's finest *eau de vie*; that they are many times blessed who have the privilege of growing the grape or distilling its fruit; and that they are traitors to an ancient tradition who fail to conserve great quantities of their precious liquid to age gracefully in the oaken casks grown from the woods of their own forests.

As he talked to us about the history and distillation of Armagnac his face took on an air of warm enthusiasm and resembled more

and more the fine portrait in the entrance hall of his ancestor
upon whom Alexandre Dumas modelled d'Artagnan, the most
famous of 'The Three Musketeers'.

The world trade for Armagnac is not at all what the Marquis
would like—Cognac is some fourteen times larger. He wants a
steady, regular, all-round-the-world trade and he wants particularly to develop the American and English markets.

Unfortunately for its reputation all Armagnac shippers are
not as meticulous as the Marquis de Montesquiou about maintain-
ing their standards by conserving large quantities of very old
brandies for blending purposes.

He told me that a few years ago the Swedes, who are great
spirit drinkers, 'discovered' Armagnac; orders poured in and
soon the distillers ran themselves out of matured stock. Swedes,
like Americans, cannot understand why some commodity they
like does not go on for ever, and they pressed and pressed for
greater quantities. Some accept all the orders, others like
Montesquiou, ration them so that their standard products can be
maintained.

During the evening we were talking about the occupation,
the last one, not the centuries old one by the British which is
constantly cropping up in conversation, and the Marquis said
that he went into the Maquis in the war because it was safer.
Seeing me smiling to myself at this apparent understatement, he
laughed and said, 'No, I really mean it. You see, people in my
kind of position in France were liable to be taken off to a concentration camp at absolutely any time. I went into the Maquis,
and well, then I knew when I was in a dangerous position and
when I was not. We had sentries and we were all friends and we
were all fighting for France; it was much better than being a
civilian and waiting for arrest.'

We went to the museum at Auch with M. Poltge, the city
archivist. It is housed in one of the most fascinating buildings
that I have ever seen as a museum, it is the old chapel of a
seminary. All the things in it have been 'won' by M. Poltge; he
has practically no money. What he does is to decide to get examples of a certain period or subject. He then writes to all other
museums asking if they will exchange anything they can spare
of this nature with him, and will they write back and say what
they want in exchange. When he finds out what they want, he
writes to the Louvre and asks them to search in their cellars for

what this other provincial or national museum wants and gets them to send it off, thereby acquiring his collection at no cost to anything except the cellars of the Louvre, which badly needs the space anyway!

He told us a most macabre story about an Egyptian mummy that he once received. It got knocked about in transit somewhat, the mummy itself went bad, and he could not make any arrangements to dispose of the corpse, which was very, very odoriferous when it arrived. The local authorities in Auch said, 'You've got no death certificate, therefore you can't bury it,' and the museum authorities said, 'Anyhow, we've got no funds for a funeral.' So he didn't know what to do with it, he couldn't keep it in the museum—it was very, very powerful—so he took it home. He did not tell his wife, and he kept it in the cellar that they had in the house.

He made feverish attempts to dispose of it; he telephoned, he wrote, and he implored, and no one would have it, until finally someone said, 'Try the hospital at Toulouse.'

He rang up the hospital at Toulouse, and they said, 'Oh yes, of course, bring it along.'

So he got hold of a friend the next night, and in the middle of the night they put this putrefying mummy into the back of his car and went to the hospital at Toulouse, a long distance away, and knocked up the concierge, but he said, 'We can't take that, we only have sick people here, we don't have any post mortems or anything like that.'

There they were with dawn approaching in a car with a stinking corpse in a city which they did not know and which did not know them.

Finally he got hold of the man who had said he would receive it, who said, 'Oh, of course I know I spoke to you on the 'phone, but I thought it was only a student ringing up and it was a joke, so I said bring it along. I never thought for a moment that you'd got a "live" mummy.'

In the end the hospital refused it, so they tried the morgue in Toulouse. At the morgue the caretaker said, 'Oh yes, if you've got a corpse, bring it in,' but when it arrived he changed his mind—'Take it away, it's too smelly.'

By then M. Poltge had really had enough and replied, 'No, this is a morgue, it's the place to receive corpses and you're going to have it,' and he went across to a large empty drawer underneath the slab on which the corpses were put. He opened the drawer, found nothing in it, put the mummy in it and ran. And that is the last he heard of the mummy. If you want to see the sarcophagus which contained that mummy, go to the museum at Auch.

The vast cathedral in Auch, first consecrated in 1548, is interestingly ugly—perhaps because it took nearly 150 years building. It is set high in the centre of the town, as is the Préfecture next door, where we were guests of the Prefect. The Préfecture, formerly the Archbishop's palace, has a curving elegant 'staircase of honour' and gardens some two or three hundred feet below house level.

The cathedral has a superb example of a seventeenth-century organ, the finest period of French organ making. All its fellows were repaired in the eighteenth century, a very bad period for that kind of work, and they were all more or less ruined. Auch, however, was either too impecunious or too lazy and its organ was never repaired. Consequently it is the only organ in France on which can be heard the absolutely true notes of the organ as it was in the seventeenth century.

Incidentally, many of the world's playing cards are made in Auch and they are very proud that the Jack, the *Valet* as they call him in France, is a Gascon.

We went to Castira Vedusan, half-way between Auch and Condom, where we saw a most extraordinary statue of a famous Gascon—Doctor L. Lannelongue, who was deputy for the Region until his death some years ago, and also a very close friend of the President of the Republic. He was a great man, but he was very proud of himself and saw to it that about six self-statues were put around his constituency during his lifetime. There was a tremendous one in the place in which he was born, but the Germans took the bronze statue away for melting down, leaving only the marble plinth. After the war the citizens felt they had to replace the doctor and M. Poltge gave them a little tiny bust of his head which they proudly mounted on the enormous marble plinth made for a bust ten times the size. It is absolutely out of proportion, just like a pinpoint at the top, and could not be more ludicrous, but the people were absolutely delighted to have it for nothing and not have to spend any money on a replacement!

The doctor also gave them a museum during his lifetime, which the state accepted because he was such an important man. Unfortunately he said it was never to be altered from the appalling style in which he laid it out. The solution is typically French—the museum has been temporarily closed[1] for the last seven years despite the fact that a curator and a caretaker are employed.

He also gave them a village hall so long as it was not touched, and the Mayor does not know what to do with it, because it is beginning to fall down.

The journey towards Condom is through pleasantly friendly villages and countryside with squat fortified churches, stilted market halls, stone colonnades and arched ramparts—a photographer's paradise.

Flowery Valence has the beautifully proportioned abbey of Flaran—incontestably the outstanding example of Cistercian architecture in the Midi.

The next village, Nerac, is where Shakespeare is said to have stayed and where, they say locally, he 'lifted' the themes of *Hamlet* and *Love's Labour's Lost* from the works of François de Belleforest and Bishop Bandello respectively. You can, in fact, see the garden alleged to be the scene of *Love's Labour's Lost* just over the Garonne as you leave Nerac.

Further on, in the museum of Armagnac at Condom, are various viticultural relics, including a bell rung to warn workers of the approach of a hailstorm. Condom changed hands between the English and the French eight times, and it does not much like the English historically. It particularly dislikes the Black Prince.

The oldest document they have here is a report of 1806 of the Department of Agriculture of Gers on progress in the art of distillation in the department, and as you come into the museum you see the words, 'Rome introduced the wine, then the vines; the Celts perfected cooperage; Moors, through the intermediary of Spaniards, taught the secrets and art of distillation; and Gascony provided the woods of its oak forests and its soft climate.' There is also a *bidon de fraudeur*, which is a large metal container shaped like a middle-aged man's stomach, made to be worn under one's clothes, in which people put their distilled eau de vie, their Armagnac, to avoid customs. There was also an *alambic de frauder*, a very small still, which could be smuggled from house to house.

They have in the museum a full bottle of 1780 Armagnac. It is the most ancient full bottle they have; there are only three of these pre-Revolution bottles of Armagnac in the world.

[1] 'Fermé au public à cause de transformation.'

In between these historic and cultural excursions we were making visits to distilleries and vineyards and learning more of this great drink Armagnac.

Armagnac ranks with cognac as the finest brandy and is produced by a special and strictly controlled process which has won it the highest award of the French government—the *Acquit d'Or* or Gold Label.

It owes its existence to the British, as Louis XI gave the wine growers of Bordeaux the privilege of exporting only their own wines to England until the feast of St Martin (November 11). The Gascons being unable to conserve their wine long enough, proceeded to distil it, so that out of an act of gross injustice comes one of the world's greatest brandies.

It is curious how often in Gers (Gascony) one comes upon traces of the ancient English occupation; one hears that the Rolls of Gascony are still in English possession; that the Gascon captains who fought for Jeanne d'Arc were called after their brandy —Armagnacaise; that the United States boycotted 'English' brandies during the war of Independence and drank enormously increased quantities of Armagnac in sympathy for these fellow 'sufferers'; that the Armagnacais have a patois phrase 'Al ri' which, according to certain philologists, comes from the English 'All right'. It means 'O.K.'! That La Fayette commanded a regiment of the Royal Dragoons stationed at Auch, and that when all is said and done—the Black Prince excepted—there exists a particularly warm affection for the British in this comparatively unknown and lovely part of France, as was shown in the war when French and British fought side by side behind the lines in the Maquis de Gascoyne.

In this land of drolleries I found surely one of the oddest of life sequences. Dominique Serres, the painter, was born at Roquelaure, near Auch, in 1731. Destined for the Church, he suddenly decided, instead, to emigrate to America. On the way his ship was captured by an English frigate and he was imprisoned in London, where one of his companions taught him to sketch. His drawings impressed both the jailer and his daughter, whom he married. In his case marriage brought freedom from bondage and he soon became a well-known painter of maritime subjects as well as being commissioned to paint the portrait of George III.

The Armagnac country covers the greater part of the Gers department as well as parts of Landes, and Lot and Garonne.

Like the Cognac region, it is divided into several parts, qualitatively different. The Bas Armagnac district produces the finest brandies with Eauze, where there is a weekly sale of eaux de vie each Thursday and on the occasion of the Fair of St Catherine on November 25, as its capital. In the centre of the Region is the next best district, Ténarèz, with Condom as its centre; thirdly, in the east comes Haut Armagnac, centred upon Auch.

The *eau de vie* is distilled in special stills called 'Armagnacais' which have not changed for a thousand years and look as if they were invented by Heath Robinson or Emmet. Unlike cognac where the spirit is made by the successive distillation of several barrels of wine, Armagnac is distilled uninterruptedly.

The stills give a maximum spirit of 63 degrees compared with a strength of 72 degrees in Charente (Cognac), the department where cognac is made.

As in Charente, the spirit is left to mature for many years in oaken caks and none leaves the shores of France until it has been passed by the College of Experts in Armagnac. In fact one usually finds more consistently good Armagnac away from France than within its borders.

Its colour is fuller and a deeper gold than Cognac and some connoisseurs prefer it to its great and more powerful neighbour.

It is, though, particularly important to buy from one of the reputed shippers and not to imagine that if you just order Armagnac you will get the same delightful drink that came your way last time—and, for once, it is more important to observe this rule in France than in England or America.

IX

Bordeaux

THE JOURNEY from Gascony to St Emilion is on a pleasant country road, the surface not always good. One sees oxen, many of them blindfolded or with hoods over them to keep the flies off, a lot of wheat, market garden produce and vines on the slopes. The road sometimes goes through woods and resembles Shakespeare's leafy Warwickshire apart from the vines. It is not a road, though, for high speeds, and in fact N.670, the road from La Réole to Libourne, is very bad but most attractive. At Lavagnac one crosses the river Dordogne, very wide and calm.

The town of St Emilion is really superb; the vines come tumbling right into it. It is a town on a hill and a wine town. Part of the hotel we stayed in is on top of the 'Monolithic' church and was frightfully noisy because one of two immense clocks strikes all the hours and all the half hours, and the other one does the hours only about 40 yards away—quite deafeningly. They go on all through the night.

Walking in the absolutely deserted town at 9.15 on our first, in fact our only, evening there, because although we returned in the day we went off to get some sleep elsewhere, we heard young people singing 'Auld Lang Syne'. We talked to them and found that they were a church choir rehearsing for a fête the following Sunday; and we talked to the *curé*, who said, 'Oh yes, that's a very well-known tune, called "It isn't farewell, it's only till we meet again".' It made this town of surpassing beauty seem very near home!

We went on to Bordeaux next morning, ending up down 10 or 12 kilometres of magnificent road—as wide as any of the Auto-bahns in Germany—crossing the river which is the lifeblood of Bordeaux, turning right-handed along the Quai de Charterons, where many of the wine merchants are, and then off that to the Cours du Médoc, where we went to J. Calvet's very large cellars.

The vineyards of Bordeaux are more confusing to the average wine-drinker than any other in the world. Most people know that there are some very special wines that are expensive; some know that all Bordeaux wines were classified as long ago as 1855 and that they nearly all carry the name of a château; and many think erroneously that any wine with the name of a château must be a good wine. This is completely wrong—it may be an artisan wine of very little merit, just a tiny part of the forty-four million gallons of wine coming from sixty thousand vineyards that flows out from the grapes of this favoured vineyard area which is said to enjoy the mildest climate in the world.

The classification of 1855 was made to ensure that only the best wines of Bordeaux should be chosen to represent the Region in the World's Fair of that year. A 'representative' committee was appointed in 1854 and when it published its findings it said that, 'it merely established a hierarchy which had been unquestionably accepted for more than a century'. The classification is:

RED WINES

First growths

Château Lafite	PAUILLAC
Barons de Rothschild	
Château Margaux	MARGAUX
Société Civile Immobilière du Château Margaux	
Château Latour	PAUILLAC
Société Civile du Château Latour	
Château Haut-Brion	PESSAC (GRAVES)
Société du Château Haut-Brion	

Second growths

Château Mouton-Rothschild . . .	PAUILLAC
Baron Philippe de Rothschild	
Château Rausan-Segla	MARGAUX
Héritiers Frédéric Cruse	
Château Rauzan-Gassies . . .	MARGAUX
Société Civile Immobilière du Château Rauzan-Gassies	
Château Léoville-Las-Cases . . .	SAINT-JULIEN
Société Civile du Domaine du Château Léoville-Las-Cases	

Château Léoville-Poyferré .   .   .   .   SAINT-JULIEN
  Société Civile des Domaines de 'Saint-Julien',
    Château Léoville-Poyferré, Propriétés Cuvelier
    fils

Château Léoville-Barton   .   .   .   .   SAINT-JULIEN
  H.-R. Barton associé de la Maison Barton et
    Guestier

Château Dufort-Vivens   .   .   .   .   MARGAUX
  Société Civile des Vignobles Ginestet

Château Gruaud-Larose   .   .   .   .   SAINT-JULIEN
  Société Civile des Propriétés de Famille D.
    Cordier

Château Lascombes .   .   .   .   .   MARGAUX
  Société Civile du Château Lascombes

Château Brane-Cantenac   .   .   .   .   CANTENAC
  François Lurton

Château Pichon-Longueville—Baron de Pichon   PAUILLAC
  Société Civile du Château Pichon-Longueville—
    Baron de Pichon

Château   Pichon-Longueville—Comtesse   de
Lalande   .   .   .   .   .   .   PAUILLAC
  Société Anonyme de Château Pichon-Longueville
    —Comtesse de Lalande

Château Ducru-Beaucaillou   .   .   .   SAINT-JULIEN
  Francis Borie

Château Cos-d'Estournel .   .   .   .   SAINT-ESTÈPHE
  Société Civile des Vignobles Ginestet

Château Montrose   .   .   .   .   SAINT-ESTÈPHE
  Héritiers Charmolüe

Third growths

Château Kirwan   .   .   .   .   .   MARGAUX
  Schroder et Schyler & Cie

Château d'Issan   .   .   .   .   .   CANTENAC
  Société Civile du Château d'Issan

Château Lagrange   .   .   .   .   SAINT-JULIEN
  Manuel Cendoya

Château Langoa . . . . . SAINT-JULIEN
  *H.-R. Barton associé de la Maison Barton et
  Guestier*

Château Giscours . . . . . LABARDE
  N. Tari

Château Malescot Saint-Exupéry . . . MARGAUX
  Seagers, Evans & Cie Ltd, Londres

Château Boyd-Cantenac . . . . CANTENAC
  P. Guillemet

Château Cantenac-Brown . . . . CANTENAC
  Société Civile du Château Cantenac-Brown

Château Palmer . . . . . CANTENAC
  Société Civile de Château Palmer

Château Grand La Lagune . . . LUDON
  Madame Albert Galy

Château Desmirail . . . . MARGAUX
  Société Civile du Château Palmer

Château Calon-Ségur . . . . SAINT-ESTÈPHE
  Gasqueton frères et Peyrelongue frères

Château Ferrière . . . . MARGAUX
  André Durand, propriétaire. L. Fouque, fermier

Château Marquis d'Alesme-Becker . . MARGAUX
  Seagers, Evans & Cie Ltd, Londres

Fourth growths

Château Saint-Pierre . . . . . SAINT-JULIEN
  Van Den Bussche fils

Château Talbot . . . . . SAINT-JULIEN
  Georges Cordier

Château Branaire (Duluc-Ducru) . . SAINT-JULIEN
  J. Tapie

Château Duhart-Milon . . . PAUILLAC
  Société Civile de Duhart-Milon

Château Pouget de Chavaille . . . CANTENAC
  L. Guillemet

Château La Tour Carnet . . . SAINT-LAURENT
  Société Civile du Château La Tour Carnet

Château Lafon-Rochet . . . . SAINT-ESTÈPHE
   Ch. Duquesnoy

Château Beychevelle . . . . . SAINT-JULIEN
   Achille-Fould

Château Prieuré-Lichine . . . CANTENAC
   Société du Château Prieuré-Lichine

Château Marquis de Termes . . . MARGAUX
   Pierre Seneclauze

Fifth growths

Château Pontet-Canet . . . . PAUILLAC
   Cruse et Fils Frères

Château Batailley . . . . . PAUILLAC
   Marcel Borie

Château Haut-Batailley . . . . PAUILLAC
   Francis Borie

Château Grand-Puy-Ducasse . . . PAUILLAC
   Société Civile du Château Grand Puy-Ducasse

Château Grand-Puy-Lacoste . . . PAUILLAC
   Raymond Dupin

Château Lynch-Bages . . . . PAUILLAC
   J.-C. Cazes

Château Lynch-Moussas . . . . PAUILLAC
   Jean Castéja

Château Dauzac . . . . . LABARDE
   H. Bernat

Château Mouton d'Armailhacq . . . PAUILLAC
   Société Anonyme du Domaine de Mouton d'Armailhacq

Château du Tertre . . . . ARSAC
   Société du Château du Tertre

Château Haut-Bages-Libéral . . . PAUILLAC
   Maugé

Château Pedesclaux . . . . . PAUILLAC
   Comte Xavier d'Erceville et Michel du Lac

Château Belgrave . . . . ._ SAINT-LAURENT
   Société du Château Belgrave

Château Camensac . . . . . SAINT-LAURENT
Cuvelier et Fils

Château Cos-Labory . . . . SAINT-ESTÈPHE
Weber

Château Clerc-Milon-Mondon . . . PAUILLAC
Mlle M. Vialard et Mme Hédon

Château Croizet-Bages . . . . PAUILLAC
Paul Quié

Château Cantemerle . . . . MACAU
P. Dubos

WHITE WINES
1st great growth

Château d'Yquem . . . . . SAUTERNES
Marquis de Lur-Saluces

First growths

Château La Tour Blanche . . . . BOMMES
Propriété de l'Etat

Château Lafaurie-Peyraguey . . . BOMMES
Société Civile des propriétés de famille D. Cordier

Clos Haut-Peyraguey . . . . BOMMES
Garbay et Pauly Frères

Château Rayne-Vigneau . . . . BOMMES
Héritiers du Vicomte de Pontac

Château Suduiraut . . . . . PREIGNAC
Léopold Fonquernie

Château Coutet . . . . . BARSAC
Rolland-Guy

Château Climens . . . . . BARSAC
Héritiers Henri Gounouilhou

Château Guiraud . . . . . SAUTERNES
Paul Rival

Château Rieussec . . . . . SAUTERNES
Pierre-Francis Berry

Château Rabaud-Promis . . . . BOMMES
Société Civile du Château Rabaud-Promis

Château Sigalas-Rabaud   .   .   .   .   BOMMES
   Comtesse de Lambert des Granges, née Sigalas

Second growths

Château de Myrat   .   .   .   .   .   BARSAC
   Comte Max de Pontac

Château Doisy-Daene   .   .   .   .   BARSAC
   G. Dubourdieu

Château Doisy-Dubroca   .   .   .   .   BARSAC
   Héritiers Marcel Dubroca

Château Doisy-Védrines   .   .   .   .   BARSAC
   Héritiers Teyssonneau

Château d'Arche   .   .   .   .   .   SAUTERNES
   A. Bastit—Saint-Martin

Château d'Arche-Lafaurie .   .   .   .   SAUTERNES
   Max Pellequer

Château Filhot   .   .   .   .   .   SAUTERNES
   Comtesse Durieu de Lacarelle

Château Broustet   .   .   .   .   .   BARSAC
   Pierre Fournier

Château Nairac   .   .   .   .   .   BARSAC
   Charles Perpezat

Château Caillou   .   .   .   .   .   BARSAC
   Ballan—Bravo

Château Suau   .   .   .   .   .   BARSAC
   Emile Garros

Château de Malle   .   .   .   .   .   PREIGNAC
   Héritiers du Comte P. de Lur-Saluces, P. et J. de
     Bournazel

Château Romer   .   .   .   .   .   PREIGNAC
   E. Farges

Château Lamothe-Espagnet   .   .   .   SAUTERNES
   A. Bastit—Saint-Martin

Château Lamothe-Tissot   .   .   .   .   SAUTERNES
   Gaston Tissot

Today there are many, like Alexis Lichine, the author of *Wines of France*, who challenge and dispute the authority of a classifica-

tion made over a hundred years ago. Lichine points out that
several of the châteaux in the 1855 classification no longer exist
or merely form part of another, possibly lower classed château.
Also he feels that some, like Château Lascombes, a second cru,
of which he is Director, and Château Cantemerle, which is a fifth,
should be raised—the latter considerably.

On the other hand a large proportion of the trade think, as does
M. Henri Binaud, Honorary President of the Wine Merchants
of Bordeaux and the Gironde and Vice-Chancellor of the Academy
of Wine of Bordeaux, that although everyone knows that there
are inaccuracies in it, it had better stay.

It must be wrong and unjust to many, he says, because only
eighty-four red and white wines were classified out of some sixty
thousand vineyards in the region. He feels that the best way
of considering the problem is to compare the classification with
a stud book in which you have race and all the things that a stud
book reveals—the only variable things are the jockey on the one
hand and the proprietor on the other. You know that you ought
to get a jolly good wine from these great *crus*, and usually you
do. Sometimes it is wrong, sometimes the outsider comes
across.

Monsieur Binaud thinks that if there were a new classification
the old ones, if they were not classified as high as formerly, would
merely say 'according to the 1855 classification', and the new ones
would put the more recent classifications on, and this would lead
to even more confusion than there is at the moment.

He reckons too that, unless a very bad proprietor takes on one
of these great properties, the depreciation would be very, very
slow and it would be reflected on the Bordeaux market. People
would know the wine was depreciating and it would not sell so
well. Its price would then go down, although it would still be
able to call itself what it was classified as in 1855. On the other
hand, certain wines not in the classification at all are so consistently
good that they always command higher prices than some of the
classified wines, though these vary very little as they have
inherited great qualities in the soil and possess great tradition.
Many vineyards are stocked with a percentage of vines forty
years old, and it is fair to say that this represents a cycle in a
vineyard. The wine that you get depends on the policy that has
gone into the stocking and the planting, as well as the wine
making, all through the forty years, because you do not get wines

from vines of any one age, you get a *mélange* from all the different vines in the particular vineyard.

In July 1935 the controlled appellations of Bordeaux were finally made law for the whole of the Gironde. The Region was divided into thirty-three appellations and these made it obligatory for all producers to abide by 'the local, loyal and constant uses proper to each production area'. In other words, if a certain district makes the best of its position, soil and climate by growing wine from a certain stock or blends of different stocks in certain proportion, and if local custom agrees that the vines are best planted at a certain density and pruned back a certain length, then these and other necessary obligations are written into the controlled appellation. It will not mean that a wine from a lesser district will become a better wine than a more famous neighbour, but it will mean, if the words *appellation contrôlée* occur on the label, that the wine if properly harvested will conform fairly to its type, whether it be a *grand cru*, an unimportant *cru bourgeois* or artisan. Categories of *appellations contrôlées* in the Region of Bordeaux are:

Red Wines—St Emilion, St Georges-St Emilion, Montagne-St Emilion, Barsac-St Emilion, Lussac-St Emilion, Puisseguin-St Emilion, Sables-St Emilion, Côtes de Fronsac and Canon-Fronsac-Pomerol, La lande de Pomerol, Néac, Médoc and Haut-Médoc, St Estèphe, St Julien, Listrac, Moulis, Margaux, Pauillac.

White Wines—Entre-deux-Mers, Côtes de Bordeaux, St Macaire, Cérons, Loupiac, Ste-Croix-du-Mont, Sauternes, Barsac.

White and Red Wines—Bordeaux, Blaye, Côtes de Blaye and First Hills of Blaye, Bourg and Côtes de Bourg, Ste-Foy, Graves de Vayres, First Côtes de Bordeaux, Graves.

THE MÉDOC

Before going off to the Médoc with M. Calvet, and again with Alexis Lichine, we visited the vast cellars of J. Calvet and Co. which house some sixty thousand hogsheads and over two million bottles. Incidentally Calvet and the following great Bordeaux firms will show visitors around their cellars except on Saturdays. They are:

A. R. Barrière Frères, 45 cours du Médoc, Bordeaux.
A. Delor and Co., 21 rue de Macau, Bordeaux.
Desca Père and Fils, 5 quai de Paludate, Bordeaux.

The cellars here are much less deep than the Burgundy ones; they are only on floor level, and like Burgundy they must be damp to avoid excessive evaporation.

The first thing we saw was the 'candling'[1] of bottles for America. In the main we found that merchants do not candle any wines except those for the American market. They say that if an American sees a tiny object in a bottle of wine, he sends it back. He seldom minds about the quality of the wine—it can be absolutely terrible, but the appearance matters enormously.

One of the merchants' great problems now is how to pack, because they want to pack their best wines in straw, but with the combine harvester the supply of straw is running out. There were two million bottles in stock there, including a large percentage of château-bottled wines in the cases. The ordinary bottles are just in racks in enormous *caves* or in libraries—which are smaller *caves* with different varieties of bottles in them. They also have fifty thousand hogs-heads of wines, so that the *caves* really are tremendously big.

M. Calvet pointed out that the Bordeaux wines are not chaptelized like the Burgundy wines where sugar is added practically every year to make up for sun deficiency in their more northern climate. In Bordeaux it is usually the other way round and there is a danger of having too much.

We saw one of the sixty-eight barrels in a sort of library of hogsheads being racked. A man stooped with a fixed lamp of about 25 watts and a small tumbler in his hand; above him a barrel with another man standing by it. The wine came out of the barrel into this glass which he held in front of the lamp, and as it filled he emptied it into a wooden funnel which passed it on to the barrel it was going to after it had been racked. He went on and on and on, missing it a bit as he was looking at it but that didn't matter as it was absolutely clear. Suddenly he stopped and he put his right hand on the tap ready to stop the flow. He sensed or he knew that he was getting to the end of the barrel, but to me the wine was just as clear as before and a few seconds later he closed it, shouted to his companion who was manipulating the top end of the barrel, and that was that.

He had seen a small cloud come into the wine, which showed that they were getting to the cloudy part at the bottom of the

---

[1] Holding the bottle in front of a strong light so that any solids in the liquid are shown up.

barrel which is known as the lees. After this no more is drawn off; what is left is put into a barrel along with the lees from lots of other barrels and allowed to settle for two to three months. At the end of two to three months this barrel full of lees is itself racked off, just as the other wine had been, not to be sold as wine, but to be put into barrels for the workers to draw off any time they wished. What is at the bottom after this final racking is then sold for distillers to make into *marc*. That is called *faire le fin*. The fining is done with gelatine except in the best growths which still use the whites of eggs.

We walked into the canteen, which is not a canteen in our sense of the word. They employ 300 workers here, and about 160 of them were sitting at two very long tables. They are given free soup and as much wine as they want. Their luncheon break is one and a half hours and it is taken in the room in which the cooperage is being done all the rest of the time. They looked a friendly lot; they were interested to see us looking at the barrels which they were working on, and lots of hands were raised and smiles came. There was the usual tremendous amount of noise.

The Médoc includes such great parishes as St Estèphe, Pauillac, St Julien and Margaux. Through their outstanding qualities and the fact that they figured so largely in the 1855 classification the wines of Médoc are the most widely known. The wines are characterized by their ruby colour, by their bouquet, aroma and keeping qualities.

The Médoc is a large triangular area some 50 miles long, and 6 wide at its base near Bordeaux. One of its other two sides is flanked by the rivers Gironde and Garonne and the other by a desolate unpopulated district of woods, sandhills and inundations flanked by the Atlantic.

The actual wine country is friendly, wooded, and bursting with vines, the names of famous Châteaux coming to meet the eye every few hundred yards. These are not vast unpeopled châteaux like those of the Loire, but smaller, more domesticated, and far more attractive.

The soil, on which so much depends, was once covered with water and consists of gravel or rolled quartz and of heavy sand about a foot deep with a subsoil of clay or alios. The vines here are replanted rather sooner than in many parts of the Gironde— every twenty-five years or so—and the land manured on an average of once every nine years—more frequently would bring a larger yield but of lower quality.

Our first visit in the Médoc was to M. Pierre Dubos, the eighty-three-year-old proprietor of Château Cantemerle, who makes magnificent wines at the Château his father bought over fifty years ago. These wines are frequently quoted as a justification for changing the 1855 classification, in which they are a fifth growth. On the other hand, the trade knows what wonderful wines M. Dubos produces and consequently they are much sought, especially by Dutch connoisseurs.

M. Dubos says that the quantity is decided after the frosts and when the flowers form in the middle of June; and that the quality of the wine is decided between July 15 and September 15—it is in that period, he said, that 'the wine is made'.

M. Dubos makes notes three times a day; he takes temperatures, the direction of the wind, and he reads the barometer. He knows in advance if he is going to make full-bodied or light wine—*corsé* or *léger*. He would not do all this if he wanted to make quantity; he is interested only in making quality wine. He keeps the records of each *charette* (that is the cart that comes up with the vintage), he makes a note of where it came from, the temperature on harvest day and the quantity of sugar in each lot of grapes. He said he keeps all these records for his grandchildren. He has a column for observations. In 1920 which was a good year, he had no observations—everything went perfectly. In 1921, another very good year, the columns were absolutely crammed—everything had been difficult, but it was worth while making notes about all the trouble.

'The troubles of wine making in the Bordelais are many,' continued M. Dubos, 'and if you look back through my notes you will find that year after year one thing or another has come along to embarrass the growers—frosts, heavy rains, thunderstorms, mildew, drought, and a score of other things. Today it costs over seven hundred thousand francs to plant $2\frac{1}{2}$ acres of vineyard, so we have great need of a steady market—but not with prices too high, else we shall lose our customers.'

I asked him about alcoholism and he laughed. 'Drunkards have always been rare in the Médoc—we eat too much! If we see a drunk man we think he has had too much rum or spirit, but we don't often see one. We like eating a lot and we like drinking a lot, but we do not get drunk!'

Before we left we tasted some of his '54 which was velvety and excellent despite being a comparatively 'off' year, though, of course, far too young. His wines all have a particularly attractive finesse, a very beautiful bouquet, and they last well, though they do not have to be kept so long as some of the great Médoc wines, notably Latour, a '34 of which I drank only a few weeks ago, to find it still hard and ungracious.

Between Cantmerle and Château Margaux I asked M. Calvet, 'How long does it take to acquire a palate?' The answer was depressing—'Everyone has a palate, of course, but it takes about five years of tasting every day to train it.' He went on to tell me that his father, uncle, cousins and himself taste samples brought in by the *courtiers* every day between twelve-thirty and two. Two of them specialize in red wine and two in white.

These great Bordeaux firms are unable to get about as much as they would like and depend to a great extent upon *courtiers* (brokers) who bring them samples of wine which they think will suit a particular merchant's trade, and if the wine is bought, come along again when the bulk is delivered to taste it with the merchant and ensure that the quality is up to the sample. These *courtiers*, very highly skilled experts, are greatly regarded in the trade. They are often very rich men, acquiring their income by charging a commission of 2 per cent on the cost price of the wine from the vineyard to the merchant.

We went on to the flat Margaux district near to the sea, where the stones are much larger than in most parts of the Gironde and so tend to conserve the sun's heat during the night. The wine of Château Margaux is more *corsé* and has more tannin in it than the districts further south. It is also lighter in colour and in body with a great delicacy and delightful flavour. The reputation of Château Margaux is world-wide and everyone agrees that if still warrants its place as one of the first *Grands Crus* of the 1855 classification. We were lucky enough to have some of their '29 at home when war was declared. It was at its peak and we quickly drank it in the first days of black-out in case it was bombed!

The cave at Château Margaux has the date 1803 on it and is long and very beautifully proportioned with eighteen pillars supporting the roof and eleven rows of barrels.

We tasted some of the 1956 wine, and the day that we tasted it was June 14. Now this was interesting as the flowers had just come out—rather late—in the vineyards outside. They had a

very, very good spring but then little sun. As a result the wine
was showing a very slight fermentation.

M. Grangeron, the *Régisseur* of this great firm, M. Calvet and
dozens of other wine people have all said that the wine does
change its character slightly like the living vine outside. It certainly changes its character in the spring as the sap comes up
in the vines. It changes its character again at the time of harvest,
as if to warn its mates of a year later that they're soon to be
imprisoned in the *fût* and will not see the sun again. The '56
Margaux with a slight fermentation that we tasted had a big
bouquet. They say here that when the wine has a wonderful nose
in the first year it is a sign that it will be good early, and this was
superb.

We then tasted some Château Margaux '55 and it was very,
very good indeed with a superb colour.

I learnt something that I may have known before but had
forgotten, that they make a small proportion of white wine at
Margaux called Pavillon Blanc du Château Margaux which is
very light, dry and individual in style.

Between Margaux and St Julien the ground is dark, damp and
marshy—good for snipe shooting. There are some vines but they
do not make big wines.

Beychevelle, a glorious Château built 200 years ago, is one
every tourist should visit. The wine is of great quality and the
Château long, low and graceful with its smooth green lawns—
how few one sees in France—accentuated by deep-red bordering
flowers and an ever-widening view to the river beyond. It was this
river which got the Château its name, as sailing ships making or
leaving Bordeaux used to dip their sails in salute to its former
owner, the Duke d'Epernon, who was a Grand Admiral of France
and the command 'baisse-voile' ('lower sails') became corrupted
into Beychevelle.

Our last visit in the Médoc was to stay with Alexis Lichine
and visit the two great vineyards which he directs—Château
Lascombes, a second *grand cru*, and Château Prieure-Lichine,
a fourth *grand cru*, of the 1855 classification.

His own home is quite lovely and everything seems in character.
He has a most elegant and attractive wife, whom we met three
weeks after their daughter was born. His table glass is by Baccarat,
the world-famous firm that makes the very, very best of the bottles
for the Armagnac, the 1893 which Montesquiou makes.

He has a firm which sells only Château-bottled wines; he has wealthy American stockholders in Château Lascombes and he is building up a very fine 'library' of wines for them in his *chai*. He uses Lascombes, which is a very lovely Château, as a guest house for V.I.P.s, and as quarters for some of his English-speaking staff, who look after the V.I.P.s, answer his large fan-mail, and write to the embassies and people whom he circularizes about wine.

Some would say that the bathroom at Lascombes is vulgar. It is painted white and half the wall is covered with labels of nearly all the great Châteaux, but most, of course, of Lascombes and Prieure Lichine, occasionally with little black strips with white letters on them saying 'Selected by Alexis Lichine'. There are some eighty of these labels around the bathroom and I think they make it very gay, very attractive and very American. I like it—it is unusual, like Lichine. He is full of enthusiasms; it was well after midnight, for instance, when he showed me the warehouse where he stocks his château-bottled wines.

He reckons he has got as big a stock of Château-bottled wine as nearly any of the big merchants in Bordeaux. He sells the wine direct to customers, direct to embassies, and also through merchants in countries where he is not allowed to sell direct.

He has tremendous contempt for the chi-chi type of writer— those who write about the unobtainable drink that they have consumed in the company of unwantable people and who use second-hand phrases about them. He thinks that vineyards are the places to find out about wines, not dinner parties nor other people's cellars, and he has shown this very well in his own book, which is quite first-class.

He, of course, enormously annoys the trade; his detractors say he is an upstart who is getting on too fast. One said to me, 'He's like a mushroom. One minute he's not there, and the next he grows bigger and bigger and is on your private lawn.' But another to whom I repeated this said, 'Rubbish—the trade should keep its lawns clean, then there would not be any mushrooms.' They just cannot understand him. Some like him; some do not like him; but they all know about him. He is to the wine industry of this part of France like a Beaverbrook or a Churchill or a Nye Bevan—you just cannot ignore him.

He thinks that tradition is enormously important in wine-making, but cannot see any reason why cellars need be dirty.

His own *chais* are absolutely admirable, each shown off with lights set in the gnarled roots of vines. The walls of most people's *chais* are dirty and sweaty, moist, horrid crumbling affairs, but his are immaculate, and I said, 'Well, doesn't that mean they're too dry?' He said, 'No, they're just as damp as other walls, but I paint them, and I keep on cleaning them, because I think it's so important to be clean, and this is done every two months.' He has a fanatic distrust of many shippers—particularly in Burgundy.

ENTRE-DEUX-MERS

An anomalous anachronism in the wine world is that whereas the quality of white wines is traditionally judged by their degree of alcohol and sugar (a fact also recognized by the customs of many countries who impose a steep rise in customs duty on wines of more than 14 or 16 degrees of alcohol), yet the buying public turns more and more to wines that are light, fruity and dry.

Producers of sweet wines are considerably worried about this trend in public taste, similar problems face those who make sweet liqueurs.

It was this fact that led the wine growers of Entre-Deux-Mers to announce on May 7, 1954, that they had unanimously decided to change over from producing a sweet wine to making dry but fruity wines by similar methods of viticulture to those of Muscadet, Chablis, Sancerre and Alsace.

The trade of Bordeaux is still divided as to whether this move was wise or not. Customers who liked the old sweet wines have been annoyed; those who might like the new dry ones are in the main unaware of the change. There is also no doubt that a good deal of the poorest of the new dry wines of the district have been bought by those who cater for the lowest priced markets, and many a customer has dismissed them for ever as poor quality 'grocers' wines.

I was therefore partiularly interested to find out what the wine growers of Entre-Deux-Mers think of things three years after the switch.

We went to visit them with M. Descaves, a Bordeaux merchant who has a great affection for the English; whose wife greeted mine with a charming bouquet of flowers and whose son was educated at Dover College.

We were met at the Château Cadillac—one of the great Châteaux of the Gironde whose owners, the d'Epernons, were considered demi-royal; whose fireplaces, of which eight remain, were among the most magnificent in Europe; whose greatest son, High Admiral d'Epernon, was by Henri IV's side when he was assassinated, and whose lovely home has recently been taken over by the Ministry of Beaux Arts and partly by the Connétablie de Guyenne, after having been left desolate after the Revolution and subsequently used as a penitentiary for 'naughty' girls.

At the great drawbridge five men stood waiting for us— representatives of the Connétablie de Guyenne, the wine growers of Entre-Deux-Mers, and the wine growers of Cadillac.

First we toured the Château, saw the fireplaces, the Queen's room with statues of the Duchess decapitated by the revolutionary mob. It is not a well-furnished Château for visitors, but it is architecturally rewarding and it has many interesting historical associations.

The part that intrigued us was where the off-duty watch lived. Here below moat level were fine quarters; large rooms with double fireplaces and a feeling of comfortable spaciousness accentuated by the beautiful proportions of a spiral staircase without any central pillars at all.

There is one room which is worth all the 100 francs that a complete visit will cost you. It is a room of about 12 square yards with a roof curving upwards like the cupola next to the leaning tower of Pisa. If two people go to opposite diagonal corners and whisper into the corner they can hear each other perfectly by putting their ear against the corner of the wall and without being able to hear any direct sound. Also, if another couple talk in a similar way from the other two diagonals they can carry on a conversation without in any way interfering with the other pair.

This kind of acoustic was used in the old days in the French Congo by priests wishing to hear confessions from lepers and other diseased people without themselves being in contact with them.

After the visit we went to the King's chamber, which with the vast waiting hall forms the present headquarters of the Connétablie de Guyenne.

In the Middle Ages, until suppressed by Henri IV, the Connétablie de Guyenne looked after the economic and communal interest of all the producers of white wines from the city of Bordeaux, along both banks of the river Garonne and extending

L

from Langon and Lormont. Their administrative headquarters were in the Château de l'Ombrière at Bordeaux, where they linked up with the similar functions of the Jurat of St Emilion.

These were the great days of the Bordeaux wine trade; when business with Great Britain was of tremendous importance and when the Connétablie used to attach a symbolic cypress branch to the masts of any ships carrying wine to Britain.

The Connétablie was reformed in 1952, its purpose to publicize and in all ways study the collective interests of the white wines of Bordeaux.

I was surprised to see that there were a number of wine bottles on the long refectory table and that a solemn dedicatory look had come over the face of the President of the Cadillac Wine Growers, who is also the senior Vice-President of the Connétablie.

He advanced towards me; took my hand and said, 'It is with great pleasure that I tell you that at its last meeting the Grand Council of the Connétablie de Guyenne decided to invite you to become an honorary member of the Connétablie.' He took a large crystal glass which one of his fellows had filled and said, 'From this day you are free to enter into all our cellars and caves, at any time of any day.' Then he handed me the large glass of wine, continuing, 'In witness of which I invite you to empty this cup of honour and of loyal friendship.' I having done my share, he removed the engraved medallion which pictures the ancient château with a British lion very rampant in a red sky; its colours red, blue, green and gold, with vintners' hands holding clusters of grapes and the words Connétablie de Guyenne around its periphery. It is threaded on to a black-and-gold silk cord which he put round my neck. He then shook my hand and now I am a member of the Connétablie de Guyenne with the right of honourable entry to all the vineyards of Guyenne, which in the main cover those of Graves and Entre-Deux-Mers.

After this unexpected and pleasurable occasion, we proceeded first to taste a number of wines in the vaulted hall and then went to the Hotel Oliver at Langon, where we lunched under sunshades in the garden, sampling bottle after bottle of delightful wines from the Deux-Mers—a Clos de Capucine made from Sauvignon grapes only, very dry, very natural; then several red Graves, including a particularly delightful Château Bouscaut '49 and a Château Jean Gervais '52 which had a wonderful nose and was a very complete wine. Then back to the whites with a première côte du Bordeaux, a Château Arnaud Juan '53 which was absolutely magnificent—it astonishes me that these comparatively little-known wines do not appear to be shipped abroad in any great numbers.

Lunch took nearly three hours and was in keeping with the high reputation of the restaurant, and afterwards we went off to do more tasting and see St Macaire, its old Roman church and ramparts, the arches running alongside its square. Most unaccountable was the protruding ruin of a pillarless spiral staircase sticking incongruously out of a crumbling building alongside an exquisite quarter-sized sculpturing of Jeanne d'Albret, Henri IV's mother, exposed to the full blast of weather, ignorance and poverty. A sad, impoverished but fascinating village.

Then on to Benauge and Targon with its views, flowers and Château. All the time talking to my fellow Connétables. I asked them if it was possible for tourists to be shown their vineyards. They smiled and showed their gnarled hands. 'Yes, it is possible, but visitors are always an embarrassment because they take us away from our work. We are not big men like they are in the Médoc or at the co-operatives—we are men who work with our hands.'

So I think that would-be visitors must remember that—visit the co-operatives or the big Châteaux. There is nearly always a syndicat d'initiative which will tell you which firms in the locality will welcome you. In Sauternes, I found later, there is a Dégustation Centre in the town of Barsac which has a list of the Châteaux which are open and ready to receive visitors on any particular day. At the moment it is only operating during the end of July and in August, but I am trying to persuade M. Rolland, President of the Society of Growers of Sauternes and Barsac, to get it opened earlier, and am also trying to make some such arrangement covering the vineyards of the Gironde as a whole at the headquarters of the Bordeaux wine trade at Bordeaux.

Those who are sceptical about faith healing should visit, as we did, the little church at Verdelais, where there are two pilgrimages a year and whose walls are covered with plaques recording cures from blind and paralysed people right through from 1366 until the present day.

After nearly a week of relentless tasting and banqueting we went from Bordeaux at 5.30 for a quiet weekend at Pyla-sur-Mer near Arcachon, some 40 miles away. Bordeaux is not an easy place to leave at that hour, so try to avoid it.

We did not like Arcachon, a town of some eighteen thousand inhabitants for forty-six weeks and a hundred and fifty thousand during the summer season. Its hotels are fine, it has good shops, there is a casino (empty in June—only croupiers when we went) dominating the town like a black church. The sands are white, the front wide. If you like to be surrounded by substantial quantities of chromium plating you may like Arcachon.

Pyla-sur-Mer, 4 miles away, where we stayed at the Hotel Brissant on the advice of M. Jacques Calvet, is quite different. The hotel is set in pine trees which border a beach of fine white sand with occasional rocks for children to go crab-hunting on. I counted about thirty people on the Sunday morning and a hundred or so in the afternoon. The hotel has a number of bungalows, each with its own little secluded garden. Occupiers have breakfasts brought over to them but other meals in the main hotel. They are very popular with honeymooners.

Lying on the sand produced the delightful aural experience of hearing the lapping of the sea blended with the song of birds. It is a spot worth thinking about for anyone wanting to combine a visit to the wine Châteaux of the Gironde with some safe warm bathing, or sailing, good food, quiet sleeping. The sea is seldom very rough as it is part of a narrow bay.

By the way—do not be put off by the quite preposterous à la carte price on the menus—thirty shillings a head for a straightforward meal with comparatively little choice. I enquired about this and found, as I suspected, that it is to keep people away who would otherwise spoil the quiet amenities of the place. The hotel is not cheap but it is most agreeable.

ST EMILION

We visited St Emilion and its vineyards with M. Philippe Dubos, nephew of the owner of Château Cantemerle. Again we were met by a deputation of growers and again we tasted many of the local wines—some on the roof of the old Monolithic church which forms the garden of the restaurant, some in the *chais* of Châteaux —all close to this picturesque, semi-subterranean town in the Dordogne valley which once echoed to the feet of pilgrims on their way to St James of Compostella.

The red wines of St Emilion, which come from the Region

immediately west of Libourne and include seven communes, have always been popular with the British—perhaps because it was English King John who gave St Emilion its first charter.

They are fat, soft and generous—some of them are great bulls of wines that make your palates hunk at them as they demand attention. Their colour starts dark but lightens with age, until at maturity they have a rich rubiness that matches the velvet of their texture. In many ways they resemble the wines of the Médoc but, to me, their flavour is more rugged, their delicacy less apparent until they have aged some twenty years in bottle.

One of the most difficult things about the wines of Bordeaux, particularly the reds of St Emilion and the Médoc, is to know when to drink them. The great merchants of England, whose reputation and integrity is renowned, know to the year, so do the shippers of Bordeaux. But do shop assistants? Waiters? You and I?

Happily the Bordeaux merchants, led by the enthusiasm of M. Edward Kressman, have devised and their trade association has had printed a vintage code chart which far supasses the outmoded vintage charts that have recently been so fashionable, By the kindness of the Bordeaux Wine Academy one of these is included in this book.

The theory behind this code is that any years when the wine is really bad—'a real dog of a wine' as they say—it is sold as 'vin ordinaire', but this seldom occurs as weather conditions in the Gironde are very favourable for wine making. All that are left are coded. Each year is divided into red and white wines symbolized by a bottle enclosed in a circle. The outline of the circle may be thick or thin, broken or steady. The bottle may be opaque or transparent or stippled. Its position in the circle may be upright or any of the five-minute periods of a clock. It will be seen that this must give an enormous number of different meanings. By the side of this chart of bottles of queer shapes and shades is a legend which tells you that bottles pointing in such or such direction show that the vintage in question is not yet ready, or must be kept for years or is not worth stocking. The shade will show if the wine is light, full-bodied, well-balanced, etc., and the constitution of the circle surrounding the bottle provides information about each year's harvest—whether it was universally successful, partially so, or very uneven.

In this company there was no danger that the wines would be anything but first-rate. Each had brought several bottles of his own and each separate bottle was discussed openly and with genuine interest as soon as the cork was drawn.

Our first wine was a Prince Noire '52, bearing the mark of the Jurade of St Emilion. The Jurade allows any of its members to submit bottles anonymously. These are given a number when they arrive—and are tasted by a commission of two merchants from Bordeaux, two *courtiers* and two proprietors. Each year between 60 and 150 proprietors submit their wines and if they make the grade they are allowed to have the stamp on them of the Jurade of St Emilion. We started this meal, incidentally, with a Pouilly-Fumé 1953, which is very popular, I find, with wine peole and is often served at dinners when the best wines of the region are not appropriate for the fish course.

We then had this Vinée du Prince Noire, followed by a Château Figeac '47, a premier *grand cru*, of great richness and very highly developed bouquet, and a Château Villemaurine. After 190 minutes of lunching and talking wine we ambulated to the monolithic church.

It is quite astonishing how nearly all the views in St Emilion end in vineyards—you walk along a road, turn an inch away, you get a new view, and always at the end of it you see vines. We even noticed that, in the Collegiate Church, with one's back to the altar the vines appear to be enframing the main entrance of the church. In fact they are across a road about 12 yards away. Everywhere one feels that the vines are clinging to the houses of the people that make them, live by them, love them.

We went from this very impressive church to the Hermit's Cave, from which St Emilion gets its name. It was called St Melion in the old days. The cave was small, as one would expect, with a little tiny part rather barricaded off in stone where the hermit slept. It seemed wrong to me that the silence and the feeling of immortality about this cave hewn in the rock was rent by a lathe working wood just a few yards away, but life is like that. I remember going into the superb church at Nancy some years ago and hearing hurdy-gurdy fair music drowning a Bach organ recital, the Cathedral walls being, in fact, used as part of the fairground.

There is a little spring on the right-hand side of the cell from which the hermit got his water. Now people throw coins there and if they make the sign of the cross with their coins it means that within the year they will be married. There is also a tiny seat hewn out of the rock on which the hermit sat, and it is said that if you sit there and wish, your wish comes true and that this particularly applies if you wish for a family.

The astonishing thing about the principal street of old St Emilion—the oldest part is within the city walls—is that during the English occupation the stone cobbles were actually brought from England, and it is still the same stone there today.

The proprietor of the Clos Jacobins, one of our luncheon hosts, 82-year-old, white bearded, alert little M. Regnier-Vauthier, let us sample his 1954 which was exceptionally good, and the 1955 which is going to be a great year in all the Bordeaux wines. In the parish church of St Emilion he showed us a painting of Christ on the cross, and the soldiers there, who should of course be Jews, are English soldiers. It was obviously painted at the time of the 'occupation' when the English were not much liked, although everyone here says that, historically, they were the kindest and the best of 'occupation' troops and their law makers were *très sympathique*.

This picture is on the altar—a little altar—at the left of the chapel dedicated to the dead of the 1914–18 war. General Talbot, who commanded the British troops here in the Middle Ages, and whose defeat at Castillon severed our political but not vinous ties with Bordeaux, very sensibly lived in the Château Belair, which has a breath-taking view across the valley and the vineyards and was owned in the fourteenth century by an Englishman— Robert Knowles, whose descendants changed their name to 'de Canolle'.

Château Belair, whose wines we tasted, is at the head of the *premier grand cru classé* and adjoins the famous Château Ausone.

We ended our long visit to this historic Region by going to its two most famous vineyards—Ausone and Cheval-Blanc, the first of the *grands* of St Emilion.

Château Ausone is said to be built on the site of the sumptuous Villa which the Roman poet Ausonius owned in the fourth century. It has an admirable exposure, its vines running down a gentle slope which shields it from the north winds. It is some- times known as 'the poet's wine', always as a wine of great qualities.

The vineyards of the Château Cheval-Blanc, despite its name

producing only red wines, is at the furthermost tip of St Emilion adjoining the Pomerol vineyards and those of another *grand cru*— Château Corbin. The by-roads are mere cart tracks here, but they lead through pleasant places—wide-open views scurrying into secretive wooded corners, ramshackle paint-blistered Châteaux surrounded by thousands of acres of naked vineyards ruined by the terrible frost of February 1956 and now being gradually replanted.

It gives an idea of how hardly they were hit that Château Cheval-Blanc, which normally produces 600 hogsheads of wine a year, made only 200 in 1956, Château Corbin none. This frost not only nearly ruined many of the great vineyard proprietors and thousands of small ones as well, but, through creating scarcity, it has also almost doubled the price of all Bordeaux wines.

At Cheval-Blanc the soil is more varied than almost any other —heavy and light, clay and gravel; as a result many different types of grapes are grown, including some on old French stock which has been successfully guarded against the dreaded phylloxera; ancient methods are still used—for example, white of egg in the fining—and the resulting wine is always good and frequently magnificent enough to win the highest awards at exhibitions all over the world.

I cannot write with anything except vicarious experience of the great neighbouring vineyards of Pomerol. We motored through them—they resemble those of St Emilion—and on a number of occasions had an opportunity of trying their wines, which their President, M. Belivier, described as having the aroma of Merlot and Cabernet in a body of exceptional strength. 'The delicacy of a great Médoc but also the sap of St Emilion.' I found it a most pleasant wine, very similar to St Emilion.

CÔTES DE BORDEAUX

St Emilion, Pomerol and many of the fine wines of the Côtes de Bordeaux are exported from the quiet wine town of Libourne, founded by an English nobleman, Roger de Leyburn, on the placid banks of the Dordogne.

Before touring its vineyards we browsed over old ledgers in the 200-years-old family firm of Horeau Beylot of Libourne— a firm which is now directed by the family's Belgian son-in-law, M. de Coninck, and by M. de Lavaux. Once again we came right up against the ancient English 'occupation' by finding that old copy invoices were not made out in francs but in pounds, shillings and pence!

Two miles from Libourne is Fronsac, where Charlemagne's hill-top fortress was destroyed by Richelieu. This is a place to visit both for its old Roman church and the panoramic view over the whole area of Entre-Deux-Mers, looking at it from the other side of the river and from exactly the opposite view that one gets from Château d'Yquem. A vast prolific valley with Libourne on your left, Bordeaux hidden on your right—and at your feet this wide, smug, slowly-slinking river which curls with the hill and suddenly broadens out into a lagoon.

I asked M. de Coninck how bad he thought the St Emilion '56, and he said, 'Well, it's no worse than the '30, the '31, or the '32' —those are the four bad years of the recent thirty or so. He finds the '47 and the '49 and the '50 very good now, and the '52 will be, and so will the '53 and '55. He said the great thing about these wines of St Emilion and the Côtes-de-Fronsac is that they are supple and complete in themselves—there's not that hardness or that coarseness which the greater wines often keep for so long. They are much softer. I, personally, enjoyed them very much more.

He cannot understand why the wines of the Côtes-de-Fronsac are so little known in England; he thinks they are wonderful wines, and the one we had at lunch really was exceedingly good. His own vineyard, the Château Canon Fronsac, is on a wonderful open south-eastern slope—a better elevation than almost any of the vineyards that I saw in this part of the world. The nearby village of St Michel de Fronsac is very beautiful from the distance —with a lovely church and the Dordogne river curling lazily round the base of it. Here the women wear large grey felt hats, whereas in St Emilion they were wearing large round straw ones.

We went up to Château Canon at Naudin on this lovely slope. The soil is clay, which gives the wine of St Emilion and Côtes-de-Fronsac its very soft quality, but is very, very 'gooey', and runs off the hill-side after rain. We had had thunderstorms the previous night, and walking in it was most unpleasant, and as one motored one noticed that the earth had been washed out of the end of the vineyards on to the roads. This all has to be picked up and taken back again to the far end of the vineyard—quite a job.

During lunch we were talking about the word 'poule', which can mean either a chicken or a prostitute or 'love-lady'. Our hostess comforted us by saying that French children were equally confused and told us of three very young children, aged about four or five, who were talking about where they had come from. One said, 'Well, I've learnt all about it, I came from a rose.' Another piped in, 'I think you're wrong, because I've learnt about it from my mummy, and I was found under a cabbage,' but the third one said, 'Well, I wasn't the same as either of you, I came from an egg from a chicken on the fifth floor.' (From a 'poule' on the fifth floor.)

A thing one keeps noticing about the French is that they are so very much more literal-minded than the English. For example, if you say you want to wash your hands, as I did in this same house, you may be taken to wash your hands in a place where only washing hands can be done. They do not go in for the euphemisms of English speech—they take you quite literally—they think that if you wanted to go to the lavatory you would say so. If you say you want to wash your hands and the kitchen is handy they will take you to the kitchen. I think that our politicians sometimes forget the literal-mindedness of the French.

GRAVES

In the Middle Ages there were vineyards within the city of Bordeaux, and the accounts of the Archbishop of Bordeaux are said by Gaston Marchou to prove that high-quality vines grew in various central streets, including the Place Dauphin (now called Place Gambetta), where the guillotine spewed its gory droppings in the Revolution.

Today the city has once more overtaken the vines and the trolley buses clatter between two of the greatest vineyards in the world: on the left, as you go towards Sauternes, the *Premier Cru* of all Graves, the Château Haut-Brion—the only vineyard outside the Médoc to be awarded first place in the classification of 1855; and on the right one of the two outstanding *crus* classed immediately following—La Mission Haut-Brion.

Seeing all this conurbation right to the very doors of the Châteaux makes 'The diary of a lady of fifty years' curious reading when it describes how, at the revolution, the Marquise de la Tour du Pin hid in a lonely house amongst a scattering of tiny vineyards just outside the city in a deserted commune called Haut-Brion!

The Graves region extends on the north to the Médoc and

Bordeaux, curves round Bordeaux, faces eastwards to the Côtes de Bordeaux across the Garonne river, sets its toe on Sauternes and Barsac, and has its western flank lined with blue pine forests.

It is an area some 30 miles long by 15 wide. An area which Montesquieu loved for its peace and its vines, an area for which he dreamed in his unhappy days as a courtier when his ambition was 'of farming my own lands and so obtaining all my fortunes from the hands of the gods'.

The English have drunk much Graves ever since the twelfth century, and in fact for some time insisted that the wines of the Médoc should also be called Graves.

Today the area consists of forty-three communes grouped together as the Syndicat Viticole des Graves, which produces up to about one hundred and ten thousand gallons of wine each year.

It is said that the special qualities of Graves come from the perfect harmony of climate and the soil, which is mostly gravel with just the right elements in its subsoil to provide complete balance.

It always amuses me to hear wiseacres shake their heads and deprecate a wine because it is blended. Was anything used by man ever more blended? In one bottle of white Graves you will have a blend of grapes from different soils that can occur in any vineyard; the grapes will come from the Semillon, Sauvignon or Muscadelle stock and there will undoubtedly be a blend of vines of different ages. All in one bottle, Sir!

Some like the reds of Graves best; others the white. The wisest seek them both!

The reds, which come from Merlot, Cabernet, Malbec, and Petit Verdot stock, are very similar to the Médocs, although their slightly greater flavour and bouquet make them a particularly good wine to accompany pheasant, partridge, or quail. Like the older Médocs, many think them best decanted, and they should certainly be brought to a warm room temperature slowly during a day or so before drinking and be allowed to 'breathe' for some hours before serving.

The Bordelais aver that white Graves, not Chablis, is the perfect accompaniment to the oysters. The wines are very delicate and pass in gentle cadences from sweet to dry. Eleanor of Aquitaine certainly brought to her marriage to Henry Plantagenet a dowry of unparalleled felicity when she brought the great wines of Bordeaux.

Our first visit was to La Mission Haut-Brion, the second most
famous of the Graves wines. The Château is very, very lovely,
not big—it does not compre with La Malle or any of the very
great Châteaux of the Loire, but it is most beautiful in the garden
and colourful (how one misses gardens in France) with roses
tumbling over very elegant wrought-iron gates. Standing in the
avenue by the front door of the *chai*, with the wrought-iron gates
in front and roses on each side, one can see across the main road
to the vineyards of Haut-Brion exactly opposite. La Mission Haut-
Brion was for many years dominated by a most unusual weather-
cock in the form of a sailing ship of Bordeaux type, bought many
years ago from the roof of the British Exhibition at Paris. It was
then mounted on the left wing of the Mission Haut-Brion for
many years, but it became dangerous and is now in the *cuverie*.
It is quite magnificent—exquisite craftmanship in very, very
heavy metal.

1956 was a disastrous year for La Mission Haut-Brion—they
made only 110 barrels instead of 400. The caves are spotless. About
the finest we saw anywhere except those of Château Lascombes,
Château d'Yquem, and those of Louis Latour in Beaune.

I asked M. Berlan, the *Maître du Chai*, when the glass bungs get
replaced with the ordinary kind of cork bungs which we know
and which are put in at a slight angle from the centre. The answer
was, 'In one year, after which the wine will no longer ferment
at all.'

The Maître thinks that '56 is going to be a very good wine,
although there is little of it. We had a *dégustation* of the '56 and '55,
both of which seemed to me to be exceedingly good, and I
personally preferred the Mission Haut-Brion '56 to the Haut-
Brion which we tasted soon afterwards, though that is not the
usual form.

The '55 Haut-Brion was very, very good indeed with a wonderful nose.

Haut-Brion itself is much more modest in appearance than
La Mission. In 1956 they lost almost 50 per cent of their crop.

I asked about their white wine, which I have been buying for
some time from the excellent firm of W. H. and J. Joule of Stone,
exported by Calvet. In fact, for some years, at the instance of the
present cellarer, Mâitre Delmas, they tried putting a certain
amount of white wine—he would not give me the exact amount—
into the red, as he said, '*Pour donner la souplesse, la finesse au vin*

rouge' (to give suppleness and finesse). They produce this white wine from Sauvignon Blanc and Le Semillion. They only did this experimentally to see if it gave it extra quality to the red wine, but they found that it made a fine white wine of its own, and that was that.

M. Delmas is a most modest man; he discounts what he does himself, he says that his recipe for a good wine is, 'C'est le terroir et le climat qui fait le vin.' (It is the earth and the climate which make the wine.) They make only 5 or 6 per cent of white wine.

In the anteroom to the *cuvée* at Haut-Brion are three very, very attractive pictures—one a panorama of the vineyard with workers harvesting; one of a vineyard worker and one of a woman. They are futuristic, impressionistic and charming. The colours are lovely. They were painted by an Englishman who spent nearly three months at Haut-Brion looking around and painting, and they were bought subsequently in 1951 by the firm's London agent and sent to the Château as a present. Unfortunately it was not possible to decipher this untrammelled colour-free painter's name—the nearest that we could get was Cullard.

The last two Graves Châteaux we saw were the philosopher Montesquieu's majestic but companionable home—La Brède—now lovingly cared for by his descendant, Madame La Comtesse de Chabannes-La Pallice, and the much more austere Château Carbonnieux, whose fine wines owe much to the story of their sale to the Sultan of Turkey.

The story goes that the wines, then produced by Benedictine monks, were introduced to Constantinople by a prisoner, who knowing that the Koran prohibited the drinking of alcohol, suggested that it should be labelled 'L'eau minérale'. The Sultan found he much enjoyed the soothing wine and, though well aware of the little chicanery, wrote back to the Reverend Fathers, 'I cannot understand why your fellow countrymen drink wine when they have this delightful mineral water!'

Montesquieu lived at La Brède when first President of the Bordeaux Parliament and subsequently wrote most of his books there. The historic building is open to the public on every day except Tuesdays, and the short tour round the library, whose original catalogues of over 7,000 books were discovered by an Oxford don, Roger Shackleton, a few years ago, takes only a quarter of an hour.

It is an enchanting, peaceful place, entered by a slender bridge over an enclosing moat, in parts almost as wide as a lake, from which enormous perch eyed us hungrily—ferocious-looking fish —and then rose with a great plop to the same flies that swallows were skimming down for, just touching the water and soaring off like a flash of lightning.

Cattle bells tolled in the distance and colourful rose gardens gave way to a broad open view with a back-cloth of woods and just occasional views through the trees of the vineyards which the philosopher loved so well—the vineyards of which he said to his great friend the Abbé Guasco, 'I don't know whether my books owe most to my wines or my wines most to my books.'

The Château is built in Cotswold type stone and its setting in fields in a forest clearing makes it both intimate and open. Everything was peaceful here except for a fugitive aeroplane fluttering futilely over head.

SAUTERNES AND BARSAC

We visited the great sweet wine districts of Sauternes and Barsac with M. Binaud, former President of the Bordeaux Wine and Spirit Trade Association.

On the way we talked wine trade economics and he mentioned that new casks have increased in cost in France almost more than anything. In 1915 they cost 15 francs, which was then 12 shillings of our money. They now cost 9,000 francs, which is £9 of our money, and there is no market for them in England—5 shillings or 10 shillings each only.

What they are doing now with the mature wine, when it does not very much matter that the wine should take up any tannin from the oak, is to put the wine into much less strong casks for shipping purposes and it is then not very important what happens to them.

New casks in fact are always best for the wine, but are not necessarily used in the bad years. In 1956, for example, it often just was not worth while, with barrels at £9 each, putting the wine into them because it was a bad year. It was one of the worst years they have ever had.

In many instances proprietors of famous Châteaux had decided not to sell that year under the name of the growth, as they must maintain their high reputations.

M. Binaud is of the opinion that the taste of eggs kills a wine.

Exceptions are omelettes with mushrooms or kidneys in them. It's best not to have wine with eggs. On the other hand, he feels one should not be too dogmatic about what wine one should have with what dishes. One does not want to frighten people; if people enjoy their wine with something the experts think inappropriate —well, good luck to them.

You have great satisfaction in any case drinking wine as long as it is a genuine wine, but you will have greater satisfaction if you follow the accepted practice. He confirms that the price of wine here in Bordeaux has doubled since the disastrous vintage of 1956, which was made not only by the rains but by the fact that the frost of February 1956 ruined some vineyards up to nearly 100 per cent—and many up to 80.

He refers to the district of Cérons as the intermediary between the dry Graves and the sweet Sauternes, which he finds delicious and supple. In Barsac we were received by M. Rolland, the President of the Sauternes Association, who owns the Château Coutet. On our way to the vineyards he told me about the way stones suddenly appear in the vineyards. They're not there one year and then they suddenly appear in no time at all. It is said, '*les pierres poussent*' (the stones 'grow').

We went to a magnificent and unlikely Château—the Château de Malle, which is built in the Italian style of the seventeenth century. It makes a most exciting visit. It is one of the most lovely Châteaux in France and is exquisitely furnished. We were most interested to see life-size figures inside cut out of wood and painted in seventeenth-century costumes. We were told they were 'scarecrows' put about the place to keep evil-doers away. In fact, I think it is much more likely that they were used as décor in the little private theatre that one sees in the grassy grounds of the Château.

Practically everything is in Italian style, the reason being that the family who built it came from near Milan and settled in France in the sixteenth or seventeenth century. They have superb mirrors and pictures, a private chapel, and a quite unique jewel box with a tremendous lock, far too heavy to carry off easily, and far too difficult even for burglars to prise open.

The vineyard which encircles the Château was 75 per cent destroyed in 1956. They have now got vast areas resting—they are not replanting it all at once, because if they did they would create a problem for their successors if they, in their turn, had to restock all their vines at the same time. Also they do not want only vines of the same age.

The Château de Malle has always been lived in; it has been in three branches of the same family—Malle, Lur-Saluces and Bournazel—for a thousand years.

The very handsome heir to the estate was recently killed in Morocco. He was a very distinguished soldier, who was so fearless and fought so bravely that the Arabs believed that they should not fire at him because the bullets rebounded on to them. He always fought wearing his red parade jacket and was called by his enemies 'L'Homme Rouge'. Then he was moved to another part of the front where he was not known, he was forbidden to wear his red jacket and was almost immediately killed. The Château is now visited only once a month on a Saturday night or Sunday by the owner. A sad story.

We then went to Château Suduirault, known as Ancien Cru du Roi, which is surrounded by a magnificent garden, and the gloriously proportioned Château Filhot where there is a note about the *pourriture noble*, which says, '*Seuls sont cueillis et triés les grains attaqués par le botrytis cinerea, qui au profane paraissent devoir être éliminés*'.[1]

The '55 was thought by all to be quite superb and complete, and our guide, M. Binaud, remarked as he passed the *Maître du Chai*, 'Bravo, pour ça, Maître.' The *Maître du Chai*, who is also known as the *Chef du Cave* or the *Chef Tonnelier*, is in charge of all the workmen on the vineyard; he is the consultant of the directorate and carries out all their orders. He must have a superb palate and be able to judge what treatment or what blend to give to his wines and stock. He supervises the grapes as they come into the *chai*; he cares for the maturing wine and decides when it should be fined. He places all orders and accounts for all purchases and meets all customers. He has to be a qualified cooper and to learn to taste and how to make wine. He is always genial and always seems to have time to help other people.

The Château d'Yquem, perhaps the most famous wine Château in the world, is an ancient twelfth-century fortress with a sixteenth-century Château within it.

It is one of the most picturesque of the Châteaux and there is a lot of colour, crimson and reds—mostly from roses—against a

[1] Only the grape berries attacked by the *Botrytis cinerea* are picked, although, to the profane, they look as if they ought to be eliminated.

background of small green lawns, great trees and vineyards coming right up to the walls. As impressive as anything were seven enormous German dogs standing some 3 feet high, whose pricked ears nearly meet on top, rather like the ear-protectors on German soldiers' uniforms of the first World War. The dogs were black or black-and-white, lovely, graceful, quick-moving animals, and had a terrier with them.

The view is quite superb; you can see over to the five *communes* of Sauternes and Barsac as if the great Château, the vast fortification housing the number one name in the wine world, is guarding in a paternal way the interests of the other lesser but beautiful wine-making districts. You see right over to Entre-Deux-Mers, you see Cadillac, you see woods and tiny hamlets, but mostly you see vines and Châteaux and red-and-white roofs.

A motor tractor was working in the vines at Château d'Yquem and it had not an inch over as it went in between the rows of vines.

The *Maître* at Château d'Yquem is M. Bureau, and the *Régisseur*, who is the manager of the place, is a very young man, M. Duhamel. He is a very lucky man, because he was taken on about a year or two back to start learning the job because the *Régisseur* was getting old. Within six months of his arrival the old *Régisseur* had died and this young man got the job just like that and is doing very well; he was there at the right moment.

We were feeling rather thirsty at this time and I mentioned this, and M. Binaud replied, 'Yes, as Rabelais says, "Drink before you are thirsty, and you will never have a thirst" ', which is very good advice particularly when you're drinking sweet wines, because it means that you really do not want to dip into them so much that they ultimately make you more thirsty still.

At Château d'Yquem everything which may touch the wine is wooden, even the cylinder, which presses the noble grapes when they arrive in from the *vendage*. Metal is never in contact with the grape or the wine. Also the crushing machine, the *emietteure*, is, almost uniquely, I think, made of wood. The wine stays three years there in new barrels.

The '54 we thought wonderful, but the '55 an absolutely extraordinary wine, as M. Binaud said, 'It is nectar of the gods.' It recalls to him particularly the '37 and to a lesser degree the '47. To him the '37 of Château d'Yquem was the greatest wine of his experience and he is a man, I suppose, of 55.

M

M. Rolland, who was my host at lunch at Château Coutet, told me another thing about Sauternes, that it is exceedingly good for people, as it has been found that it contains penicillin; it therefore cures many ills, especially those we do not know we have.

We went with M. Lalonde of the Ambassade du Vin de Sauternes from there to lunch with him at Château Coutet, passing through very wooded country whose vines are hidden by the trees.

I noticed that uniquely in the vineyards of this part of the world they have started signposting 'Route du Vin' at the crossroads. They also put up the words 'Circuit de Sauternes', and if there are historic Châteaux nearby they mark those, although you can follow the circuit on the card of the three main wine circuits that you can get from the Syndicat d'Initiative in the middle of Bordeaux or the Syndicat d'Initiative in any of the smaller towns. All the Châteaux have them as well.

We were received by M. Rolland's wife and other guests at the Château Coutet and we saw, apart from the lovely *caves*, a most interesting framed letter from the late Sacha Guitry.

A friend of his sent him two cases of Château Coutet as a present. Next time he was in Paris he rang up Sacha Guitry to say that he was there and was coming out to see him, which reminded Guitry that he had not drunk any of the wine, so he got down to it.

When the friend arrived Sacha Guitry was in a very shaky state —as they say here, he had found the wine very 'fatigant', but all the same he sat down and he wrote to M. Rolland the letter which is framed there for anyone to see. The letters wander all over the page—it's only two or three sentences—just like a person who has dined too well might wander over the streets, and it ends up with the words, '*ivre mort grace à eux à eux*,'[1] and underneath in enormous letters which take up nearly half the paper, but always descending, the words, 'Vive le Château Coutet'.

It appeared he and a friend who was lunching with him drank a bottle between them, and they liked it so much that they then drank another bottle, and it was a very powerful wine—21 degrees of alcohol!

At lunch we talked about the 'stretching' of wine, and they told me that when Curnonsky, the Prince of Gastronomes, was told that Algeria had revolted, he cried, 'Good heavens, if we lose Algeria, how can we make Burgundy?'

[1] Dead drunk, thanks to them ...

In the Sauternes Region one is constantly impressed with the care and quality and more care which go to making the wines— it is also very obvious that producers are much worried both at present world trends towards drier wines and by the fact that so few people now spend time preparing or eating the dishes which used to come at the end of a substantial meal—the sweets and fruits to which these incomparably sweet wines are the perfect complement.

In case you do not have time either to seek the advice of the staff of the Conseil Interprofessionnel du Vin de Bordeaux or to visit their exhibition and *dégustation* centre at 1 Cours du XXX Juillet, I copied down two verses of a complaint written in 1680 by 'a person of quality' at the time when shipments of Bordeaux wine to Britain were stopped owing to the quarrel between Colbert and William of Orange.

It was presented to the Conseil by the Grand Old Man of the British wine trade—M. André Simon:

THE CLARET DRINKER'S SONG
or
THE GOOD FELLOW'S DESIGN

By a Person of Quality

A pox on the fooling and plotting of late,
What a pother and stir has it kept in this state?
Let the rabble run mad with suspicions and fears;
Let 'em scuffle and fan, till they go by the ears;
Their grievances never shall trouble my pate,
So I can but enjoy my dear bottle at quiet.

A friend and a bottle is all my design,
Has no room for treason, that's top-full of wine,
I mind not the members and makers of laws,
Let 'em sit or prorogue as His Majesty please;
Let 'em damn us to woollen, I'll never repine
At my lodging when dead, for alive I have wine.
Yet oft in my drink I can hardly forbear
To curse 'em, for making my claret so dear.

It is not inappropriate now, is it?
On our last day in Bordeaux we lunched with Madame Dubos,

whose daughter-in-law had been an expert guide to both Haut-Brion and La Mission Haut-Brion, which she had known since childhood. During a gay meal enlivened by her daughter's enthusiasm she told us a sweet story about the ages of a man (or of a woman)—twenty years is '*un jeune homme*', at thirty years '*un homme ieune*', at forty years '*un homme très jeune*', at fifty years '*un homme encore jeune*', at sixty years '*un homme toujours jeune*', at seventy '*un homme toujours très jeune*', and at eighty or when writing his obituary '*un homme éternellement jeune*'.

After ten days of almost overwhelmingly generous welcome I was feeling tired, very grateful, but very nearly 'eternally young'!

X

Cognac

OTORING INTO Cognac and Charente from Bordeaux, one notices much cereal, a lot of market gardens and a certain amount of wood. Only a proportion of the area is planted with vines. The reason is that after phylloxera, when tens of thousands of small distillers and growers were very badly hit, the areas known in patois as *gelif*—that is subject to *la gelée*, were not replanted.

These small growers in unfavourable positions had been warring against frost for years and years, but once their stock was destroyed they saw the light and went over to the safer occupation of cereal production. Also, of course, they could not afford to wait and did not know that France was soon going to get immune American stock.

Seeing the 'town' for the first time, as we did, from the slopes of the Grande Champagne region, which lies south of Cognac, the view is very like Ay near Epernay—vine-covered slopes rolling down to fertile plain.

The road is an undulating one, and when you are on the top of the 'undles' you have vines on either side; when you go down into the troughs there are only cereals. It is just those few feet which make all the difference between an area that is *gelif* and one which is not.

The discoloration of walls and buildings in the streets in Cognac and Jarnac is quite astonishing. For some feet up, the wall looks just like the inside of a chimney, the dirty sooty appearance coming from the brandy fumes which leak out at the rate of twenty-six thousand bottles a day, and percolate everywhere. On hot evenings it was almost as if somewhere quite near a chimney had been swept and a little bit of brandy had been poured on the soot, and you had that kind of smell coming in through the window. I even noticed as I passed a churchyard outside Cognac that the walls around it were slightly blackened. Perhaps the fumes are wafted over from the city or maybe it comes from the bones of brandy drinkers and inspired the old song, 'When I die don't bury me at all, just pickle my bones in alcohol.'

Great firms like Martell and Hennessy encourage visitors—Martell's receive up to twenty-five thousand a year. They get shown round by French, English, German or Spanish speaking guides, and the tour takes an hour to an hour and a half.

King François I was born in Cognac—it is said locally under a tree by the river Charente opposite the island which houses the Restaurant Robinson. There are many Restaurant Robinsons on islands in France and you get wound over to this in a little boat—shaped like a gondola and illuminated by the lights of the restaurant reflected on the water. It really is most attractive.

Cognac is proud of its many open places, its fine parks and the graceful River Charente which winds around it, the river that François I thought the most charming in the whole of his beautiful land. Up till 1939 barges used to take the barrels and cases of Cognac down to La Rochelle for export, but they have now been replaced by lorries. Running up from the river is one of the most attractive and gracious streets in Cognac, the Rue Saulnier.

It was, inevitably, the Romans who brought the cultivation of the vine to Charente; but it was economic expediency rather than resourcefulness that led to the hard white wine being distilled, and it was near-disaster which showed the astonishing improvement brought by allowing the brandy to mature in oaken barrels.

In the Middle Ages the English imported large quantities of wines from different sources and distilled them into fierce, fiery liquids which warmed the heart's cockles when diluted with water (which it was said to purify) and sweetened by products of the apothecary's art.

In the sixteenth century shipping space became scarcer and scarcer, economic conditions in the Charente became desperate and the vintners petitioned their Governor to lighten taxation, as bad wine sales were ruining them and they were forced to pass their wines through alembics and make them into brandy or else use them for vinegar.

At this time they obviously considered that distilling wine was a sacrilege and, as Robert Delamain records, in his fine *History of Cognac*, they considered it an entirely unworthy expedient 'which risked denuding all the country of firewood'.

However, there was nothing for it but distillation, and this was carried out in the same way and with similar alembics to those used by the ancient Egyptians—a method little altered even today.

Gradually the trade expanded and barges took the unmatured white liquid down the Charente to La Rochelle, from whence it was shipped to all parts of the world.

Another disaster presaged fabulous prosperity for Charente— this was the Spanish Wars of Succession which so diminished their export trade that great piles of barrels of *eau de vie* had to be stocked in warehouses and distilleries throughout the Region.

When trade routes opened up again after the signing of the Treaty of Utrecht the merchants, hastening to export their eau de vie again, found that it had changed by ageing in the oaken barrels, from white to golden, had lost most of its fire and had acquired something of the perfume and bouquet that all the world admires today. From then onwards their fortune was assured.

Since then the art of blending has been added to the principle of maturing; rigorous laws have been made defining the areas from which the grapes may come and others to see that only the finest product of the distillation—the heart—is allowed to mature. The beginning and end of the distilled liquid, called heads and tails, is put on one side for redistillation, as its flavour is not perfect.

Cognac, which like champagne owes much to its climate and rich, chalky soil, is made from the wine of three main plants— the Folle Blanche, the Colombar and—ever increasingly—the St Emilion; to these as 'make up' stock may be added Semillon, Sauvignon, Blanc Rame, Jurançon, Jurançon Blanc, and Montils, but these are only allowed up to a density of 10 per cent of the planting.

The vines cover an area of one hundred and sixty thousand acres with seventy thousand vineyards producing some fifty-five million gallons of wine and sub-divided in hierarchical order into the districts of Grande Champagne, Petite Champagne, Borderies, Fins Bois, Bons Bois, Bois Ordinaires, and Bois Communs. As with champagne, the price you pay reflects very fairly the percentage of the finest wines that have gone into the making of your particular brand of cognac.

The grapes are harvested about the end of September, crushed very slowly to prevent any 'linen' (grape fibre and juice from pips) getting into the wine, and allowed to ferment entirely naturally.

Distillation begins immediately after fermentation and goes

on for six months between the end of October and the end of May.

The first 'cooking' or 'run' of the wine gives a 28 per cent distillate called the *brouillis*; the 'heads and tails' are put on one side to be distilled again and the heart is given its second distillation. Again only the heart is taken and this is called the cream and is in fact the raw unmatured cognac. This second distillation is a difficult, delicate, and important operation fascinating to watch with the low fire, the slow trickle of the liquid, and the keen, watchful concentration of the *distillateur*—a craft handed down from father to son.

We tried some of the new, uncasked brandy—at this stage it is always called *La Vigne en Fleur*—the vine in flower. It was fiery and heady though it already had a distinctive bouquet. You either put it in your mouth and spit it straight out or else rub it in your hands—in either case the perfume lingers for some time.

The cognac now goes into superb new barrels of Limousin or Troncais oak—barrels made as carefully as furniture—notchless and smooth. Martell's, who do about 70 per cent of the English trade, which they call the home trade as the family come from the Channel Islands, have in stock about one hundred thousand of these valuable barrels containing about one-sixth of all the cognac made, and they lose the equivalent of one and a quarter million bottles a year by evaporation. Their oldest *chai* looks just like a church—vaulted and dark, solemn and very impressive and permeated with a damp, sooty smell. Martell's call it 'paradise'!

After a year the cognac will be transferred into older casks which will continue to give it its colour of golden amber, whilst the evaporation through its pores slowly reduces its fierceness and alcoholic content at a rate of about 40 per cent in fifteen years and there it will stay between three and seventy years.

Time and again I was enjoined to pay attention to the brand rather than to any alleged age.

The words 'Napoleon brandy' and an aged-looking bottle mean little or nothing. Certainly they may mean that it is the oldest cognac the firm handles, but it certainly does not mean that the wine was distilled prior to July 13, 1815, when Napoleon gave himself up to the British on the nearby island of Aix by placing himself under the protection of the Prince Regent—'the greatest, the most constant and most generous of my enemies'.

If, in fact, the brandy had been distilled in or before 1815 and had not been bottled within fifty or at the most sixty years it would have quickly deteriorated and all its alcohol would by now be merely a stain on a wall in Cognac. In fact, today, all the great cognacs are bottled within seventy years as they are then considered to be at their peak. They are taken out of the wood in which they would thereafter have deteriorated and put into very broad-based thin-necked glass containers—the first cousins of those used by the greatest of the sweet-wine makers of Roussillon. And there they can remain as long as maybe without in any way losing their quality.

The oldest of many cognacs we had the privilege of tasting at Martell's were an 1875 and an 1848, each had been in wood for about sixty years, the '75 being undoubtedly much the finer of two astonishingly delicate brandies.

Before blending, the brandy is filtered at a controlled temperature to stop expansion and then the difficult art of blending commences whereby the cognacs from different districts and ages are made into an entity which will maintain the tradition for which the firm has acquired a reputation. Incidentally, the only metal the brandy touches is red copper, if it is running quickly over it from, say one cask to another or from barrel to bottle, or silver plate if it is to be in contact for any appreciable time. Only in this way is the subtle bouquet and perfume preserved for the eventual consumer.

There is a great deal of muddle and confusion over the marking of brandies and the best thing to do is to buy a renowned make at the highest price you can afford. As in every other trade there are some who exist to meet the demands of those who are always seeking 'bargains'.

They sell their wares in fascinating bottles embellished with exciting labels. They add a little flavouring, blend greater quantities of soft but not very delicate brandy and, in fact, produce just what those with a keen eye for a 'bargain' are seeking. On the other hand, there are scores of fine brandies made and distributed by firms who are proud to be of honest service to those who look upon cognac as incomparably the finest *eau de vie* in the world.

The following stars and marking have become traditional, though they vary from firm to firm, the object of each firm being to maintain exactly the same quality and type under the same markings year by year:

***	Cognac 3 to 15 years old
V.O.	Very old
V.O.P.	Very Old Pale (15 to 30 years old)
V.S.O.	Very Superior Old (25 years old)
V.S.O.P.	Very Superior Old Pale (30 years old)

Some firms employ the following lettering:

V.V.O.	Very Very Old
X.O.	Extra Old
V.V.S.O.	Very Very Superior Old (Reserve)
V.V.S.O.P.	Very Very Superior Old Pale

(Vintage Cognac)

There are three main trade groups in the Charente: those who own vineyards and make wine and also distil; those who buy grapes, make wine and also distil; and those who buy wine and distil it. Nearly all the great firms belong to the third category.

It is worth while visiting all three types, and visitors can arrange to travel through the lovely countryside calling on these men of Cognac, large or small; can admire the neatness of their vineyards; hear how proud the cultivators are of their cognac; how they deplore abuse in the drinking of it, and how disgusted they are with the designation given it in certain American states of 'intoxicating liquor', which also applies to methylated spirits if you care to drink it.

One notices that the women wear long sunbonnets coming down over their shoulders like spaniels' ears, sometimes hiding their shoulders, sometimes their faces, and called in patois 'kiss nots'—a relic of the English occupation brought about by Elainore of Aquitaine's marriage to King Henry II and designed, presumably, to encourage the shy English soldiers—or were they?

Both in Armagnac and Cognac I found a certain fear that the present restlessness and rush of modern life and the change of taste would mean an end of the after-dinner coffee and liqueur habit which meant so much to earlier generations of the thriven.

This so worried the Marquis de Montesquiou that a few years ago he started marketing Armagnac as a 'long drink'.

More recently Martell's have carried out an intensive market research campaign in England and the results have convinced them that they, too, should try to popularize the idea of drinking cognac as a long drink. The brandy and soda of our father's generation drunk as a 'reviver' must come, they fear, in this age to a certain extent to take the place of finer cognac. There may well be a diminishing place for cognac in a world in which less and less time is being devoted to the social graces of eating and drinking—more and more to consuming cocktails, chicory and tinned food, which is not a way of life but a living insult to our metabolism.

They also discovered to their surprise that their best customers in England are those people who keep a half-bottle of three star brandy in their houses for use in emergencies and who, like the Dutch with their gin and Danes with their Schnapps, find that they pretty often need them!

XI

Wines of the Loire

MUSCADET

THE ROAD from Cognac to La Rochelle is very pleasant, very much like England's countryside—green hedges and trees, a certain amount of vines, a lot of cereal and market garden land and many slopes.

The busy, thriving port of La Rochelle disappointed us enormously. The two forts each side of the harbour are interesting, the sixteenth-century Hôtel de Ville is worth a look if you are keen on architecture; the city ramparts are thick and remarkable; but from the point of view of a holiday this almost beachless place is a complete loss.

The good thing we found in La Rochelle, apart from the liveliness of the place (if you want to see a French provincial port really bursting at the seams on a Saturday night, go there), was the excellent Restaurant de la Marine, which looks on to the busy harbour. It was absolutely full of American servicemen from a nearby aerodrome, mostly talking politics with an altogether endearing enthusiasm.

We liked the place so little that we beat a hasty retreat and eventually pulled up at Pornic, which is a small fishing port about 35 miles due west of Nantes.

On our journey from La Rochelle we went through place after place where they were celebrating the *Fête Dieu* (The Corpus Christi procession of First Communicants to church and to the shrine of the Virgin Mary). It was a most moving sight, solemn-faced girls wearing elaborate white dresses and boys also in white or their best black and carrying white banners and posies of white silk or flowers. The whole of the population must have worked from dawn making the intricate patterns of flowers—down each side of the street and in some cases down the middle as well, just leaving room for the children and their parents to walk after church to the shrine of the Virgin Mary, which they had made absolutely lovely—a riot of flowers knit in delicate patterns. On the streets were used roses, marguerites, daisies, rambler roses, rushes, green stuff from the fields and branches of trees. Each person seemed to be doing his own little bit of road. It was quite heart-breaking to have to crush the flowers in the car, but they did not mind. They just smiled, said, 'Go along', and built it up again after we passed.

Whilst the children are in church, activity is redoubled. Parents bring out bunting and gay colours—mostly the colours of France —and drape them all round the outside of their houses, so that after their spiritual experience the children come out into a changed world—one very much *en fête*, a day of great rejoicing and tremendous family celebrations which some, I was told, keep up for two or three days.

Personally, I liked Pornic. It is very French and in four days we met no other foreigners. Like most seaside resorts the beaches are somewhat inadequate at weekends, but everyone was friendly and invited us to join in their beach games. It is a family place and there are no sophistications, but there is an excellent nine-hole golf course and tennis courts. We were very comfortable and well fed at the Plage and Golf Hotel, where we had to stay an extra day as the Cycle Race of France was starting from Nantes and every hotel was full up.

We were met at the luxurious and comfortable hotel at Nantes by M. Guillon Verne, Regional Director of Tourism, who assured us that we should have stayed at La Baule, which he says has the largest stretch of sands in Europe, though it gets very crowded like everywhere else from the middle of July until towards the end of August.

He thinks, personally, that the best months in this part of the world are May and June, though the sea then is rather cold for bathing, and then again from the end of August up till about September 10, when a lot of the hotels close down and it really becomes rather a deserted place.

Muscadet, which with Gros Plant is the wine of Nantes, is a dry, fruity wine with a minimum of 10 degrees of alcohol. It is usually between $10\frac{1}{2}$ and $12\frac{1}{2}$ and best when it is between 11 and 12. As it is both light and fragrant it is a delightful wine to drink in hot weather and with shell-fish. At home we often drink it before meals. In my opinion it travels well but is not popular with the trade, as the vineyards will sell direct to you and me.

Colonel Leonard Dennis disagreed with this statement when he read the chapter in draft, and says, 'The real truth is that it is a wine which is very little known in this country and is always imported in bottle and, therefore, carries a higher rate of duty, with the result that the price when offered to the public is rather higher than they are prepared to pay for a wine with which they are not conversant.'

We first went to see M. Verlynde, who is Vice-President of the Committee of the Vins du Pays Nantais and is the Mayor of his little village. He told me that in the Loire they drink the Muscadet the year after the harvest, in England and in Paris two years, and in America if the labels are attractive. His wine is the Château de Gillières. Of quality he says, 'No sun, no sugar; no sugar, no bouquet,' that was when we mentioned that we had much more bouquet in the Muscadet wine that we have at home than in any we had so far drunk. He answered that it was because we were drinking the 1956 vintage, which was not a sun-blessed year. So always try a sample bottle of muscadet before ordering any quantity, as it will vary from year to year more than wines which come from further south.

I asked if the wine kept in hot climates and got the answer, 'It goes through the Red Sea and it is very agreeable at the end—it was also in perfect condition when drunk in a bathyscope thousands of feet under the sea.'

The vine stock is Muscadet de Bourgogne. It is said to have come to these parts in 1709 packed within the marrow bone of an ox. The year before there was a terrible frost, they had no vines left, everyone was dispirited and none was being replanted. Someone tried out the root which they had found in the bone, and hence Muscadet, which gives an entirely different flavour and different wine from the same stock when planted in Burgundy. M. Verlynde says, 'a good wine rejoices man's heart'—he has this saying over his mantelpiece in his Château. He has eleven children, so it seems not only to rejoice but to revitalize man. He is a very cheerful person.

We went next to the first of two M. Charpentiers, M. Roger at La Chapelle Heulin, whose wine is called La Domaine des Aveneaux. We went out to see his 25 acres of vineyards. I asked him about harvesting, he replied, 'The 1957 harvest is finished.' In other words, he had lost nearly the whole of his, though the work has to go on in the vineyards just the same. The weeds have to be kept down, they have to spray against diseases carried by egg, diseases dropped by fly—and they have to spray several times against mildew, to which Muscadet is very susceptible—all for no reward at all. Overheads are in fact exactly the same, except for the labour of harvesting, which will be practically nothing. M. Charpentier has no sort of mechanization on his farm at all—there are just two horses, himself and a little labour.

We then went to see his father, M. Emile Charpentier of La Cognardière at Le Pallet. His wine we thought very good, though the '56 as in every *dégustation* that we enjoyed again was not quite so *bouqueté* as the '55; and then on to M. Lusseau of La Galissonnière, also at Le Pallet. His *caves* are very small, the *caves* of the little man—very different from the great world of Champagne and Cognac and from the co-operatives of the south. This is a land of individual little farmers, of which there are some twenty thousand in the Muscadet *Appellation Contrôlée* area alone.

His *cave* had several very nice *cuvées* of wine all next to each other. My guide, M. de Bettignies the Regional Controller of Appellation d'Origines, pointed out to him that he should have had their capacity painted on the side of these newly-painted *cuvées*. M. Charpentier ignored the remark. M. de Bettignies looked nettled and said somewhat curtly, 'It must be done,' and he got the reply quick as a knife from the proprietor, 'It's always—one must!' Then he looked at me, we laughed and he said, 'There's always tomorrow,'—very much like the Spanish 'Mañana, mañana!' It reminded me of Dumas' story of two Tourangeaux: 'Would you like some soup?' 'Yes.' 'Come and fetch it, then.' 'Thank you, I don't think I want soup any more.'

They have a reputation for laziness in these parts, but their well-cultivated vineyards give the lie to it though, as one grower said to me, 'Of course, we usually tend the vineyards in these parts better than the gardens.'

There is a great difference in the types of owners of Muscadet vineyards—some are solely vintners, others make a little wine and also do other jobs quite outside the wine industry, tending their vines in the mornings and the evenings. In the Beaujolais, where I once lived, I have sometimes seen them working at 4 a.m.

The working day in these parts is from 6 a.m.–12 noon and from 2–6 p.m.—a twelve-hour day with two hours off for lunch. Just sometimes in very, very hot weather the luncheon hour is extended to three hours.

M. de Couesbouc, President of the Regional Wine Growers lives at Le Coin St Fiacre and grows 37 acres in muscadet and 2 in vin rouge for consumption by his workpeople. He told me how bothered he is about what happens to Muscadet wine after it leaves their shores in the wood and how he wished the various countries' Customs would permit them to export wine in bottle more cheaply. Apart from other disasters that may happen to it in dark cellars, he finds that a slight secondary fermentation is often set up through the voyage and that none the less certain merchants still bottle it instead of waiting a few weeks. M. Couesbouc again emphasized that in Muscadet wine differences are due more to the year than to soil as the soil and slopes are very similar thoughout the region. There are no hills with a south-east exposure and all the vines get about the same amount of sun, and it is the sun which makes the wine and brings its variation in fruitiness and dryness. Just opposite M. Couesbouc's Château is a lovely scene—just like the West Midlands. Very small, intimate fields, the only difference being that where you would see hops in Herefordshire, here you see vines. The river is as tranquil, as slow, as lazy as the Wye and there are fewer cattle—no red soil and white faces certainly, and the sky was bluer but it had a happy Herefordshire feel.

We spent a morning visiting the Cathedral and the magnificent Château of the Dukes of Brittany in Nantes. The Cathedral is one of the most lovely I have ever seen. It is lovely because you *can* see it. I had a similar experience once in Evesham Abbey, when it was brightly lit because a television programme was to come from it, the lights revealing parts of the Abbey that had never before been seen by living man.

The gracious fifteenth-century Cathedral of Nantes with its enormously high arches, its towering nave, its Gothic façade which resembles Reims, is most beautifully light—light for a sad reason—as nearly all its glass was destroyed during the war. Half of the windows are filled with plain glass and four-fifths of the rest has merely got cardboard or some kind of opaque cover over it, but the result, as Edward Fitzgerald says, 'is all truth and daylight'.

In a side chapel on the right is the tomb of François II and his two wives; alongside it is a memorial which you never get far away from in France—to British dead. In this case to the million British dead of the 1914–18 war who, as the words say, nearly all left their bodies on French soil.

The glorious fifteenth-century Château in the centre of Nantes, where François II accepted from the Duc de Bretagne the alliance for ever between Bretagne and France, contrasts sharply with the gloomy and terrible cell in which the political prisoners of the Revolution were put in their hundreds with only a little tiny walk a few yards across in which to exercise. The cell was illumined by a feeble light near which these about-to-die aristocrats passed their time carving quite beautiful memorials on the stone window-sills, some religious, some figments of the imagination, some models of their own homes.

One of Muscadet's greatest vintners, the Marquis de Goulaine, unlike most of the proprietors here, keeps all his wine in barrels and not in large glass or cement-lined cuvées. His cellars are in two ancient vaulted kitchens, perfectly cool on the hottest day of the year, which are part of the lovely Château which has been in his family for over 1,100 years.

There are two very attractive chimneys, fourteenth and fifteenth century, in the *cave*, and it was here that we heard, on the 28th day of June 1957, a second fermentation taking place in one of the barrels, which was making a guggling noise like a fish rising. M. Lusseau told us that this 'talking' wine always comes from the same corner, the same *clos* of a vineyard. Also that that corner is shared; it is on the extremity of his and someone else's vineyard and the other man's wine also 'talks'. In other words, it starts fermenting again when all the others have finished and it does it every year.

We drank out of glass tastevins, first of all some Gros Plant, which is a Vin Délimité de Qualité Supérieure. It is very light, very dry, and very good with fish. Locally, they say it is even better with oysters than Muscadet, because it is drier, and oysters require the driest wine. Perhaps the best wine with oysters is Chablis, the second best very dry champagne, and the third best Gros Plant, though the list would be disputed by many. Whilst we were tasting it I noticed a plaque in the cellar to the heroic memory of Jules André Ripoche, gardener and wine grower at Château de Goulaine, with the words, 'killed for his fidelity 1794'. It really makes one think. Here was this man, their gardener, their wine grower, who fought for them in the Revolu-

N

tion and gave his life fighting against his apparent interests but according to the dictates of his conscience.

We lunched with M. Sautejeau, Mayor of Vallet, and his son-in-law, M. Beauguin, and saw the *pipette d'argent*, which he had won as the Grand Prix d'Honneur at the Foire de Vallet. He told us that all wine judging, whether locally or in a big city like Nantes or in Paris, is done by a team of four people, which always includes a merchant, a wine grower, and a broker, who do not know any of the bottles, which are completely hidden, and yet year after year one of the great wines will always get chosen as being the best. At lunch we had a 1955, 1949, and 1937 in that order. The greatest marks went to the '49, the '37 was just 'over the hill', the '55 coming up. The great thing about this Muscadet wine is that you must not leave it in your cellar for long.

Our last visit was to M. Barre at Gorges, where we drank some Muscadet *sur Lies*. This is put in bottles just before the fermentation has ended knowing that this will leave some 'lees' in the bottle. It will eat its own 'lees' which will give a slightly more mature, more full, more round flavour than if it had been allowed to ferment and then been racked and drawn off. It is not made commercially, but we were twice offered it and good it was.

We were very sad to leave Nantes and Muscadet.

ANGERS

By the time we arrived at Angers we were captivated, ensnared and seduced. Seduced by hamlets in valleys, by vines climbing up slopes rising gently to wooded hill-tops, by Châteaux, by gardens, by fortresses, by friendly people, and most of all by quiet streams and rivers flowing through verdant meadows or avenues of trees.

We liked the Dive banked with gentle, luscious fields and farmsteads; we found the Layon more often rush than river yet always friendly, but best of all the Loire, wide and serene, bejewelled with wooded islets and the reflections of its subject Châteaux.

The Loire valley has been called 'the smile of France', 'the garden of France', and has inspired innumerable graceful tributes from romantics like Ronsard and Du Bellay, from Jules Lemaitre, Remi Bellau, and, of course, from Rabelais!

To me it typifies the charm of France and I would return to it again and again.

From Nantes one enters Angers by a steep hill dominated by the squat and famous castle which in Shakespeare's *King John* has seen many a shape and stage, but which here stands seemingly indestructible. It must surely have inspired the recent designer of the hock-type, foreshortened glasses in which the local wine is served. Ugly glasses unworthy of fine wines.

The gardens inside the castle walls wear a somewhat pretentious air—the French find it difficult to achieve planned informality which, I suppose carries an Anglo-Saxon hall-mark—but this is somewhat relieved by a charming building, tucked away in the shade of a corner, known as 'the little château'.

The inside walls of one length of the castle are used as a gigantic back-cloth for open-air productions in the annual festival of dramatic art. It makes a most impressive set with scenes played along some 30 yards of castle wall or on the well-shrubbed ground 60 feet below, the two linked by long inter-crossing diagonal paths, the whole lit with French brilliance. We saw some mock Shakespeare written about thirty years after the dramatist's death —poor stuff, well acted.

Part of the castle was destroyed by allied bombers during the last war, but this merely inspired the authorities to build an impressive new wing to house, in perfect conditions of light and spaciousness, the world-famous tapestries of the Apocalypse. These beautiful, soft colours woven nearly 600 years ago, and the fierce 'futuristic' devils and human forms accentuate the timelessness of great art; is there here something that once inspired Bruegel?

The finest wines of Anjou are white and are divided into four Appellations d'Origine: Coteaux de L'Aubance, Coteaux du Layon, Coteaux de la Loire and Coteaux de Saumur.

It is most important to remember with Loire wines that there is usually a tremendous difference between the wines of any two years and also that wines from similar vine stock can taste quite different. My advice is always try a sample bottle before giving a repeat order.

The reason for this difference is twofold. Firstly the vineyards are at the northern end of the district in which the vine can be cultivated for wine production and therefore the grapes are apt to lack sugar in a summer in which there has been a shortfall of sunshine. Secondly, because the type of soil and subsoil varies from gravel to chalk over many parts of the area.

The famous Rosé of Anjou, for example, is only at its best, fragrant, brilliant and light, when its Cabernet stock is growing in flinty soil. Put it on clay and it still produces many grapes, but the quality is gone, the wine becomes heavier and lacks finesse and much of its fragrance. If you want to be sure of drinking the finest of these rosé wines always look for ones marked '*appellation contrôlée*'.

The white wines of Anjou all come from a single stock, the Pinot de la Loire or Chenin Blanc, the rosé from the Cabernet Sauvignon, le Groslot de Cinq-Mars, le Gamay and le Got; the reds from the Cabernet Franc, also called Breton.

One soon learns that one has to be very careful not to drink too much Rosé Cabernet as its fragrant lightness hides an alcohol content of 13 degrees compared with the much smaller amount of Muscadet.

As in Muscadet we found this predominantly a land of little properties and we visited many of them with M. André Auger, a leading vine grower and Vice-President of I.V.A.S., the organization which looks after the communal problems of all the vine growers of Anjou and Saumur.

On our way from Angers to the vineyards we visited the charming riverside village of Behaud. It was easy to see why this was the favourite village church of Louis XI and Charles VIII. It is quite fascinating, partly hewn out of the hill-side rock with the building starting at all sorts of different levels. This happens not only with the outer walls, as even the altar is partly carved out of the rock and partly the work of stonemasons. It is small, simple and lovely.

We lunched at *Le Relais du Château*. This famous restaurant is at Brissac, but it is also only about 25 inches from Quincé as the two communes join, and the restaurant links them. There are ten tables under the trees—well spaced out and very delightful. It is a very, very good restaurant.

According to M. Auger the Anjou vines probably came with the Romans in about the year 200, the Church needing them for Mass, for the sick and for the elderly. They were not like vines as we know them today, they were uncultivated and straggly and their grapes would have produced vinegary wine.

He is certain, even if A.D. 200 is too early, that they had the vines in 400, when it is said that much-travelled St Martin, when Bishop of Angers, went to Marmoutiers to visit a monastery under his care. He left his very famous ass outside the monastery, and when he came out it had gone. Apparently the ass had said to himself, 'This is pretty poor—I'm hot and tired and thirsty,' and had managed to make off to the cool vineyards, where he found the grapes so refreshing that by the time the monks found him he had levelled the lot down to about knee height. The monks were pretty upset about this, but there was nothing they could say.

Later they were astonished to find that the grapes which had been left below the level of the ass's knees, the ones that he could not get at or had not time to eat, produced absolutely magnificent wine. The grapes were very much bigger than any they had had in the past and gave almost the same amount of wine as four times the quantity of the smaller grapes, whilst the quality was infinitely higher. They scratched their shaven heads and thought a bit, as monks do, and that was the beginning of the system of pruning the vine and keeping it down below a certain height. Or so the story goes!

St Martin is a very much loved and respected Saint in the wine world and nowhere more so than in the Loire, where everyone lets themselves go at the annual Fête de St Martin which takes place at the end of January. To *faire la St Martin* is to have no ordinary party, and if one does have such a celebration one has to take care to guard against *le mal de St Martin*, which is drunkenness—a great crime in any wine district. You will often be warned here that the wine is *tres fatigant* (very tiring), a polite euphemism for saying that it is fairly strong and will make you tiddly if you don't look out.

With our lunch we each had a delightful little melon decapitated like a boiled egg, the pips scooped out, the aperture filled with port and the original piece replaced. The flesh is delightful, the juice unbelievable!

During our 'tastings' we soon found some of the many differences in the Angevin wines. We found light wines and 'fleshy' wines, dry, medium-dry and sweet; still wines, *pétillant* (slightly sparkling) wines and sparkling wines; wines with rich fruity bouquet and others with a delicateness that was almost aloof.

It was soon evident that the Angevins think most of their white wines, then their rosé, and least of all their reds, although some of the latter, like Champigny, are highly regarded.

The whites were already famous in the fifteenth century and the vintage from warm and sunny years will usually keep a very long while—1893, 1906, 1921, and 1933 still being in excellent condition—almost like liqueurs, coloured gold or amber and with a bouquet that is a floral symphony in itself.

The wine is bottled about six months after harvesting, but should then be allowed to mature for several years before drinking.

In the main we found that the wines of Coteaux de l'Aubance were very delicate, fine and fruity. We drank them principally in the shadow of the famous Château de Brissac, whose owner way back in the fifteenth century had to pay a due three times a year of cakes and his famous wine to the local Bishop, and where, at a visit after the war, the Mayoress of Angers slipped unobserved into the moat whilst leaning forward to admire an angle of the lovely building, and had to remain clinging to a part of a draw-bridge until her absence was remarked several hours later. With a sang-froid more often attributed to those of Anglo-Saxon origin, she went quickly home, changed and was soon at her place, happy and welcoming, at a reception the town was giving to some distinguished visitors.

The wines of the Coteaux du Layon and the Coteaux de la Loire are very full. Many wine makers set out to produce very sweet, 'chewable' wines from grapes harvested after the *pourriture noble* has set in, but there are some who always make a dryish wine which is none the less magnificently fruity in taste.

In between visiting vineyards we went to some of the most beautiful of the Angevin châteaux and you must, too, as travel books and brochures can only do less than justice to them. Remember, though, that corridors are long, the cobblestones of the approaches are tiring, and the magnitude of new experience so great that if you try to visit more than about one interior a day you will soon be exhausted.

Try, too, to learn something about these great châteaux before you visit them; each has a history that is a novel in itself.

One that particularly appealed to us was the formidable Château of Montgeoffroy which seems to have acquired something of the ruggedness of the old General who built it.

The Maréchal de Contades was Governor of Strasbourg before building Montgeoffroy. He had long been enamoured of his sergeant's wife and took her with him to the Château, which was neither sacked nor destroyed at the time of the Revolution because the son of this strange misalliance had risen to important rank in the Revolutionary Army and had taken unto himself the protection of his natural father's vast home.

In the end it was the Revolution, though, which accelerated the old soldier's death, as his servants, whom he had always treated with disdain, finally formed themselves into a tribunal and sent him a message telling him that their first duty would be to try him for consistently maltreating them. This so enraged the old man that he started to say exactly what he thought of them, had a heart attack and died. Apart from the Louis XVI style Château and its surprisingly 'new' sixteenth-century furniture, there is a wonderful collection of harnesses worn by the Alsatian dogs which used to drag his hunting sleighs in Alsace, several magnificently preserved ceremonial and private coaches, and, if you can get round the friendly lady whose job it is to show you around, a fascinating collection of copper kitchen dishes.

As one approaches Saumur one sees more and more of the inhabited rock-holes called *tuffeaux*. Some houses we visited had their front rooms with brick or stone facing and their back rooms cut out of the solid rocks, and most are associated with wine storing. Here, on the hottest day, wine or worker can feel cool and sheltered. Emerging, one almost inevitably sees the huge castle set high above the Loire and the gentle town it once guarded. Saumur castle is famous for housing the world's only horse museum—a tribute both to man's friend and to the famous French cavalry school whose cadets and instructors fought so gallantly between Montsoreau and Gennes in 1940.

Saumur, the 'pearl' of Anjou, is best known for its sparkling wine, but its still whites which are often exported and its reds which seldom are, although very light in flavour, are superbly coloured, and with 13 degrees of alcohol make very acceptable table wines.

Limestone soil makes the wines dry and light and they have a marked tendency to become *pétillant*, or slightly sparkling. This tendency, which they share with the wines of Champagne, is obviously what led them to make wines of a champagne type known as Vins Mousseux.

These sparkling wines have to remain in bottle for at least one year before they are allowed to be sold. They resemble champagne in many ways, though missing something of its finesse and flavour. Not everyone can afford Champagne for a celebration and this wine makes a very satisfactory alternative.

TOURS

The heart of 'the garden of France' was twice seared during the war—first during the gallant defence of the city by French troops and subsequently by allied bombing of its bridges.

Today the city of Tours is a curious hotchpotch of old and new. Its fine Cathedral and impressive town hall remain and so do many parts of the picturesque old quarter, some of it still held together only by wires and guy ropes. Many new buildings have appeared, but the total effect is far less attractive than Angers or Nantes, though it is an intriguing city with several magnificent hotels in one of which, the Metropole, we had the great pleasure of staying.

The Hoteliers of France have a warranted reputation for professional expertise. Nowhere, though, have we been made more unobtrusively welcome than by M. Audemard and his staff at the Metropole, which probably explains why the clientèle when we were there in early July was international in character and happy in appearance.

Our first visit in Tours was to an astonishing kind of *Son et Lumière*. This consisted of entering the lovely vaulted crypt of an old church rediscovered after an American bombardment in the war, called the Celliers St Julien. The 'sound and light' consisted of about a dozen small tableaux which were illuminated in different parts of the vault, whilst a voice and 'appropriate' music initiated one into the history, specialities, anecdotes and traditions of the various Tourraine vineyards. It is all very noisy, very informative, if your French is good, and will appeal strongly to those who cherish four-in-hand cocktail cabinets.

The road from Tours to Montlouis winds between the Loire and a succession of attractive villages overhanging the road, many of their houses cut out of the cool chalk cliffs and all joined by walnut and apple trees, and by their love for the velvety and *gouleyant* wine which the pinot blanc, the soft, lukewarm climate and generations of care have turned into captive sunshine ranging in shade from silver gilt to amber.

These are wines which keep for years—the 1834, the greatest year ever, is still good as are other great years—1870, 1893, and 1900. Their qualities are very similar to the wines of Vouvray—

and like other wines of the Loire they vary greatly from year to year. Montlouis may be mellow, sweet, demi-sec, or sparkling; it always has a brilliant colour and fruitiness.

The best years for these fine white wines are those which give between 11 and 12 degrees of alcohol; at this strength there is a fascinating flinty taste about the wine which is called *pierre fusil* by the French. When it has more than 12 degrees it loses some of its bouquet and finesse.

The great variations in all the Loire wines make the job of the merchants particularly important as, by holding back stocks of many different years, they can achieve a blend which ensures that their customers get a similar wine from purchase to purchase.

Time and again in the Loire as elsewhere, I found wine men who feel very stongly about the question of vast differences in Customs duty on wines in bottle and in barrel. It is not just that the French trade is fearful that counterfeit wine may be sold in foreign countries, but because often the journey of the wine in the barrel sets up a very slight second fermentation which is not spotted in the importing country. The second fermentation leaves a tiny deposit in the bottle which annoys the ultimate customer.

Montlouis, perched on its pedestal of chalk, and Vouvray are divided only by a kilometre and by the Loire, whose waters, sometimes swift, mostly placid, are unnavigable and whose sandy, picturesque islets are dangerous through quicksands and water holes which drag bathers down when the river is high.

A railway bridge spans the river and Spitfire pilots had to drop bombs on it after high altitude bombing had—as so often in these parts—destroyed much but left the vital objective unscathed.

At the end of the war the inhabitants of Montlouis and Vouvray said, 'Good—when the bridge is rebuilt it will have a motor and pedestrian section on it and we shall be spared the drive of 9 miles every time we want to go from one town to the other.' Not a bit of it: the railway bridge was rebuilt, but despite many protests it is a railway bridge only and the twin towns a few thousand yards apart are still separated by 15 kilometres of road!

On our way from Montlouis to Vouvray we passed through Amboise, whose Château recalls young Charles VIII's ephemeral Italian conquests and whose magnificence inspired the Franco-Italian Renaissance which François I continued in the valley of the Loire.

It is sad that these great châteaux are seldom lived in now except in a token way, simply because there are practically no families who can afford even to heat them in the winter months. At Blois, beloved by La Fontaine, who found it 'laughing and agreeable', we were told that le Comte de Paris does in fact come to the Château for a few weeks in the summer, and we learned, too, how much the French admire this man, who as 'Pretender' to the French throne is not allowed to serve in the French Armed Forces but whose love for France is such that he enlisted in the French Foreign Legion in the last war. His Château of Blois with its astonishing exterior staircase is one of the most wonderful sights in France.

At Vouvray we met M. Jules Delaleu, proprietor, wine maker and President of the Vouvray wine syndicate, who makes, under the name Clos Dubois, all the wines of Vouvray—the tranquil, the *pétillant* and the sparkling. When we got there, his wife was labelling bottles; Granny was holding baby on a 'potty', and the usual pack of dogs was in the courtyard. The house is a very fine example of a rock building with a very nice façade flanked with the cellars and a little room for bottling.

It was a tremendous surprise when we went down to the *cave* and found ourselves in a museum. The family has owned this property for seven generations and in the musueum are all the things they have collected during the course of turning the soil or which they have had handed down from father to son. It is well lit and fascinating, containing, amongst much else, a very interesting set of exhibits of fossilized objects found in the vineyards during ploughing. There are many shell seafish, showing that the sea covered these parts at one time; there are fossilized assess' bones, keys, and even fossilized sponges.

We had a *pétillant* Vouvray with M. Delaleu—a 1956—which was very nice; a *pétillant* wine is far less bubbly than a Mousseaux.

After lunch we went to the immense *caves* of Marc Brédif at Rochecorbon, between Vouvray and Tours. The firm buys grapes from the same—ten to twenty—vineyards every year and makes either *pétillant*, champagne type, or still wine. They have a stock of about one hundred thousand bottles of sparkling wine in gay *caves* finely laid out and illuminated. Originally all these holes in the rock were made because stone was taken from them to build great houses, great châteaux and great cathedrals. Later, the poor went to live in them, found they were very good for storing wine, and so the custom started.

In the first of these deep, elegant *caves* we saw an enormous seventeenth-century press and then an even bigger sixteenth-century one with a horizontal wheel all made of wood and weighing some 6 tons, which came originally from the Domaines de Chenonceaux and which were being worked until 1927. It looked like a guillotine but was squatter.

By law Mousseaux wine has to be kept one year in bottle. This firm always keeps it for two. Finally, after touring the caves we—and you, if you wish, as all these Loiraine firms sell direct and welcome possible customers—ended up in their *dégustation* room.

Incidentally the heat inside was 50 degrees and the heat outside was over 90—an absolutely exhausting difference when one went out.

The sample room is circled with little bins with a lovely marble-topped table in the centre with the traditional Vouvray litre glass in the middle. All the way round it was the remaining stock of the great vintage years, and I made a note of them. They were 1874, 1893 (the greatest of any of the last hundred), 1895, 1900, 1906, 1911, 1914, 1919, 1921, 1922, 1924, 1928, 1933, 1937, 1943, 1945, (which was superb), 1946, 1947 (equally fine), 1949, 1953, and 1955. Of these we tasted many.

We ended up by having a 1947 Vouvray Naturel; it was at least 15 degrees and was like a very good Sauternes, and as you opened it you could smell it—it had a tremendous nose and was very soft and delicate. It is very popular with Dutch and Belgians. M. Brede thinks that Vouvray is best from its fourth year up to ten years, and in the very great years, up to fifty.

The road that runs from Tours to Chenonceaux is very beautiful. It goes down by the river Cher, much smaller than the Loire and less obtrusive. The land on each side of the Cher has all the serenity of an ageing but still beautiful woman, a mixture of trees and peace and ponds and corn and backwaters and lived-in houses.

Veretz has a lovely Romanesque church with an exceedingly slender steeple, and there is a smell all round this district of thyme, wild flowers and rambler roses. Twelve kilometres from Tours one can loop off the main road to Vallet. A narrow road goes down through vineyards, with just occasionally a man or woman working, backs bent, skin almost sun-blacked, tending the vines, and then you come to Vallet, which is a dream village with neither restaurant, shop, nor any signs of commerce. It is on the river and here wealthy men—people from Paris and Tours—have built or acquired summer houses—very, very lovely.

First we came to a garden of pinks surrounding a modern Château built in eighteenth-century style, quite small and exceedingly elegant. Then, on our left, a farmhouse which had been converted, and this was near an old mill, again made into a lovely country house with a backcloth of trees and river lapping up to the lawns and little runways into the Cher from which to launch boats. The Cher is not a dangerous river and a lot of rowing happens on it.

Having loved the loop we continued this delightful journey to Chenonceaux. As one approaches the village, one sees a very, very long avenue of immense plane trees, several hundred yards long, which meet at the top and which have a simple beauty either in daylight or when each one is illuminated at night.

On summer evenings many of the great châteaux of the Loire come to vicarious life. *Son et Lumière* started in the Loire in 1952 and since then the degree of sophistication of these pageants has rapidly increased.

Today, if you walk down the towering avenue of plane trees towards the Château of Chenonceaux your roof of verdant green will be bathed in golden light. You come to the gardens: the Château, whose five elegant arches bridge the gracious Cher, lies massive, impressive in front of you, its finest lines and most graceful curves hidden in night's cloak.

Then comes music, the right music and superbly reproduced: then the Château appears in a full blaze of light; thereafter appropriate voices, deep one, light ones, husky ones, bosky ones, take up the tale of the Ladies of Chenonceaux; Catherine Briçonnet and Catherine de Medici, who made its story but found little happiness there; Diane de Poitiers who found too much; Louise of Lorraine, the White Queen who mourned there for ten dull years, and finally Madame Dupin who was so beloved by the villagers that this most precious place was allowed to stand, when many another was destroyed in the Revolution.

There is nothing vulgar about the presentation of these festivals of sound and light, but I am told that in future years they will be even more 'up-to-date'—the lights will be coloured instead of golden and change according to the story. I wonder! Did the moon change to purple when Diane de Poitiers had her day, and to green when Catherine de Medici packed her off to the comparative austerity of Chaumont?

On our last day in the Loire we went to Chinon, whose Château was largely destroyed by Richelieu. History says that this was avarice on his part as he wanted to build a château for himself out of the stones—but is it not more likely that he set out to break up all the fortified positions that could be used against him in the religious wars?

Chinon is a most impressive ruin. One can still imagine here the death of an English King; the pomp of a French court; and the solemn moment when a maiden shyly advanced upon a King to launch a crusade which meant the beginning of the end of the English 'occupation' of France and brought her to her death at the stake.

The royal quarters at Chinon are most royally guarded in an inner sanctum with great towers at each corner, a drawbridge across its entrance, and from its walls a peaceful view over the slate-grey roofs of Chinon to the languid Loire rippling slyly past with never a ship nor a boat to do it honour—just occasionally a poor looking shell and a bent figure fishing dangerously for eels.

The characteristics of the wines of Chinon and of Bourgeuil are very similar, though some say that Bourgeuil's flavour is raspberry and Chinon's of violet. I am told you have to be an absolutely outstanding expert to be able to note the difference, and then I suspect that probably you cannot for certain because the same grape, similar soil and identical appellation laws govern the two districts.

Chinon should be drunk a little less *chambré* than a Burgundy or Bordeaux—just slightly less warm. It keeps well, but there is the possibility of a second fermentation if the wine gets up to a temperature of 65 to 70 degrees, which, of course, it never does in local caves, but which it can do when en route to a foreign market.

The second fermentation will cease almost directly the fût gets back into a cellar of 50 to 53 degrees, but it will have become more dry, because sugar will have been lost in the fermentation and it will be cloudy. To me the Chinon has just the same qualities as the Bourgeuil and they are both good pleasant, fruity wines to drink with meat, but not earlier in the meal. They are a little bit more *dur*, a bit harder, than the Bordeaux wines and have a nice nose, the most enjoyable we had was a St Nicholas Bourgeuil that we drank in the Metropole in Tours.

After Chinon we went to vineyards in Bourgeuil. There are various communes within the Bourgeuil district and St Nicholas Bourgeuil is a separate appellation on its own. The wines vary within the different communes, and also some of the communes are different within themselves, as some are on the sand made when the Loire flowed over this land and some are not. For example, St Nicolas and Bourgeuil themselves are half sand and half limestone, whereas Restigne is sand and Benais is limestone. So here you have all these wine districts making almost exactly similar wine, the same grapes and the same sun, but not from the same soil, so you will always get some variation.

Bourgeuil is a very light, fruity wine, slightly finer than the other Bourgeuils, which is why it got its own appellation. It is about 11 degrees in an average year, rising to about 12 or 13 in a very good year with a minimum for *Appellation Contrôlée* of 9½.

As in most vineyard areas, one finds frequent references in ancient literature to the part played by the Church in tending the vines of Touraine. Here as far back as the eleventh century the Benedictine monks were proudly recording that their wines of Bourgeuil were abundant and 'brought rejoicing to a sad heart'.

Before loading ourselves, our experiences, and one hundred and fifty thousand words of Dictaphoned 'documentation' on to our T.R.2 and making for Havre (remember when you do that the Seine is a wide river and one has to be ferried across), we made a quick visit to sample the full-bodied and rather mellow wines of Sancerre, which are excellent with cooked fish and pork dishes, and finally to taste the dry white wines of Quincy, which go well with oysters, shellfish, and goatsmilk cheese.

Our visit had taken just on three months and it had been preceded by many others, by much reading and a good deal of tasting.

We had met the kindliness of quiet, contented people whose wine is a way of life and we had realized, long before the end, how very little any Anglo-Saxon can normally expect to know about wine and what a fascinating study it makes.

APPENDIX I

Champagne

IN 1956, the sale of Champagne in France increased by 22 per cent over 1955, that in overseas countries by 8 per cent.

38,500,000 bottles were made by the great Champagne firms which largely buy their grapes from vineyards they do not own; 5,800,000 by vineyard owners from their own stock or co-operatives.

The names of principal champagne makers with approximate figures of production in 1952 are as follows:

	bottles
Moët et Chandon	3,500,000
Mercier	1,950,000
Pommery-Greno	1,600,000
G. H. Mumm	1,600,000
Veuve Clicquot	1,600,000
Heidsieck Monopole . . .	1,300,000
Charles Heidsieck	1,250,000
Lanson	1,150,000
Ayala-Montebello-Duminy . . .	1,000,000
Piper-Heidsieck	1,000,000
De Castellane	1,000,000
Gauthier	850,000
S.A.M.E.	800,000
Perrier-Jouet	700,000
Louis Roederer	700,000
Bollinger	600,000
Taittinger	550,000
Ernest Irroy	500,000
Pol Roger	450,000
Henriot (3)	350,000
Philipponnat	300,000
Krug	250,000
Delbeck	250,000
Deutz et Gelderman . . .	225,000
Billecart-Salmon	225,000
Veuve Laurent-Perrier . . .	200,000
Georges Goulet	150,000
Salon	40,000

31,278,718 bottles were sold in France.
13,165,558 bottles went to foreign markets
1,906,976 bottles went to French Colonial markets.

The principal buyers were:

	1956	1955	1954
England . .	2,766,465	2,645,826	2,195,833
U.S.A. . .	2,684,723	2,558,016	2,178,054
Belgium . .	1,584,700	1,581,311	1,453,317
Algeria . .	733,450	460,452	398,036
Italy . .	508,860	485,393	372,526
Venezuela .	372,644	324,439	304,522
Morocco .	360,212	342,855	357,743
Switzerland .	331,481	263,927	243,922
Canada .	233,974	191,908	178,117
Sweden .	226,263	238,329	178,173
Holland .	215,299	184,959	167,835
Germany T.O. .	201,594	198,796	151,805
Germany Civile	163,023	133,288	92,621
Belgian Congo .	142,147	149,640	158,630
Senegal .	126,251	131,473	137,806
Indo-China . .	69,216	199,322	416,542

The recent outstanding vintage years were 1945, 1947, 1949 and 1952.

The Names and Contents of bottles

Quarter bottle . .	6½ fluid oz.
Half bottle . . .	13 ,, ,,
Imperial Pint . .	19½ ,, ,,
Bottle . . .	26 ,, ,,
Magnum . . .	2 bottles
Jeroboam . . .	4 ,, or Double Magnum
Rehoboam . . .	6 ,, or Triple Magnum
Methuselah . . .	8 ,, or Quadruple Magnum
Salmanazar . . .	12 ,,
Balthazar . . .	16 ,, }No longer produced.
Nebuchadnezzar . .	20 ,,

How to be sure that a Wine is genuine Champagne

The name 'Champagne', also the words 'Produce of France' must be printed in conspicuous type on the *label* or on the *neck label*. It must also appear in full on the part of the *cork* inserted in the neck of the bottle.

When to drink Champagne

As often as possible! Non-vintage as an apéritif and with the hors d'oeuvres and fish. Mature and full-bodied vintage wines with meat, game or poultry. Dry or demi-sec with sweet courses.

At what Temperature should Champagne be served?

At 44 to 48 degrees Fahrenheit. It should not be iced but cooled.

How to Open

Gently. There is nothing clever in making the cork pop loudly, though admittedly it is fun.

What kind of Glasses are best?

Flute or tulip-shaped. Never dry them with cotton cloths.

APPENDIX II

The Royal Family of the Wines of Burgundy

The King
Le Chambertin

The Queen
La Romanée Conti

The Dauphin
Le Musigny

The Royal Children
Le Richebourg; Le Clos de Vougeot; Le Corton; Le Montrachet

The Royal Princes
Les Romanées; Le Clos de Tart; Le Clos Saint-Jacques;
Les Échezeaux; Les Bonnes Mares; Le Clos des Lampreys

The Dukes and Duchesses
Gevrey Chambertin; Chambolle-Musigny; Vougeot; Vosne-Romanée;
Nuits-Saint-Georges; Aloxe-Corton; Pernand-Vergelesses; Savigny-
les-Beaune; Beaune; Pommard; Volnay; Mersault; Monthelie;
Auxey-Duresses; Puligny-Montrachet; Chassagne-Montrachet;
Santenay.

Traditional

APPENDIX III

Recipes

POULET A L'ESTRAGON

Prepare a stock with ½ litre of dry white wine, ½ litre of water, 4 ounces of lean bacon, the insides of the chicken and stems of tarragon (the leaves are kept aside). Cook for ½ hour, dip the chicken in this stock and let it cook for ½ hour.

Prepare separately some butter in a pan with the tarragon leaves finely chopped, let it cook for a minute or two but it must not brown, add a pinch of flour, then some stock.

Before serving add 3 yokes of egg. Cut up the chicken. Add lean bacon and cover with the sauce.

PÂTÉ DE PIGEON

The day before:

Prepare some minced pork seasoned with salt, pepper, and finely chopped shallots.

Cut each pigeon in four, season them with salt and pepper only.

On the day:

Prepare a dough with: 12 grs. yeast
> 1 lb. flour
> ¼ lb. lard
> ½ lb. butter
> Salt
> A glass of water

Let it stand for 2 hours.

Prepare cake tins; in each of them put one thin coat of minced pork, the pigeon, then another coat of minced pork. Cover well with the dough, cook for 1¼ hours in moderate oven.

Hotel du Cheval Blanc,
Sept Saulx,
Nr. Reims.

POULET AU CHAMPAGNE

Cut chicken in four. Brown lightly in oil. Place in sauté pan without any fat; cover with liquid:

$\frac{3}{4}$ champagne
$\frac{1}{4}$ stock in which mushrooms have been cooked

Add salt, pepper, thyme, bay leaf. Cook slowly. Then strain.

Later thicken the liquid in which the chicken has been cooked with: a 'roux', meat jelly, fresh cream and, finally, cooked mushrooms.

La Chaumière,
Reims.

JAMBON EN CROÛTE

This is a magnificent way of serving ham, as all the juices are preserved in the crust. The ham should be one that has been quick-salted; if not, soak it for 10 hours. Remove the bone from the ham, put in cold water without seasoning, bring to boil and allow to simmer for about 2 hours (10-12 lb. ham). Let it cool in the water.

Prepare pastry (3 lb. flour, 1 oz. salt, 1 lb. lukewarm lard, $\frac{1}{3}$ pint warm water) and allow it to stand for about 3 hours. When the ham is cold, remove rind and excess fat, wrap in rolled pastry, coat with egg yolk, and season according to taste, leaving an opening for steam. Cook in a hot oven for about $1\frac{1}{2}$ hours and pour some Madeira through the opening a few minutes before removing from the oven.

Traditional Alsatian recipe.

BOEUF BOURGUIGNON

Cut 2 lb. of stewing steak into small cubes, cover for 24 hours in red wine seasoned with herbs. Remove and dry the steak and brown in frying pan with 2 tablespoonfuls of fat. Add 2 chopped shallots and 1 clove garlic, add 2 teaspoonfuls of flour and let brown. Strain the wine marinade and add to the beef with enough stock to cover meat well. Fry $\frac{1}{4}$ lb. of fat bacon and add to pot. Brown a few small onions in the bacon fat, add these to pot, cover and let simmer until meat is tender. The meat is excellent, the juice superb!

Traditional Burgundian recipe.

JAMBON CHAUD MODE DE L'ETOILE

Boil down 1 cup Chablis or other white wine with 1 or 2 shallots and a sprig of tarragon. When only a little liquid is left in the pan add 2 cups good stock. Add 3 tablespoonfuls tomato purée and cook covered for 1 hour at the lowest possible simmer. Add an equal quantity of cream and cook for 10 minutes. Strain sauce and stir in 1 teaspoonful butter. Pour over slices of hot ham and serve.

SOLES AU CHABLIS

Take 4 soles. Take off both skins, cut off the fins, clean them and cut through the bone in the middle so that they stay flat. Butter the bottom of a baking dish, add 4 or 5 rings of onion, and lay the soles on them so that they hardly touch; salt and pepper lightly. Add ½ glass of Chablis and enough water barely to cover the soles. Cover with buttered paper. Cook for 10-15 minutes.

SAUCE

Drain the juices into a casserole, keep the soles hot, reduce the liquid by half, add a little flour and butter, cook for 5 minutes. Take away from fire, mix in quickly with a little beating 2 egg yolks which have been mixed with a little water. Put back on the fire and bring to the boil, stirring very quickly (which stops the sauce from curdling). Add the juice of half a lemon and some butter which one mixes in by stirring (without letting it boil).

Dishing up: Put the soles on a baking dish, sauce on top, and glaze in a bain-marie in a very hot oven. Serve quickly.

M. Bergerand,
Hotel de l'Etoile,
Chablis.

SALMIS DE CANARD TRUFFE

Prepare a tender and plump duck. Roast it 25 minutes in a hot oven.

Cut the duck in five pieces: 2 legs, 2 wings, 1 centre.

Keep the body. Keep the pieces warm in a saucepan.

Cut the body in fine little pieces and put in a saucepan with 2 or 3 minced shallots and 2 glasses of good red or white wine. Reduce till it is nearly dry, then moisten with enough thin good gravy. Then thicken with butter worked with flour. Let it cook 20 minutes on the side of the stove.

Pour through a fine sieve, squeezing the minced body. Put this sauce on to the pieces of duck. Add a glass of good Madeira and a big truffle, sliced. Let it simmer 20 minutes and keep it hot.

Serve very hot with a smoothly thickened sauce, not too thick. Add a pinch of sugar if the sauce is a little acid.

M. Bergerand,
Hotel de l'Etoile,
Chablis.

SOUFFLÉ A L'ORANGE (for two emptied oranges)

Put in a saucepan 2 knobs of butter, 2 coffee-spoonfuls of flour, and cook this mixture for ½ minute. Add ½ glass of milk, previously boiled, cook for a minute, take away from the fire, stir in 2 egg yolks and bring to the boil again. Add a handful of sugar, ½ liqueur glass of strong curaçao and 2 lumps of sugar previously rubbed against the lid of the emptied oranges. (Melt these 2 lumps in a drop of hot water before adding to the mixture.) The mixture must be fairly thick.

Beat up the 2 whites of eggs stiffly, fold them into the mixture which you now put in the emptied oranges, sprinkle with sugar and put in a hot oven for 5 minutes.

M. Bergerand,
Hotel de l'Etoile,
Chablis.

FONDUE DE POULET A LA CRÈME

Cut a tender chicken as for a fricassée; put the pieces with a good knob of butter in a shallow saucepan. Add a large onion, or two smaller ones, previously finely sliced, a little table salt, and a pinch of pepper. Put the lid on the saucepan and let it 'sweat' for about 20 minutes on the side of the stove. Three-quarters of the way through the cooking add a small glass of good 'Fine Champagne', a good pinch of curry powder, and a pint of double cream; leave it on the stove till the chicken is cooked. Then take out the pieces of chicken, reduce the sauce till it is quite smooth, add a piece of fresh butter and pour this sauce on the chicken through a sieve, squeezing the onions.

Keep hot without letting it come to the boil. This dish must be served very hot.

Restaurant des Gourmets,
Marsannay-La Côte,
Nr. Dijon.

CRÊPES PARMENTIER

Cook 3 potatoes in salt water and mash with milk. Allow to cool and add 2 tablespoonfuls of flour plus 6 unbeaten eggs and 3 tablespoonfuls of thick cream. Mix until it has the consistency of ordinary cream. Heat some butter in an omelette pan, pour in ¾ tablespoonful of the mixture and allow to form into round like a pancake. Turn over, sprinkle with cheese and serve.

VOLAILLE À LA CRÈME DU CHAPON FIN

Cut a good-sized chicken into eight pieces. Fry them in butter with a sliced onion, salt and pepper; when the pieces are lightly browned sprinkle in a tablespoonful of flour, brown it and mix with about ⅓ litre of water. Cover it and cook slowly for ½ hour.

In the meantime, prepare a mixture of 4 egg yolks and ⅓ litre of double cream and just before serving pour this mixture into the pan in which the chicken is cooking and cook rapidly until it thickens without letting it boil. Dish up at once.

M. Blanc,
Chapon Fin,
Thoissey.

A DELIGHTFUL PORK DISH

Take a piece of pork fillet weighing about 2 lb. and marinade it for a day in a dish containing the following ingredients:

> a large glass of white wine
> juice of a lemon
> a little olive oil
> a few leaves of thyme
> sage, salt and pepper

Turn the pork several times during the day. Next day wipe the pork and put in a baking dish in the oven (it takes about 40 minutes in a hot oven for a piece of this size). If the pork gets too dry, baste it with a little of the liquid used for the marinade.

Serve it with sauté potatoes and sliced tomatoes fried with garlic and parsley.

Hotel Templiers,
Collioure.

QUENELLES LYONNAISE (to make thirty 'pieces')

Ingredients:

> For the 'panade': ¼ litre water
> 100 grs. butter
> 400 grs. flour
> Salt, pepper, nutmeg
> Fish: 1 lb. raw pike flesh

In a rather shallow thick saucepan put water, butter, salt, pepper and nutmeg. Bring to the boil, throw in the flour, and stir vigorously with wooden spoon till the mixture forms one whole and does not stick to the saucepan. Leave it on a slow fire to get as dry as possible without sticking to the pan. Allow to cool, and then add, one by one, 3 eggs.

Pass the fish meat two or three times through a mixer.

Add to the panade, then add, one by one, 10 whites of eggs. Let this stand for about 5 minutes. Add 1 lb. of butter. Allow to stand for 5 minutes. Lastly, incorporate the egg yolks.

Put the mixture so obtained on a floured board. Take portions and roll them in the shape of long thick sausages, and then cut them in sections about 3 inches long; or you may shape your quenelles like eggs with the help of 2 dessert spoons. Lay them on a flat dish and place in frig. till needed.

When required poach for about 10 minutes in water just simmering. Remove very carefully; allow water to drip. Put a little butter at the bottom of an oven dish and lay quenelles in this.

SAUCE

Make a Bechamel sauce, add small white mushrooms (do not wash, but peel and cut very thinly). Pour this sauce over the quenelles in the oven dish, and place in slow oven until hot.

La Tante Alice Restaurant,
Lyon.

FILET DE SOLE TANTE ALICE

Butter a shallow baking dish, put in a few shallots cut up finely and salt and pepper. Lay the fillets of sole in it, just cover with white wine and fish stock and boil for 3 or 4 minutes. Take out the fillets, add sliced tomatoes and some cream to the liquid and reduce it by one quarter. Make a thick sauce with the liquid in the usual way, and finally add 2 beaten egg yolks and a few drops of lemon. Serve the fish on a flat dish with the sauce poured over it.

Tante Alice,
Lyon.

FILETS DE SOLE BEAU RIVAGE

Poach 2 good-sized fillets of sole in lobster stock. After they are cooked arrange them on a hot dish and garnish with mushrooms and pieces of lobster.

Reduce the stock until it thickens and add fresh cream, finish by mixing it with a little Hollandaise sauce.

M. R. Castaing,
Hotel Beau-Rivage,
Condrieu.

FRICASSEE DE POULET A L'ANGEVINE

Cut up a chicken into eight pieces. Put in a frying pan with a largish piece of butter and a few small onions. Fry the chicken on both sides without browning it and add 6 oz. of mushrooms. Pour in a bottle of dry white Anjou wine and let it simmer until the chicken is cooked. Then take out the chicken, onions, and mushrooms and place on a dish. Put ½ pint of very thick cream into the liquid in which the chicken was cooked, let it cook, add salt and pepper to taste and pour over the chicken.

M. Gillet,
Le Vert d'Eau Restaurant,
Angers.

BROCHET AU BEURRE BLANC

To 1 quart water add 1 cup white wine, ½ cup vinegar, 1 carrot and 1 onion both sliced, salt, peppercorns, a pinch of thyme, a bay leaf, and a sprig of parsley. Simmer for 30 minutes and then poach a 2 lb. pike in this stock.

Chop 4 or 5 shallots and simmer in a casserole with ¼ cup each of vinegar and white wine until the liquid is almost evaporated. Add bit by bit ½ lb. butter over low heat so that the butter does not boil, stirring continually with a whisk to get a creamy result. Season with a little salt, pepper, and a pinch of cayenne. Spread this beurre blanc on the fish at the moment of serving.

CANARD À LA NANTAISE

Roast a duck in the usual way. While it is in the oven sauté 12 small onions in butter until golden. Add 2 or 3 tablespoonfuls diced lean bacon to the onions and sauté together for 3 minutes. Cook separately 2 lb. peas in boiling water for 5 minutes.

M. E. Moreau,
Chef de Cuisine,
Rôtisserie Le Bonniec,
Nantes.

SWEETBREAD WITH PORT

Quantities: 1 sweetbread a person. Soak them so that all the blood sticking to them is out. Blanch them, putting them in the water when cold; take them out, drain dry, clean them of all skins, etc., put them under press. In an oven dish melt knobs of butter, add sliced carrots, sliced onions, parsley stems, ¼ bay-leaf, 4 sticks of thyme, fresh mushroom stalks and a crushed tomato, add the sweetbread, cover the dish, put in the oven for 10 minutes.

Take dish out, pour some brandy over sweetbread, set it alight, then water with a rich stock, ½ glass of wine (dry) and a liqueur glass of port, bring to the boil, then put back in the oven for 30 minutes. Then take the sweetbread out of the dish, put them in a cocotte (a heavy cast-iron saucepan), add a few drops of port, some mushrooms previously cooked in butter, keep warm.

Strain the sauce, let it boil down to half its quantity, check the seasoning, then work it with butter béarnaise fashion. Pour this smooth sauce over the sweetbread already placed on serving dish, decorate with one slice of truffle and two for each person.

With this dish you may serve: Spinach, peas, bottoms of artichokes or even potatoes.

From: '*Le Bon Laboureur*',
Chenonceaux.

APPENDIX IV

Bibliography

WINE BOOKS

English

Natural Red Wines, by H. Warner Allen (Constable)
White Wines and Cognac, by H. Warner Allen (Constable)
The Vade-Mecum of the Wine Lover, by William Buckley and Claude Landry (La Conception Publicitaire)
The Vineyards of France, by J. M. Scott, illustrated by Keith Baynes (Hodder & Stoughton)
The Wines of France, by Alexis Lichine and W. C. Massée (Cassell)
Stay me with Flagons, by Maurice Healey (Michael Joseph)

French

Grands Crus de Bourgogne, by E. D. Moucheron (Jean Dupin of Beaune)
Connaissance du Vin de Champagne, by M. Maurice Holland (C.F.P.P.)
Le Viticulture et le Vin de Colmar a Travers les Siècles, by Lucien Sittler (Editions Alsatia)
Les Vins de Loire, by Pierre Bréjoux (Collection 'Cuisine et Vins de France 1956')
Les Vins de Bourgogne, by Pierre Poupon and Pierre Forgeot (Presses Universitaires)
Le Vin de Nos Vignes, by Leon Foillard (Cuvier of Villefranche)
Le Bourgogne Tastevin en Main, by Georges Rozet (La Confrerie des Chevaliers du Tastevin). Editions Epic 1951—Horizons de France.
Les Origines du Vignobles Français, by Jean Mommessin (Protat Frères, Mâcon)
Contes du Tastevin (Bourgogne) (Coll. Folklore), by Maurice Chervet (Editions du Rocer-Monaco)
Les Vins de Bordeaux, by L. Larmat (Larmat, Paris)
Les Grands Vins de Bordeaux, by Société de l'Annuaire de la Gironde, Bordeaux
Monseigneur le Vin—Establissements Nicolas, Paris
Almanach du Beaujolais, by Jean Guillermet (Guillermet, Villefranche)
Histoire du Cognac, by Robert Delamain (Editions Stock)

HISTORICAL AND TOPOGRAPHICAL
English

Burgundy Past and Present, by Evelyn M. Hatch (Methuen)
Prospects of France, by Alan Houghton Brodrick (Hutchinson)
Three Rivers of France, by Freda White (Faber & Faber)
The Spirit of France, by Paul Cohen-Portheim, translated by Altan Harris (Duckworth)
French Life and Landscape, by Alfred Firth—2 volumes (Elek)
Châteaux of the Loire, by Vivian Rowe (Putnam)
Provence by Marcel Brion, translated by S. G. Colverson (Kaye)
Aspects of Provence, by James Pope Hennessy (Longmans)

French

Châteaux en Gironde, by Jacques J. Mérillan (Dumas)
Notre Dame de Cîteaux (Watson of St Etienne)

LITERARY
English

The Lamartine Ladies, by Laura M. Ragg (Macdonald)
Dear Theo, by Irving Stone (Autobiography of Vincent van Gogh). Ed. by Stone (Constable)
Portrait of Vincent, by Lawrence and Elizabeth Hanson (Chatto & Windus)
Letters from Madame de Sévigné, selected, translated and introduced by Violet Hammersley (Secker & Warburg)
Cézanne, by Roger Fry (Hogarth Press)

French

Les Confidences, by Lamartine (Petite Bibliotheque Littéraire) (Lemerre)
Anthologie du Sacavan, by Marc Leclerc (André Bruel of Angers)
La Cathédrale de Reims, (Charm of France series) (Challamel)
Lettres de Mon Moulin, by Alphonse Daudet (Editions du Verseau)

PERIODICALS

La Journée Vinicole
La Revue Vinicole (whose friendly interest has been most encouraging)
Revue du Vin de France
Saisons d'Alsace—Antoine Fischer, Strassbourg
La France à Table
L'Opinion
Pavilion Français
Richesses de France

Acknowledgments

WRITING this book has only been made possible through the help of many people, all of whom love France.

I am particularly indebted to Colonel Leonard Dennis, Master of wines and Managing Director of Smith and Hoey of London, who made out my itinerary, whose good name unlocked many a precious chai, and who read this book in draft except for the chapters on Champagne, Alsace, Burgundy, Bordeaux and Cognac, which were 'vetted' for errors in fact or inference by Monsieur Etienne Lanson, Madame Schlumberger and Monsieur Brion, Monsieur Poupon of J. Calvet, Monsieur Binaud, former President of the Bordeaux Wine and Spirits Trade Association, and Monsieur Maurice Firino Martell, respectively, to all of whom I am very grateful both for this and for all the time they gave me when I visited them.

That writer of delightful books Mr Vivian Rowe of the French Tourist Board helped me greatly, as did Mr Stanley Blood of W. and J. Joule of Stone, Mr 'Tubby' Ionides of Percy Fox of London, and Mr Vaughan Reynolds, editor of the *Birmingham Post*, who encouraged me to write about my 'hobby'.

The Linguaphone Company brushed up my French, as did Mrs Hellings of Birmingham; my T.R.2 gave me 'time in hand' and my Dictaphone saved innumerable hours of one-fingered typing.

Beyond all other books on wine I enjoyed reading and studying Alexis Lichine's *The Wines of France*, and to meet him was as stimulating as to read him.

It was a great privilege to be enabled to meet 'the little men' as well as the proprietors of world-famous Châteaux, and for this and much else I owe thanks to Baron le Roy de Boiseaumarie, President of the Wine Growers of France and his Regional Controllers.

My thanks go to Thelma Couch, who transcribed 160,000 Dictaphoned words, and to Angela Bishop, who ultimately typed the book and collated many scraps of almost illegible writing.

Many others helped me, and I should particularly like to record my gratitude to—

L'Ambassade de Sauternes-Barsac
M. Audebert of Bourgueil
M. Audemard of Hotel Metropole, Tours
M. P. Beauvilain of Chinon

M. Bergerand of L'Etoile, Chablis

M. Albert Besombes of Bourgueil

M. de Bettignies of Nantes, Technical Councillor for Muscadet of the Institut National des Appellations d'Origine

M. Albert Bichot of Beaune

Professor Thomas Bodkin

M. Boeckel of Mittelberheim

M. François Bouchard of Beaune

M. Marc Bredif of Rochecorbon

M. Louis Budin of Epernay

M. Jean Calvet of Bordeaux

The Hon. Moyra Campbell of Epernay

M. Emille Charpentier of Le Pallet

M. Roger Charpentier of Le Chappelle Heulin

M. de Coninck of Libourne

Le Connétablie de la Guyenne

Le Connétablie de la Jurade de Saint-Emilion

M. E. Cruse of Bordeaux

M. Dargent, Director of the Comité Interprofessionnel of the Wine of Champagne

M. Jules Delaleu of Vouvray

M. and Madame Jean Descaves of Bordeaux

Dunlop Rubber Co. of Birmingham

M. Deschaux of Valence, Technical Councillor for Côtes du Rhône of the Institut National des Appellations d'Origine

M. and Madame René Dourdicolle of Bordeaux

M. R. Dourthe of Bordeaux

M. Dubern of Restaurant Dubern, Bordeaux

Messieurs René and Philippe Dubos of Bordeaux

M. de Fonrocque, Secrétaire Général Académie du Vin de Bordeaux

M. Pierre Forgeot of Beaune

M. Fould of Château Beychevelle

The French Embassy, London

M. Claude Geoffray, President of the Wine Growers of the Beaujolais

M. Geoffroy de Couësbouc of St Fiacre

M. Émile Gerbault of Montlouis

M. Gillet of Le Vert d'Eau Restaurant, Angers

Comte G. de Goulaine of Haute-Goulaine

M. Gruninger of Colmar

M. Jean Marc Heidsieck of Reims

The Hon. F. Hennessey of London

M. Louis Jadot of Beaune

Mrs Helen Jones of Birmingham

M. Jourdon of Givrieux d'Azergues

M. Klipfel of Barr

M. Labbé of Angers

M. J. Lafargue of Hotel-Restaurant 'Robinson', Esconac-Quinsac

M. Louis Latour of Beaune

M. Roger Michel, Director of Tourism at Beaune

M. Jean Mommessin of Mâcon

Marquis de Montesquiou of Auch

M. Jean Morin of Nuits-St-Georges

M. Andre Oger of Château Fresivaye, Maine-et-Loire

M. Onzit, Technical Councillor for Mâcon of the Institut National des Appellations d'Origine

M. Polge, Archivist of Auch

M. Camille Rodier of Burgundy

M. Rose of Tours

M. René Sabbe of Epernay

M. Tharaux of Borgueil

M. Toutchkov, Technical Councillor for Roussillon of the Institut National des Appellations d'Origine

M. Verlynde, Vice-President of C.I.V.N.

M. D. Guillon Verne, General Secretary of Comité Regional de Tourisme, Nantes

M. Daniel Viollette, the Secretary General of C.I.V.T., Tours

M. Henri Vourloud of Lyon

Baron de Willermin

W. A. H. Shaw of London

F. R. Palengat of London

L. E. de Rouet of London

Robertson Villar and Watson Limited of London

S. F. Hallgarten of London

W. S. Hick of London

Guy Prince of London

H. T. Penell of London

Hugh Gladstone of Birmingham

and

The Wine and Spirit Association of Great Britain